'Rarely have I come across such an extraordinarily comprehensive book that details three key stages of a business – buying, growing and exiting. Joanna Oakey clearly has a great deal of knowledge and expertise as well as a very practical approach to maximising opportunity in every stage. To me, this is a book that all business owners need to read and keep close, using it as a valuable resource. A very impressive book.'

Andrew Griffiths, International Bestselling Author and Global Speaker

'Completing four successful acquisitions didn't just double our revenue, it doubled our multiple. None of these deals required any cash or debt which, more than any other deal I've done, made me realise that while value is created serving customers, wealth is created in the deal room. Joanna is a master – read this book and read it again.'

Glen Carlson, Co-Founder, Dent.Global

'Joanna Oakey is a proven leader in the Australian SME legal space. This is a book that captures her deep experience and passion for working with owners across all aspects of M&A, and is something every business owner should have in their hands.'

Edward Chan, Non-Executive Chairman and Founder,
Chan & Naylor, Wize Mentoring

'This book is entrepreneurship at the next level and I applaud Joanna Oakey for putting it all together. There is so much wisdom, strategy and so many secrets in here. Seriously, for the cost of a pub dinner it can be yours and you can use it to make millions. Now that's a good deal.'

Dale Beaumont, Founder & CEO, Business Blueprint

'Joanna Oakey and Aspect Legal have supported the Australian business sale industry and our association (AIBB) for many years. Her thought leadership and pragmatic advice reflects her experience dealing with SME businesses and their owners, and contributes not only to the professionalism of our brokers but the Australian M&A and business sale sector more broadly.'

Ian Jones, Director, Merchant Business Brokers
President and National Chair of Australian Institute of
Business Brokers (AIBB) 2022

'Joanna's book is a goldmine of practical, down-to-earth information and application of concepts used in the business world, often not understood by small business owners. If you want to grow, acquisition is a great way to do that, and a true wealth builder. To avoid the trips and traps – no matter what stage you're at with your business – Joanna's book is a "must read".'

Kerry Boulton, Entrepreneur, CEO & Founder, The Exit Strategy Group

'Joanna's expertise comes with a commercial and practical approach to the law. It is refreshing, and her work has supported our 30%+ growth year on year!'

Oliver Lazarevic, CEO, Supply Clusters

'Any business owner looking for pragmatic SME advice should get to know Joanna, Aspect Legal, and their methodology.'

Simon Bedard, CEO, Exit Advisory Group

BUY, GROW, EXIT.

The Ultimate Guide to Using Business as a Wealth-Creation Vehicle

Joanna Oakey

First published in 2022 by Joanna Oakey

A catalogue entry for this book is available from the National Library of Australia.

ISBN: 978-1-922764-05-8

Printed in Australia by McPherson's Printing
Book production and text design by Publish Central
Cover design by Pipeline Design

The paper this book is printed on is certified as environmentally friendly.

Disclaimer
The material in this publication is of the nature of general comment only, and does not represent professional advice. It is not intended to provide specific guidance for particular circumstances and it should not be relied on as the basis for any decision to take action or not take action on any matter which it covers. Readers should obtain professional advice where appropriate, before making any such decision. To the maximum extent permitted by law, the author and publisher disclaim all responsibility and liability to any person, arising directly or indirectly from any person taking or not taking action based on the information in this publication.

CONTENTS

PREFACE IX

It can go wrong ix

When it goes right x

Turning the discussion on its head xi

A disclaimer . . . of sorts xiv

How to use this book xv

PART I: BUY

CHAPTER 1: HOW AND WHY BUSINESSES ARE BOUGHT 3

Acquisition entrepreneurship 4

Acquisition as a supercharged path to growth 4

Acquisitions to increase your multiple for exit 15

Acquisitions for roll ups 18

Acquisitions for investment 19

Management buyouts 19

CHAPTER 2: WHY ACQUISITIONS FAIL 21

The most common reasons why deals don't succeed 22

Transaction failure 26

CHAPTER 3: THE FIVE ESSENTIAL DRIVERS OF A SUCCESSFUL PURCHASE ... 31

The 5Ps Driving Great Purchases 31

CHAPTER 4: PREPARATION: BEING ACQUISITION READY   **33**

Defining what success looks like   35

Preparing a strategy   35

Assembling your deal team   37

Establishing your process   38

Organising finance   40

Understanding the acquisition structure and agreements   41

Assessing your current business   41

CHAPTER 5: PRIMARY VALUE: ENSURING THE TRANSFER OF KEY VALUE   **43**

How to approach the transfer of value   43

What is the value in a business?   50

CHAPTER 6: PROTECTION: IDENTIFYING AND CONTROLLING RISK   **61**

The different types of risk   62

Identifying transaction risks through careful planning   62

Identifying landmine risks through due diligence   63

The key areas of due diligence   70

When due diligence goes wrong   77

Other ways of controlling and minimising risk   80

CHAPTER 7: PROCESS: MAKING THE DEAL HAPPEN   **86**

What happens when there is no pre-defined clear process   86

The processes required for a smooth sale   89

CHAPTER 8: PURCHASE STRUCTURE: MAKING THE TRANSFER WORK   **95**

The structure of the purchase   96

The timing of payment   100

How the purchase price is paid   102

CHAPTER 9: YOU'VE BOUGHT THE BUSINESS, NOW WHAT?   **110**

Final buying tips   110

PART II: GROW

CHAPTER 10: BUILDING THE FORTRESS TO PROTECT YOUR GROWING BUSINESS   115

The Fortify methodology   122

CHAPTER 11: IDENTIFY AND PROTECT: FINDING AND SECURING THE VALUE IN YOUR BUSINESS   123

Identify (key value assets)   123

Protect (lock in value)   124

The areas of your business you must identify and protect   125

Using insurance to manage risk   148

CHAPTER 12: PREDICT: ANTICIPATING THE LANDMINES BEFORE THEY BLOW YOU UP   150

Areas of core risk in a business   151

Early warning systems   153

CHAPTER 13: PREVENT: ADDRESSING THE CORE SYSTEMS AND PROCESSES FOR GROWING AND PRESERVING VALUE   157

David and Goliath   157

Approaches to risk prevention   159

The areas of your business that present risk during growth   160

Personal risks   194

CHAPTER 14: UNDERSTAND YOUR ENDGAME   197

A strongly fortified business   197

PART III: EXIT

CHAPTER 15: EXITING IN STYLE   201

Common sale problems   202

How businesses are sold   208

CHAPTER 16: THE FIVE ESSENTIAL DRIVERS OF A SUCCESSFUL SALE   212

A deal salvaged . . . barely   213

Almost a million dollars lost   216

CHAPTER 17: PREPARATION: THE MOST CRITICAL COMPONENT   **219**

The areas of your business you must consider for your exit   220

CHAPTER 18: DEAL STRUCTURE: THE FOUNDATION OF A SUCCESSFUL SALE   **240**

Share sale versus business sale   241

Deferred payments, earnouts and retentions   249

Sales in stages and partial sales   260

Taking shares as part of the purchase price   269

CHAPTER 19: TRANSFERRING VALUE: MAXIMISING WHAT BUYERS WANT   **273**

The customer base   274

Key relationships within the business   275

Intellectual property   277

Lease maximisation   281

Key people   282

CHAPTER 20: PROTECTION: MINIMISING YOUR RISK   **286**

Pre-sale risk   287

Transaction risk   291

Post-sale risk   294

Risk protection   303

CHAPTER 21: PROCESS: SEEING THE DEAL THROUGH   **304**

The top causes of slow deals   305

How to achieve the nirvana of speed and tight processes   307

Understanding the hidden element: emotion   310

CHAPTER 22: THE END OF THE STORY   **316**

A coming flood of competition on exit?   316

One final note   317

It's not as hard as it all may seem   319

CHAPTER 23: JARGON BUSTER: TERMINOLOGY EXPLAINED   **321**

ACKNOWLEDGEMENTS   **329**

ABOUT THE AUTHOR   **331**

PREFACE

Every business acquisition is the birth of something new – a new lease on life, a new opportunity in new hands. And every exit is the opportunity for business owners to realise their dreams of liquidating the asset they have built for often a very long time, through literal sweat and tears (hopefully, not blood as well . . .). This is why I love working with businesses at acquisition and exit.

In other areas, being a lawyer is often centred around conflict and risk, which – to be perfectly frank – is really not something that ever floated my boat. But working at the point of acquisitions and exits gives me an incredible insight into the point where years of hopes, dreams and toil crystalise into a sale for these hard-working owners, after which they sail off into the sunset, clutching their bag of cash and revelling in their new life. It's also where deals done in a single signature can add years of growth to a business.

IT CAN GO WRONG

I love this area so much I built a podcast around it.[1] But over time I began to realise clearly that this is not the story for every business owner. While I saw the happy stories, I also saw that the point of

---

1   Check out the *Deal Room Podcast* on your favourite podcast app. There are hundreds of episodes devoted entirely to the world of buying and selling businesses.

exit can be a time of shattered dreams. Very often there is a massive disparity in what a business owner thinks their business is worth versus what they actually achieve.

Or sometimes business owners don't even realise the missed opportunity at the day of exit – the reality they are facing versus what they *could* have achieved had they understood value drivers and exit preparation a little more. The intrinsic value in their business has been depleted both by stepping on landmines along the way and through the failure to have built the business in a way that creates value for a buyer.

Or worse still, in so many cases I've seen people who have not even made it to exit – they have blown up the business before reaching this point.

In all of these instances, these people devoted *so much* time and effort to their businesses. But ultimately, they have missed out on having their business deliver them the value that could have been.

And as the tapestry of experiences in dealing with these businesses started to unfold for me over the years, it became hugely apparent there were a number of key elements that contribute to the ultimate success of our clients: in acquiring businesses, in growing them, and in their ultimate exit.

WHEN IT GOES RIGHT

My clients who found their own nirvana at exit had a number of things in common:

- They **acquired** (either as a beginning, or as a growth tool for their business) with a clear vision of the value they were after, how to maximise that value during the transaction and after, and how to minimise and manage the risks in the transaction and ongoing business.
- They **grew** the business understanding what creates value – future return, not just current-day return. And as they grew, they fiercely protected that value by building the foundations

of their business in a way that allowed them to weather the inevitable storms along the way.

- And finally, as they approached **exit**, they primed their business for market based on their understanding of the value that a buyer would be looking for and the risks that would diminish value in a buyer's eyes. They understood how to play the game of exit, to extract maximum value for themselves, on terms that worked for them.

And so it is that we have our business cycle of buy, grow (and often buying again! Followed by more growth . . .) and exit. Where the understanding of each of these elements, and their interaction with each other, is the secret sauce to **ensuring that the years of effort of growing a business can truly be leveraged.** Where **today's work produces not just today's gains, but also feeds into increasing the underlying value of the asset along the way,** so that at exit there is substantial value that can be extracted. And where **running a business in a sale-ready state ironically provides not just the best business at exit but also the best business to run in the meantime**.

In this book, we examine not just the three phases but the *interaction* of the three phases of business in acquisition, growth and exit. I am always amazed at how many businesses are started (or acquired), grown and sold without ever having properly considered this trilogy in an integrated way. Because understanding the interaction of these three areas is the key to using a business to effectively build wealth, and ultimately, freedom.

TURNING THE DISCUSSION ON ITS HEAD

Buy, Grow, Exit. is about turning the usual business discussion on its head. It is about how to approach these three different phases of business with long-term vision. The underpinning insight requires understanding core value and core risk. It also requires establishing systems and procedures to identify and protect that value and the

The understanding
and interaction
of the cycle of
BUY, GROW and **EXIT**
is the secret sauce to
ensuring you are
BUILDING A BUSINESS
that can truly be
leveraged, so at exit
there is substantial
value that can be
extracted.

assets underpinning it, while predicting and preventing problems before they occur. This book takes you through the process of digging into these areas and working out how at each phase you can maximise value and minimise risk.

Your progression through this book may not be linear.

If you are at (or close to) the point of sale, you may not think you are interested in acquisition.

If you are at the position of newly entering into a business through acquisition, or looking at acquisition as a growth tool, you may not think you are interested in the topic of exit.

And in the midst of growth, you might not be thinking about either acquisition or exit.

But this is precisely the point. While this book is designed so that you can flip to the stage that is relevant to where your business is now, the book as a whole gives the required context to fully understand and make the most of each stage.

When you are exiting, you will benefit from understanding what's in the minds of your buyer.

When you are acquiring, you will benefit from understanding how to protect the assets you have bought, and in truly understanding what will provide value for you once you take this business you are acquiring to exit.

When you are in growth mode, you will benefit from understanding how acquisition can help to achieve growth, and how running in an exit-ready state makes for a better business to run. And most importantly, you will absolutely benefit from understanding what creates value at exit, so that the decisions you are making today take into account (and maximise) the endgame.

And while *Buy, Grow, Exit.* contains lots of long-term strategies, it also contains nuggets of gold that will provide immediate assistance in each phase.

Wherever you are in the process, it's never too late to understand the principles behind driving great deals – and ultimately in maximising the value and minimising the risk in using business acquisition, growth and sale as your ultimate wealth-creation vehicle.

Ultimately, the point of this book is to dive deeply into why the interaction between buying, growing and selling will help pave the way in driving highly successful deals in acquisitions and exits, and in protecting and enhancing the value of the business between acquisition and exit by building a legal fortress around the core assets.

A DISCLAIMER . . . OF SORTS

Firstly, before we dig into how to use this book, I want to make a disclaimer . . . because I am after all a lawyer (so I just can't help myself).

I want to make it clear that I am writing this book from my perspective as a lawyer.

I'm not a marketing consultant, I'm not a growth specialist, I'm not a business coach. And I've never formally studied any of those areas.

I have however worked with businesses for decades during their periods of buying, growing and exiting, and have seen very clearly what has worked and what hasn't.

I have interviewed hundreds of professionals on my podcast digging into these issues, and I am constantly involved in discussions about the conundrum of the wave of baby boomer businesses that are now starting to hit the market and are set to create market saturation.

I have spoken ad nauseum to literally thousands of accountants, business brokers and corporate advisers who also – like me – deal with businesses every day at the points of acquisition, growth and exit, so many of whom are dealing with sellers who are disappointed at the true value of their business (or more particularly, the amount they will end up having in their pocket). Or sellers who don't even make it to an exit because the intrinsic value in their business has been depleted as it wasn't built with a mind to what creates value for a buyer.

And so, in this book, I'm not pretending to hold all the answers about how to grow a business and extract the maximum value from it. But I am providing an insight into how to look at that value in a way that you may not have considered before. And into how viewing your current business, or any acquisition targets, through that lens will help you:

- buy the right business in the right way
- grow your business so that you maximise its value and so that value is protected along the way
- exit in a grand fashion, to extract the wealth you deserve.

HOW TO USE THIS BOOK

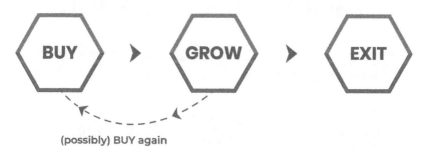

This book has three parts: Buy, Grow and Exit. And each of these charts a different point in the lifecycle of a business.

Part I, Buy, is most relevant if you are . . . buying – *go figure!*

You might be starting out in business and are at the point of that initial acquisition, or perhaps you are in growth mode and are using acquisitions as a growth tool. This is where you need to understand the strategy of acquisition. What you need to look out for. How to maximise the value you can extract, and minimise the risk. And how to ensure the processes along the way support, rather than under-mine, this approach.

Part II, Grow, describes the necessary phases of growth and consol-idation. This is an extremely important phase to come back to after every acquisition, during any period of fast growth, and before exit.

Part II, Grow, describes the necessary phases of growth and consolidation. This is an **EXTREMELY IMPORTANT** phase to come back to after every acquisition, during any period of fast growth, and before exit.

It's the phase that protects the assets you have bought and built, and locks in that value. It's also the phase where you get to set the business up in a way that will maximise its value, and the value you will be able to extract.

The decisions made in this phase impact your tax outcomes, and therefore the ultimate cash you will see out of a sale. But they also impact whether you will even make it to a sale. Because this is the critical phase for a business, of testing the strength of the fortress that has been built around the business.

During the growth and consolidation phase, every business faces repeated and often unexpected landmines along the way. Those landmines will threaten not just to erode the value in a business, but sometimes threaten its very existence. So in this phase, we lay the right foundations for maximising value, and we build the fortress around the business to fiercely protect that value.

And in part III, Exit, you are in the final phase of value extraction. This is the pointy end, where it's imperative to understand the methodology of the sale process, and to understand the potential bumps along the way so they don't throw you off course. It's also where it's important to understand the levers you can pull, and ultimately how to control the deal and the risks, so you can maximise the pot of gold at the end of that business rainbow.

So your progress through this book will most likely not be linear. You may be at a specific point in the business where one of these phases is most relevant.

Where are you in this cycle?

And so without further ado, I bring you part I, Buy.

Part 1

BUY

CHAPTER 1: HOW AND WHY BUSINESSES ARE BOUGHT   3

CHAPTER 2: WHY ACQUISITIONS FAIL   21

CHAPTER 3: THE FIVE ESSENTIAL DRIVERS OF A SUCCESSFUL PURCHASE   31

CHAPTER 4: PREPARATION: BEING ACQUISITION READY   33

CHAPTER 5: PRIMARY VALUE: ENSURING THE TRANSFER OF KEY VALUE   43

CHAPTER 6: PROTECTION: IDENTIFYING AND CONTROLLING RISK   61

CHAPTER 7: PROCESS: MAKING THE DEAL HAPPEN   86

CHAPTER 8: PURCHASE STRUCTURE: MAKING THE TRANSFER WORK   95

CHAPTER 9: YOU'VE BOUGHT THE BUSINESS, NOW WHAT?   110

Before you delve into this part, I recommend that you start by measuring your acquisition readiness by taking our very short scorecard. Find the scorecard at our resources hub at www.buygrowexit.com.au.

Chapter 1

HOW AND WHY BUSINESSES ARE BOUGHT

Acquisitions, done right, provide the ultimate opportunity to build extraordinary wealth.

The reasons for buying a business (or into a business) vary. You might be acquiring to start out in business, or replacing a job with a business, sometimes referred to as 'acquisition entrepreneurship'. Or you might be acquiring a business for the growth of your existing business. You might be setting out on a directed path of consolidating businesses, perhaps to eventually sell them in a trade sale or through an initial public offering (IPO). Or you might be acquiring a parcel of shares in a company as an investor, or in a business you are already working for.

Whatever your reason for the acquisition, and whatever the size of your acquisition 'target' (the business you are buying, or buying into), the fundamentals of acquisition remain the same. In this part, we investigate what those fundamentals are to help you drive acquisition success.

Let's look at some of the different ways business are acquired.

ACQUISITION ENTREPRENEURSHIP

'Acquisition entrepreneurship' is a term that describes starting an entrepreneurial journey by acquiring and building up an existing business (or series of businesses) rather than by starting a new business from the ground up.

By acquiring a business that's already generating revenue, you can avoid the pain and hard work of startup, and also a lot of the associated risk (given the high rate of failure for startups).

Buying a business gives you access to established systems and customer and supplier bases which have already stood the test of time. You get to confirm in advance that there is a market for the product or service (by the proven revenue base). And it gives you an ability to evaluate the business and its current processes, and to work out how you might inject new ideas to optimise it.

By buying a business you also avoid the often long lead time involved with starting from scratch, and can simply focus on implementing improvements, scaling the business, or any other growth strategy.

ACQUISITION AS A SUPERCHARGED PATH TO GROWTH

Acquisition can also be an extremely powerful move even if you already have an existing business – as a supercharged path to growth.

This is one of my absolute favourite topics. I am an entrepreneur at heart, and the opportunities for SMEs to grow exponentially through acquisition excite me. But this is so often overlooked by businesses that spend years and decades in the grind of slow organic growth, completely overlooking the power of this alternative pathway.

The power of acquisitions to add years of growth in a single signature is widely understood by large corporations, who consistently use M&A[2] and bolt-on acquisitions to grow.

---

2   Mergers and acquisitions. Check out chapter 23 for more jargon busting!

Statista reports that in 2019, the global value of M&A deals amounted to US$3.4 trillion. What's more astounding is that in 2020, despite the COVID-19 pandemic ravaging countries all over the world, global M&A deals still totalled a whopping US$2.8 trillion. And in a recent report, McKinsey & Company reveal research that confirms companies that regularly and systematically pursue moderately sized M&A deliver better shareholder returns than companies that don't.

But it is a little-known secret that this strategy can work just as well for SMEs to grow. And indeed, the size of a business can be critical not just to growth, but also to survival. Recent statistics in Australia, compiled by the Australian Bureau of Statistics and the Australian Small Business and Family Enterprise Ombudsman, have painted a very clear picture that when looking at the survival of businesses over a four-year period, the greater the size of a business, the higher its rate of survival.

Thus, ultimately for many small businesses, acquisitions can play a crucial role in determining their commercial success and, ultimately, survival.

So let's investigate why acquisition is such a killer growth strategy.

ORGANIC GROWTH VS ACQUISITION GROWTH

In the main, SMEs focus on organic approaches to growth. But the one overarching issue with organic growth is that it's slow! On the other hand, strategic acquisitions can (if done right) achieve growth rapidly. So, while organic growth offers control, the reality is that years of organic growth can be achieved in a single deal through a strategic acquisition.

I have had some fabulous discussions with clients who have looked over their years (often decades) of business building and finally come to this realisation after their first or second acquisition. One client in particular comes to mind: Jerry. Jerry recently recounted the story to me of the history of his consulting business, which had seen him spend a decade in long, hard growth. On the outside his business looked like a success, but the grind of their focus on organic growth had worn him and his business partners down. On the advice of an adviser, they decided to look at alternative strategies for growth and started pursuing acquisitions. Jerry recounted to me that he had a pivotal moment on the day he signed the contract for his first acquisition – when it suddenly struck him that he was now doubling his revenue in a single signature. His first millions took him a decade. But through acquisition, his next millions happened in just a few months. Of course, it came with a price, but the leverage it brought him and his partners allowed them to scale in a way they couldn't possibly have achieved organically in even a fraction of the time, and ultimately the business quickly went from strength to strength off the back of that acquisition, and he went on to do many more in the future.

This lightbulb moment is just not seen very often in the SME business world.

Some of the most successful business owners I know work religiously with this acquisition approach, and continue to build empires around them – empires that run with much less effort and grind than the rest of my clients that I see who are stuck in organic growth mode.

So many businesses continue the daily struggle to clamber their way to growth to try to make it to a size that will sustain them. You will soon read the stories of some of the minority that have discovered the power of acquisition for growth and that are now revelling in the spoils that it can bring.

While I won't pretend that acquisitions are just as simple as turning up and signing a document, the reality is that an acquisition done well will immediately increase revenue, but the biggest win is the impact on the value of the business. So, while an acquisition of a similar-sized business might double the revenue, the goal is to triple

So many businesses continue the

DAILY STRUGGLE

to clamber their way to growth to try to make it to a size that will sustain them.

or quadruple the ultimate value – to achieve an uplift in the value of the business you have just acquired simply from the benefits you can now access from the increased size.

Let's take a closer look at what these benefits are.

THE BENEFITS OF ACQUISITION FOR GROWTH

The top three benefits of acquisition for growth that we see being utilised most fully by our SME clients are:

- the ability to add clients and revenue while being able to strip costs out of the acquired business
- the ability to add to their current service or product set (to enable cross-selling and upselling, the provision of a fuller solution to both client bases, and to make clients more 'sticky')
- the ability to access business value arbitrage.

Let's examine these three.

A CHEAPER WAY TO ADD CLIENTS AND ACCESS ECONOMIES OF SCALE

Many of our clients who are pursuing an acquisition strategy have as their main driver the ability to add to their client base immediately, thus increasing their total revenue, while being able to strip out costs that are sitting in the target business (such as reception, administration, accounting, marketing and other services that can be often partly or fully absorbed into the existing business's overheads).

Often where the price for the target business is based on the current profit in that business, the **profit** in that business will jump immediately after many of the costs are ripped out on the basis that the acquiring business can take them over with their current over-heads. Therefore, the **value** of the acquired business also immediately increases providing a fabulous, almost immediate, uplift in the value of the asset you have just purchased.

For example, we work with many accounting practices who adopt an acquisition strategy for growth. Generally when they acquire an additional accounting practice, they are able to strip out a lot of the costs of the acquired accounting practice by moving them into their current infrastructure. This allows a massive acceleration in the profit from the acquired entity, and greater return overall.

Obviously some costs can't be entirely absorbed by the current business, but many of those types of costs can be paired with the spending of the current business and together – due to greater buying power – this can achieve better pricing through economies of scale.

A LEVERAGED WAY TO PROVIDE MORE SERVICES OR PRODUCTS
Acquisitions can give you the platform to offer a better solution to your clients through giving them access to more holistic services, where your acquisition serves to add new services or products to your current offerings.

The addition of extra services or products also provides a highly leveraged opportunity to upsell and cross-sell to the customer base of both businesses. You will have a new set of products and services to offer your current clients from the offerings provided by the acquired business. And you will also then have an opportunity to upsell and cross-sell to the customers of the acquired business with the services or products of your current business.

This ultimately results in not only a massive opportunity to increase the leads and revenue for each business separately, but it also produces a better, more complete, customer solution for both sets of client bases. The other benefit of adding more products and services is that it makes your clients more 'sticky'.

Examples of how to apply this strategy well include seeking a target that has services to complement your existing products, or vice versa. Or simply to add on to your existing service or product offering.

If we use the example again of accounting practices, typical acquisitions in this industry revolve around adding financial planning, mortgage and insurance businesses, which not only enable an accounting practice to extend the services they can offer their current clients but also provide them with the client bases of each of these additional businesses to sell their accounting services to.

This shows how acquisitions can provide incredible leverage. And of course if you are acquiring multiple businesses, this ability to cross-sell can provide exponential increases in value for each additional type of service or product business you add.

A WAY TO CREATE BUSINESS VALUE ARBITRAGE

Most businesses simply think about profit in considering the value of their business, but another essential consideration is the **multiplier** that will be applied to the profit to arrive at a sale value.[3] There is a general rule of thumb that SMEs are valued at around about 3× profit. But in reality, the multipliers used for each individual business can vary hugely. Generally speaking, our SME clients can sell or buy somewhere in the range of a multiplier between as low as 1, all the way up to about 10.[4]

There are lots of considerations behind what multiplier will apply to a particular business, and one of those considerations is size. Often the greater the size, the higher the multiple that will apply. In very simple terms, this means that you might be able to acquire a business for 2× profit but once you merge it into your existing larger business, the value of that business jumps to 3× profit. So if the business you

---

3   When I say 'profit' or 'earnings' in this book, I mean operating profit (revenue minus the operating expenses) which is essentially for our purposes the same as the term EBITDA – a term that is used in the world of business acquisitions. See chapter 23 – the jargon buster – for the definitions of EBIT and EBITDA. You will need to get used to these terms if you venture into buying or selling a business, as they are standard terms industry wide, but for simplicity in this book I'll use the everyday terms of 'earnings' and 'profit'.

4   As an aside, there are certain types of businesses where there may not be any profit yet, or where value sits in something other than revenue or profit, so value will be calculated in other ways.

are acquiring has a profit of $500k, and you are buying it at a multiple of 2 – you will purchase it for $1m.

If by adding it to your existing business, you are then able to increase the multiple from 2 to 3 because of the increase in size, the value of that business suddenly becomes $1.5m (3 × profit of $500k = $1.5m). As opposed to the old valuation based on the smaller size of 2× profit. So there is an almost immediate increase in value of $500k, just by the multiplier moving.

But wait, there's more! Your **existing** business may also increase its multiple. If your business prior to acquisition also has $500k in profit with a 2× multiple then prior to the acquisition it also had a value of $1m. And if its multiple increases to 3× because of the uplift in size, then its value will also increase to $1.5m.

So when you add the two uplifts together you can see that you may have **paid $1m for an acquisition**, but have suddenly **added $2m to the business** (when you add together the value of the initial $1m + another $500k uplift from each entity due to the increased multiple).

Now if you can achieve that sort of increase in price (business value arbitrage), I think anyone would agree that is good buying!

		BEFORE ACQUISITION		AFTER ACQUISITION	
	PROFIT	MULTIPLE	VALUE (PROFIT × MULTIPLE)	HIGHER MULTIPLE DUE TO COMBINED SIZE	VALUE (PROFIT × MULTIPLE)
Existing Business	$500,000	2	$1,000,000	3	$1,500,000
Acquisition Target	$500,000	2	$1,000,000	3	$1,500,000
	Total value of the individual businesses		$2,000,000	Total value of the combined business after acquisition	$3,000,000
				Cost of acquisition	$1,000,000
				Increased value from acquisition	$2,000,000

Of course, I have oversimplified this for the purposes of explanation of the concept, and you will have to do work to dig into what the drivers are of the valuation multipliers in your industry and how size is likely to impact those drivers. But these figures illustrate the concept that so many businesses miss entirely.

We have many clients who have clicked onto the power of this approach, across many industries. For example, one of our clients is a dental aggregator. There is often very little sale value in each individual practice that they acquire. But when aggregated, each of these small practices add up to a whole that will ultimately provide a rich opportunity for IPO, or just a much higher multiple for a trade sale due to the ultimate size achieved with the practices aggregated together. This particular aggregator uses a model which often encourages the sellers to maintain some equity in the business, so that they too get to participate in the uplift of the value that is brought by the increased size of the whole business together. Genius.

––––––

Here are a bunch of other benefits that an acquisition for growth can bring:

- **Access to new markets (or quicker access to new markets) and expansion of geographical reach.** Acquisition of a business that's based in another location instantly allows the acquiring company to gain a foothold in that area for distributing its original products or services. In addition to this, combining the assets of both businesses often enables the resulting business to expand into new locations that were previously not served by either entity.
- **Cost reduction by targeting upstream or downstream of the supply chain (vertical integration).** Acquiring a business that's part of your supply chain (for example, a furniture retailer buying a business that manufactures furniture) can lead to huge savings in overhead expenses and costs. Aside from simple costs

savings, acquisitions within your supply chain can also help to reduce supply chain risk, and increase operational efficiency.

- **Access to more advanced technology.** Acquisition gives businesses the opportunity to upgrade their technology or access new technology that would otherwise require a long process to create organically.
- **Increased workforce.** Acquisitions typically increase personnel size. Each team member comes with their own unique set of industry knowledge, skills and experience – all of which are valuable in propelling the business to greater success. These employees are also very likely to have an already existing network of industry contacts, which further widens the business's potential reach and impact. This value in talent acquisition has recently become more important as we have moved into a tight labour market, a trend which is likely to increase into the future.
- **Access new expertise.** Acquisitions are a great way to add new expertise to your business. Many of our clients' acquisitions of very small businesses are driven simply by wanting to scoop up talented staff – sometimes referred to as 'aqui-hire' (hiring through acquisition).
- **Greater market share.** When you acquire a business that is related to or complements your own products and services, you will also increase your share of the market by taking out competitors. Ultimately larger market share is generally tied to improved value through increased efficiency, and easier brand recognition in the market.

GIVE ME SOME EXAMPLES!

I have so many examples of businesses where acquisition for growth has achieved incredible outcomes.

We've already examined our clients in the accounting industry, who have achieved amazing results from using acquisitions to quickly expand their client base and their service offering. This not only nets them an uplift in revenue, but given they are able to rip out significant costs in the acquired entities due to duplication, they also get an uplift in the value of the acquired entity after those costs have been stripped out – providing an immediate return on their acquisition spend. And when the acquired entities provide new service offerings, they have also been able to get a further uplift from the upsell and cross-sell opportunities.

We have also seen great returns with clients who run gyms and health centres. This is another industry where multiple sites can be a licence to print money. And while it can always be an option to open a brand-new site[5], acquiring an existing business with an existing client base is generally the much faster route to adding locations. And this is particularly attractive when the cost of the acquisition can be quickly offset with the gains that can be made through being able to run the acquired business cheaper through economies of scale and the absorption of many running costs like being able to share management (and take on higher quality management personnel as a shared resource) and overheads (like accounting, bookkeeping, CFO, administration and marketing).

We have clients who run business coaching, who have added on acquisitions of complementary businesses such as marketing and recruitment. These additional business units have given them the power to offer their clients incredible holistic growth services (rather than just business coaching) while also using the client bases of each individual business to upsell and cross-sell to the other merged businesses – contributing to a massive and fast increase in the size and reach of each of those merged businesses.

Our clients have also reported great uplifts in the performance of both the acquired and the acquiring businesses through greater business insights – for example:

---

5   Often referred to as a 'greenfield' site or business.

- marketing that has worked well for one business
- management techniques that lead to strong team performance
- approaches used by one team that could be replicated across the other in dealing with customers.

Essentially our clients have reported that acquisitions have enabled them to pull the best out of each business and replicate it across the others.

We have clients in the dental industry who are successfully using this growth through acquisition approach. There are aggregators who do this on a large scale, but also the smaller practices who have clicked on to the benefits of bolting a few practices together to get the benefits of greater scale. They often:

- share specialists between practices (increasing the service offering of each practice to enable upsells)
- achieve greater buying power and use shared resources to reduce costs
- share insights from one practice to the other (for example, successful marketing techniques).

We also have clients in recruitment, marketing, technology, software as a service (SAAS), retail, manufacturing, home services, professional services and many other industries who have achieved so many of these benefits.

The opportunities are real, but they are missed by so many businesses who just haven't even considered the possibilities.

Are you one of them . . . ?

ACQUISITIONS TO INCREASE YOUR MULTIPLE FOR EXIT

Contrarian advice: before you exit it might be a good idea to look at acquisitions as a way to increase your size, or fill out your service or product offering.

In an earlier section on business value arbitrage we considered the concept of how value at sale is often based on the multiplier that

Contrarian advice: before you exit it might be a good idea to look at acquisitions as a way to INCREASE YOUR SIZE, or fill out your service or product offering.

is applied to the earnings, and how that multiplier can often increase as the size of the business increases. For example, micro businesses can sell as low as 1× earnings. But larger SMEs can attract multiples of at least 3× or 4× earnings, and often much more depending on the industry.

Very simply, this means that sometimes if you are gearing up to exit, you can use acquisitions to add value quickly to your business prior to exit. Those acquisitions can potentially provide three benefits on the sale value, by:

- increasing the profit that a multiplier will be applied to
- increasing the multiple that will apply to the earnings in your current business
- increasing the multiplier to be applied to the part of the business that you have just acquired.

So you might find that you can spend a bit of money prior to exit acquiring businesses to increase your size (and multiple), and achieve an exponential uplift in total value.

As I write, our team is working with two clients who are doing exactly this. One of those clients is in engineering, and spent 14 years slowly growing his business. He came to us as he started to consider selling the business, having been approached by buyers at around about a multiple of 4× profit. But in the process of sale he came to the realisation that there were a bunch of businesses on the market in his industry that were smaller and were selling at less than half his multiple. Being good with numbers, he realised very quickly that he could buy one of these smaller entities and immediately double its value (given he would buy it at a multiple of less than 2, but then roll it into his current entity that was being valued by prospective buyers at a multiple of more than 4). So he cleverly decided to acquire one of those smaller players and double the acquisition price overnight, in addition to adding a lot of extra general value in the business through extra technology and personnel from the acquisition.

It's so exciting to see businesses come across opportunities like this that can greatly increase their value at sale, but just sad that often the idea hadn't come far earlier in the lifecycle of the business to enable them to use the strategy multiple times over to maximise the impact.

ACQUISITIONS FOR ROLL UPS

Another approach to acquisitions is a directed path of consolidating fragmented industries through a 'roll up'. A roll up is when an investor buys up multiple small companies in the same market and combines them into a larger entity. This provides economies of scale, expanded geographic coverage, great brand recognition (if the acquired entities are re-branded), and can also sometimes be used to merge companies with complementary capabilities that will enable them to together provide more products or services than they could as smaller, independent businesses.

It can lead to significant cost reductions in the long run as well as a greater share of the market.

Consolidated businesses can also get cheaper financing if the new entity is more stable, more profitable, or has more assets that can serve as collateral. (But, sometimes financing can be more difficult in a roll up than in an acquisition of a single business, as it can involve more complex financing considerations.) Being larger, the new company can likewise negotiate better terms with suppliers and offer a wider range of products or services.

Given that larger businesses are generally valued at a higher multiple of earnings than smaller businesses, this consolidation of smaller businesses can provide an immediate uplift in the value of the acquired entities (simply because as part of a bigger business, their earnings are now valued at this higher multiple – on the basis of the business value arbitrage approach we discussed earlier).

Roll ups are a favourite tool of private equity firms, which have earned billions using it. And we have clients using this approach to varying degrees. Some are only aiming for a handful of acquisitions to roll up over a number of years, whereas others have their sights on a more aggressive acquisition path, working through hundreds and hundreds of targets, aiming towards tens of acquisitions (or in some cases 50 or more) over a short time span.

Ultimately the end game for roll ups is generally a timed exit (often over a short-term period of five to seven years) via a trade sale or through an IPO.

ACQUISITIONS FOR INVESTMENT

Acquiring shares in an SME can also be a great form of investment without needing to necessarily be part of the management or operation of the business.

Most SMEs will aim for a profit level of between 10% and 25%, and of course many SMEs will achieve far higher (but also possibly lower!) than this. By choosing a solid business to hold equity in, you have the opportunity for not just distributions out of the profit each year, but also (and often most lucratively) a stake in the pie of the future sale value of the business.

This is a favoured form of investment by investors who have a willingness to contribute capital to help fund expansion of a business, or who have business experience that they are willing to offer in the form of mentorship for the management of the business – with the aim of the capital and (or) the mentorship intended to help fuel expansion of the size and value of the business.

We work with many buyers who are investors in businesses, and many businesses who sell part of their equity to investors, to achieve fast and strong growth – and have seen this enrich both the founders and the investors.

MANAGEMENT BUYOUTS

Acquisitions will often also be made by employees.

The term 'management buyout' (MBO) is often used for this sort of transaction – where the management team purchases the business.

But for many SMEs this is not necessarily limited to the management team (given many SMEs often don't have a structured management team) – so often in SME world this terminology is more broadly used to refer to an acquisition by an employee or group of employees.

A sale to employees makes a lot of sense for both the founder and the employees buying in. The business is known to the buyers, and therefore the level of due diligence required and operational handover post sale is far reduced. This approach also provides the employee buyers the potential for far greater control and rewards financially than they had as employees. This can be a great succession strategy for a business owner, and also a fabulous retention strategy to keep on board the best players by offering them ownership over time.

This type of acquisition will in some cases be funded by the seller through payments agreed to be made over time. Sometimes this might even be negotiated by the employee buyers to be paid slowly enough to enable it to be funded to a large degree by dividends (coming from the profits of the business).

Chapter 2

WHY ACQUISITIONS FAIL

While there is obviously so much opportunity in acquisitions, there is also another side: not every acquisition is a success. Indeed, there are many well-known studies on large M&A deals that report failure rates of up to 70% of M&A deals – so, almost three out of four deals are deemed a 'failure' by the organisations involved.

Most of these studies relate to public companies and large deals, and my anecdotal evidence is that 'failure' rates in SME world are significantly lower than this figure. But I have certainly seen many examples of deals that would probably be seen as not meeting the goals that buyers had in mind for their acquisitions.

I have seen countless people buy businesses in new industries, having one impression of the industry, only to decide to sell soon after (sometimes less than a year after) when they realised the reality was different to their dreams of it.

I have had clients who have gone into a business acquisition in partnerships, where the relationship between the partners has failed and the business needs to be re-sold. And I've also seen many instances where the dreams and plans haven't quite come to fruition, often caused by issues that were avoidable.

While there are many advantages in acquiring for growth, it can also come with disadvantages. It can be costly and complicated at the outset. It may also result in culture clashes in the combined workforce. Management also need to deal with possible redundancies in personnel, look into the need to sell assets, and prepare for branding the new company.

THE MOST COMMON REASONS WHY DEALS DON'T SUCCEED

So, I have over time created a list of the most common reasons why deals don't achieve the success that was planned:

LACK OF INDUSTRY EXPERIENCE

If a buyer lacks deep experience in the industry that they are buying into, this can create a significant risk that the buyers miss key elements of the evaluation of the business they are acquiring. It can also result in the buyer's ideas about what may increase the post-acquisition performance of the business not coming to fruition.

I have seen many acquisitions fall into this category.

Of course, one of the reasons for acquisitions is to gain access to skillsets and perhaps also coverage in industries that you have not had previously. But if you are looking at an acquisition in a completely new industry, you need to tread with caution and ensure that protections you are making on how the acquired business will perform are based on sound principles rather than assumptions. You need to ensure you have the right team around you who do understand the industry you are buying into. That can help you make a realistic assessment of the target business and future projections, and identify value and risk in the target to ensure these are properly dealt with during the acquisition and in the post-acquisition transition.

MAKING CHANGES TOO QUICKLY

I find that this is a common issue – buyers come in full of energy and exuberance to implement their ideas of what the business should look like. However, often they have no idea how destructive rapid change can be in causing destabilisation of staff, customers and particularly the prior owners if those sellers will continue to be connected to the business in some way.

Sellers will often continue to be connected to the business after deal completion if there is a transition phase from the seller to the buyer, or an earnout or retention or other deferred payment arrangement where the seller continues to be invested in the performance of the business.

I have seen some explosive examples of sellers and buyers in this phase having terrible fallouts, substantially impacting the client base and the staff.

The seller often has an emotional connection not just to the business but the way in which the business is run. And when they have money on the line connected to the ongoing performance, it is very common that too many changes too quickly will put them offside and potentially create a damaging environment that can impede a smooth transition.

The clients and the staff also often have an emotional connection to the business as it was pre-sale.

So, changes should be implemented slowly and carefully. And most importantly, only after a significant settling in period.

TENSION FROM KEEPING PREVIOUS OWNERS IN (OR INVESTED IN) THE BUSINESS FOR TOO LONG AFTER THE SALE

As discussed above, many acquisitions will be based around the seller being invested in the business for a period after completion through an earnout, deferred payment or by having them continue to hold onto a minority equity holding. The reason behind this is generally an effort to preserve and transition the core value in the business, where that value has some connection to the seller. For example, if the core value is in the client base and the buyer believes that the seller will need to personally help transition clients over time. Or where the core value sits in the transfer of knowledge.

But the risk here for both parties is that the seller does not integrate well with the buyer or how the buyer runs the business.

The reality is that many sellers have built their business over multiple years (often decades) without being answerable to anyone – and in doing so they have made themselves (and often see themselves) as unemployable. They really don't want to be answering to anyone, and often they just aren't good at playing that role. And while they may submit to this for a short period to secure the sale, the reality is that tension often sets in very quickly.

I've spoken to many owners who have exited but been required to stay around for an earnout, and they often call this one of the most stressful periods they have had. And if they are stressed, everyone is stressed! So, it's critical that as a buyer, if you are using an earnout or some other mechanism to keep the seller in the business, you understand this issue and find ways to set up the relationship from the beginning to minimise the potential for problems.

A FALLING OUT AMONG THE BUYER GROUP

This is often simply because of a lack of clarity between the group of buyers on critical issues such as decision making, risk appetite, future direction and how (and when) any of the parties – or all of them – can orchestrate an exit. Fortunately, this can be prevented to a large extent by ensuring a proper shareholders' agreement is in place, and that the right issues have been discussed and agreed in advance. (We cover this is much greater detail in part II.)

LACK OF DUE DILIGENCE AND GENERAL UNDERSTANDING OF THE BUSINESS

A lack of due diligence can be a massive risk in an acquisition, and can lead to either the purchase of a business with issues lurking in it that haven't been obvious from the surface, or the purchase of a business that doesn't provide the intended outcome. Examples of problems caused by risks in a business that haven't been identified from the outset are numerous, and there are countless stories of buyers who have ended up with massive ongoing problems as a result of issues that could have been identified through proper due diligence.

We have also seen many examples of business acquisitions that just don't generate the benefits that were intended. For example, we've acted for a number of buyers who have bought businesses as part of a push into new markets who have wanted to save costs by limiting due diligence and subsequently based a lot of their investigations on discussions with the seller. They were often focused almost entirely on the purchase price, not the ongoing running of the business or ongoing risk.

In many cases the buyers have lasted only a few years in the business (and as mentioned previously, we have seen buyers even last less than 12 months!) before they turned around and re-sold the business (usually at a lower price than they bought it for) because the business didn't match their dream for it. And of course in the process, they lost not just all the time and cost involved in the transaction itself, but also often suffered a decrease in the capital value, simply because they didn't want to spend money at the front end checking properly.

———

As I have said, studies on M&A success rates (or more particularly, failure rates) revolve around large acquisitions, and mostly on the activity of public companies. There is a massive lack of data on the success rates of SMEs in this area.

There are many reasons for this lack of data.

Firstly, SME M&A is a smaller market. M&A is a strategy used regularly by listed entities to enable their organisations to continue to grow. But, as we have discussed, SMEs are often completely unaware of this as an option for growth for them.

The second reason is that data from public companies is much easier to obtain, given they have reporting obligations to the market, whereas private companies have no similar reporting requirements.

The final reason I believe also lies in the approach of SMEs. Reporting on 'failure' rates suggests that there is some measure that has been established to indicate whether there has been success or failure, and that someone has the ability to analyse this and come up with an answer. In my experience, many SMEs who are acquiring don't have a predefined measure of what 'success' looks like. They don't have KPIs that they are looking to meet. And they often lack a clearly defined plan for the acquisition and transition so that they can ultimately reflect on it as a success or a failure. And this is in itself perhaps the biggest failure of all.

So if you are intending to embark on an acquisition (or multiple acquisitions), take note of this high reported 'failure' rate. While I don't believe that this number is fully representative of what SMEs would report from their acquisitions, these statistics do serve as a reminder that if you are going to look to utilise acquisition as part of your growth plan, you need to take care to do it right and you must have in mind a clear vision of what success looks like.

TRANSACTION FAILURE

But it's not just about 'failure' of the acquisition after completion; the other important consideration (and the reality for many deals) is the failure of the transaction process itself. For example, the deal hits some speedbumps and then takes much more time, energy and money than had been anticipated and is allowed to languish for months and months, wearing down both buyer and seller to a point where they lose trust in each other and lose all the momentum in the deal. Or the deal hits problems that ultimately kill it.

HOW EMOTIONS CAN KILL A DEAL

Often transaction failure is driven by a lack of understanding of the role that emotion plays in a deal. Emotion is such an important part of understanding the potential issues that may arise in a deal that I am now of the opinion that it is one of the largest causes of deals falling over before they get to completion where either the buyer or the seller (or both!) has not regularly been involved in M&A transactions.

It's critical for you to understand as a buyer what the motivations of the sellers are as to why they are selling. If it is a business that the sellers have built up over a long period, there can be a lot of unexpected emotion for them in letting go of the business that has formed such a large part of their life.

I have seen many deals hit an impasse because, on the face of it, a seller is overly concerned about certain elements of the deal, but ultimately the emotion (coming from the process of major change in their life) is driving the belligerence. This is a regularly repeated issue, and is of critical importance for a buyer to understand. At these times, sellers need to be moved quickly through the process to ensure deal momentum is helping to override any bouts of emotion that creep up.

It is why the process as a whole is extremely important, as we will discuss in later chapters.

But as a buyer it is also important to understand your emotions as well. Emotions generally play out in one of two ways for buyers – they can either be caught up in the emotion of deal fever and just want to get the deal done at all costs. This of course can be dangerous. But on the flipside is the nervous buyer, who can become too easily distracted and overwhelmed by risks.

A great example of how this can play out is a recent deal that involved the sale of a manufacturing business. The deal involved a first-time buyer who initially was extremely motivated to purchase and to move forward quickly. A terms sheet had been agreed, he had gone to great lengths to appoint expensive lawyers and accountants, and he looked ready to go. But as a first-time buyer he was extremely cautious, and he had no-one keeping him to a timeframe or providing the reassurance he needed that the deal could achieve his goals for success.

When he and his deal team commenced due diligence, the deal then languished in that stage for months and months as he and his deal team very slowly worked through every nook and cranny of the business. He over-thought everything, and the time that it was taking his lawyers and accountants seemed to just add to his nervousness. Ultimately he and his team lost perspective of what was normal commercial risk, and he worked himself into a frenzy of concern.

So in the end, of course, the deal fell through – leaving the seller having to start the process all over again. This was a terrible outcome for both parties. The business was hugely impacted by this extended and fruitless sale process, as they had diverted a lot of their attention to dealing with the process and this buyer. And the buyer lost out on a good deal, having spent all this time and presumably massive adviser costs without having anything to show for it.

It was a sad example of what can go wrong when a nervous buyer hasn't worked to a timeframe and hasn't been surrounded by advisers who could reassure him about how he could minimise and manage his risk, rather than him feeling that the risks he was seeing were insurmountable.

———

Of course, emotions are not the only cause of transaction failure. In fact, there is a long list! It includes:

- **Lack of planning and preparation.** The most common cause for a deal falling over before the finish line is a lack of planning and preparation by one (or both) of the parties. For example, often the seller simply will not have due diligence information ready as it is requested, forcing a long delay as they scrape together items from often a long buyer due diligence list.

This engenders distrust immediately in the mind of the buyer, sets the deal off on the wrong course, and creates early speedbumps that can ultimately be the downfall of the deal. Alternatively, we often see instances where a buyer walks into a deal but doesn't have finance or their deal team in place, or simply has not taken the time to properly educate themselves about what they will need to see the deal to conclusion. The consequence is that the process slows down, and never regains momentum (and in some instances where the business is in high demand, buyers can lose the deal to another buyer who is ready to go). Finance is a particular issue in the current market, and buyers that haven't properly secured money in advance can find that finance might be a lot more difficult and time consuming than they had initially anticipated, and in many instances can't be resolved in time to save the deal.

- **The wrong advisers on a deal team.** The advisers for one or both of the parties are slow, uncommercial or aggressive in their dealings, and end up creating so many barriers to the deal that the parties never reach agreement and the deal falls over. (I talk about this issue in detail in chapter 21 on the sale process, and provide some examples of how this issue often plays out.)

- **Adverse outcomes from due diligence.** The buyer's investigations find that the value that was expected in the business is not there, or that the risk in the deal is too high. This however can sometimes be a good reason for transaction failure. If during the deal it comes to light that the business is not as expected, and the failings can't be dealt with by commercial or legal means, often it is appropriate that the transaction is abandoned.

- **Seller disharmony.** Disputes can emerge among the selling party if there are multiple sellers who don't agree on key terms. This can also occur with buyers if there are multiple parties forming a buyer group. But this is much more rare than issues of alignment among multiple sellers.

- **Third-party consent issues.** Third-party consents required for the transfer of contracts in the business (for example franchise agreements, key distribution agreements, supplier contracts, large client contracts, leases) that haven't been planned out properly in advance can block the transfer of key value in the business.
- **Lack of process.** Failure can occur when there is a lack of process for the deal and no-one driving a timeline for due diligence and contract negotiations.
- **Communication issues.** If the communication between the parties is inefficient and driven by emails forwards and backwards, with drafts and redrafts taking months, the parties can slowly lose trust in each other until the deal ultimately falls over.

In our next chapters we look at how to tackle these risk factors, and how to drive your deal to success!

Chapter 3

THE FIVE ESSENTIAL DRIVERS OF A SUCCESSFUL PURCHASE

As you have seen, the list for why deals might fail to achieve their success metrics is quite long. The way to minimise the likelihood of issues impacting your acquisition is to have a clear focus on the drivers of success of the transaction itself, and of the business after completion.

THE 5Ps DRIVING GREAT PURCHASES

In my decades of experience in this industry I have observed a number of these key drivers for buyers, which I have summarised as the 5Ps Driving Great Purchases:

- **Preparation:** being ready to buy when you find the right business. Being ready to pounce!
- **Primary value:** understanding the key value in the business, and how that value will transfer.
- **Protection:** understanding the risks in the transaction and in the business, and putting in place the right elements to manage and minimise that risk.
- **Process:** ensuring you are approaching the deal, the due diligence and the contractual components with the right process in place.
- **Purchase structure:** a critical consideration in structuring the offer, with consideration of:
  - what the sale is – share sale, unit sale, business sale or asset sale
  - the timing of payment
  - how the purchase price is paid. Will it be paid in full at completion, or partly deferred? Is it a set payment, or will it be partly contingent on future performance, or some sort of milestone? Will there be a retention sum to protect against future risk?

Given that an acquisition could be one of the biggest investments you are ever going to make as a business, it's critical that you take the time to understand the drivers for making it a success. We'll dive into each of these in detail in the following chapters.

Chapter 4

PREPARATION: BEING ACQUISITION READY

Being *ready to acquire* is the key to ensuring you are looking for the **right** business, and that you are ready to go when you find it. This is a step that is most often forgotten, but is likely to be the highest predictor of the ultimate success of your new business.[6]

It's important not to launch into a business acquisition on pure emotion, or just based on the meticulous workings you have come to in a spreadsheet. There is so much more to buying and transitioning a business than the pure numbers from your forecasted assumptions.

---

6   If you haven't already taken the acquisition ready scorecard, head over to the resources hub at www.buygrowexit.com.au to get a score now of how acquisition ready you are.

Preparation is a step most often **FORGOTTEN**, but it is likely to be the highest predictor of the **ULTIMATE SUCCESS** of an acquisition.

DEFINING WHAT SUCCESS LOOKS LIKE

Success metrics for acquisitions are often broken down into three focuses: strategic success, financial success, and operational success. Therefore you should be thinking of setting your acquisition goals in this context.

Strategic success is about reflecting on the strategic goals you are looking to achieve, and your own metrics of success:

- What is the purpose of your acquisition?
- What time investment do you want to put in?
- What is your end goal, and how quickly do you want to get there?

Financial success metrics are about setting a goal for the 'shareholder value' that you are looking to achieve:

- What return on investment are you aiming for?
- What revenue do you need from the new acquisition?
- Where this is an acquisition for growth, what revenue do you expect to achieve in the combined entity, and over what period?
- What are you expecting from an uplift in multiple, and the ultimate enterprise value?

And the third criteria of success is **operational success**. In other words:

- What operational goals do you have?
- How might an acquisition help to achieve improved execution of the operations of the business, greater value for the client base, and improvements in the goods or services provided or the way in which they are provided?

PREPARING A STRATEGY

The next step is ensuring you have prepared a solid strategy for the acquisition, based on your understanding of the industry of the target business. Let's consider what this means for first-time buyers and existing business owners.

FIRST-TIME BUYERS

For first-time buyers it's imperative that you take your time to fully understand the industry you are buying into.

Do you know what it takes to work in that industry and to achieve success?

If you are already working within the industry, the next step to the strategy is understanding what makes a business successful within that industry and what your own metrics of success are (as discussed earlier).

Often first-time buyers will have worked as employees in an industry, rather than as business owners. It is critical to understand how owning and running a business might be different to your experience as an employee. Having this understanding will help enormously in being able to identify a business that can be run and grown successfully, and that will meet your expectations of business ownership.

EXISTING BUSINESS OWNERS

If you are acquiring for the growth of an existing business, the questions you need to answer revolve around your strategy for how an acquisition will help you achieve your business objectives. You should ask yourself a few critical questions:

- What are my business goals?
- What specifically will I need in an acquisition target to deliver these goals?
- Do I want to diversify?
- Do I need to cut labour costs? Or administrative costs? Or other costs?
- Do I need to add services or products to my current offerings to enable cross-selling, upselling, and a more holistic solution?
- How much money am I willing to spend on the acquisition, and how quickly do I want to see results?

One of the often-missed considerations by buyers who intend to integrate a target into an existing business is culture.[7] This should start with a consideration of the existing culture in your current business, which can then be used as a basis to analyse the target to determine if it is a good fit – both from a culture perspective and from a synergy perspective.

Ultimately you will need to evaluate if the target not only matches with your acquisition strategy but also improves your company's overall synergistic performance. To do this, you need to fully understand how the acquisition will fit together with your current business strategically, in terms of your markets, customers and operational systems.

ASSEMBLING YOUR DEAL TEAM

If you want to complete a deal that achieves your success metrics, you will need expert assistance in:

- the evaluation of the target business
- due diligence
- the strategy of the offer
- negotiation of the deal and the contract
- integration.

So, make sure you have skilled, experienced people on hand who have passed through the fire before. This is one of the most important steps in preparing for the success of your acquisition – ensuring you are surrounded by people who fully understand the journey you are on, and who can provide intelligent guidance along the way.[8]

---

7   There is a good discussion of this in episodes 163 and 164 of *The Deal Room* podcast, where I talk with one of our clients who is an aggregator and has run the gauntlet of business acquisitions many times over. It's a great couple of episodes to listen to if you are looking to acquire to add to an existing business or businesses.

8   If you would like a lawyer buying guide and checklist to help guide you through what to consider when you are appointing a lawyer to assist you in this process, check out our resources hub here: www.buygrowexit.com.au.

Often there is a misperception that all lawyers, accountants and professional advisers understand the M&A environment. But the reality is this is a specialist space that many professionals only have passing experience of.

When you build your deal team, this is the team that will be tasked with guiding you on the journey. It will be who you turn to for advice, knowledge and skills in your deal. In addition to your M&A expert legal and accounting team, you will also need to have a financier to help you finance the deal, and sometimes also a corporate adviser, broker or buyer's agent to help you find your acquisition targets.

And the final step in considering your deal team – if you are acquiring for growth – is your own internal team. This will be a change for them, and the transition and new environment will often require many of your current team to expand their own skillsets. Even if they aren't directly involved in the acquisition, you will often have many of them involved in integration. So it's important that you think about how you will guide them through that change, and sell them on the bigger opportunities available to them through the success of the acquisition.

ESTABLISHING YOUR PROCESS

The next step in preparing for your acquisition is to ensure you have a clear process in place that you will commit to following. We dive into this subject in much more detail in later chapters, but from a high-level perspective you should be establishing your process with your deal team right from the beginning. It will need to include the way in which you will find your target, how you will analyse and evaluate the value and risk in the target and in the transaction, and the timelines you need to meet.

Once you are in a deal, sometimes the emotion of the acquisition grabs hold, and takes over. This is known as '**deal fever**', where the excitement of the deal and the commitment to the end goal takes

Once you are in a deal, sometimes the emotion of the acquisition grabs hold, and takes over. This is known as

'DEAL FEVER'.

On the flipside is the reality of

'DEAL FATIGUE',

where the deal drags on and on and on.

over rational processes, and results in a deal going ahead without proper due diligence and analysis. And if you have one person on the team who has deal fever, often that fever can start spreading. So you need a really clear process mapped out to take you from the beginning of the deal all the way to the very end to combat the risk of deal fever taking over, and a commitment by the deal team to go through the process step by step.

On the flipside is the reality of '**deal fatigue**', where the deal drags on and on and on due to lack of a process (or lack of commitment to the process if there is one). Deal fatigue can leave you at risk of the deal falling over, or being too eager to make concessions just to get it across the line.

ORGANISING FINANCE

It perhaps goes without saying that having your finance lined up is a critical step in preparation for acquisition. But it is often the simple things that are missed. Over the past decade we have seen an often changing credit environment. The impact of regulation and changing market players can impact the availability and speed of finance, so it's important to start your finance investigations early and get clear on the options available, the associated timings, and the process. Once your search for a target commences, things can move quickly, so you want to get on the front foot and ensure you start this work early in the acquisition journey.

Another financial consideration if you are acquiring for growth is how prepared your current business is for taking on new finance. This should include a consideration also of current and projected future financial stability – will your business be financially stable enough to deal with something as big as an acquisition? Assess your budget, and understand what this will look like into the future post-acquisition, ensuring you have built in appropriate buffers for working capital for both entities and the costs involved in the acquisition itself.

UNDERSTANDING THE ACQUISITION STRUCTURE AND AGREEMENTS

It is imperative that you consider from the outset the structure and vehicle you will be using for the acquisition, so that when you find a target you will be ready to jump into gear immediately.

If the acquisition will involve multiple parties in the buying entity, you will also want to ensure that you have in place the right agreements to govern that relationship. For example, if your buying structure is a company, this will require a shareholders' agreement.

This document should contain provisions relating to decision making (including who has the right to be a director, and the levels of decisions that will be made by directors versus the shareholders), dispute resolution and, perhaps most importantly, exit – which should include both provisions relating to how to deal with voluntary exit by a party, and provisions relating to when exit might be forced (for example, through drag along clauses, which we discuss later).

This document need to be in place before the sale agreement is signed for the acquisition to ensure that everyone is aligned from the outset. It's important to bear in mind that the process of finalising a shareholders' (or other partner) agreement can take time, so it is important that you start this process as early as possible so as not to impact your ability to act quickly with the acquisition.

We discuss structure and partner agreements in detail in part II.

ASSESSING YOUR CURRENT BUSINESS

The final step in preparation for an acquisition, if the acquisition is for growth, is the assessment of your current business and its fundamental strength. If you have holes in the protection or operation in your current business, adding the integration of a new business into the mix could be an extremely dangerous move. It's critical to ensure your structure is fully in order and your foundations are in place before you look to add to it.

You should critically consider if your current business is strong enough. Is your current legal infrastructure strong enough to ward off attacks while you are focused on the acquisition and integration? Can your business run sufficiently while your attention is diverted?

This is where the cycle of buy, grow, and exit really starts to kick in. This is the stage where you need to ensure that your business is fortified, before (and then indeed again after) acquisition. In part II we discuss the key elements you should be reflecting on to ensure that your business is legally sound and protected as it grows.

Chapter 5

PRIMARY VALUE: ENSURING THE TRANSFER OF KEY VALUE

One of the most important steps in evaluating the business you are looking to acquire is understanding what it is that forms the core value you are seeking out of the acquisition, and ensuring that this value will be transferred. This seems obvious, but so often buyers (and their lawyers) become so caught up in the details of the transaction that they miss the wood for the trees.

HOW TO APPROACH THE TRANSFER OF VALUE

Stand back and assess what the value really is that you are looking for in this acquisition. It will be different for each business. The key value might be in the clients. Or in the staff. Is it in the suppliers, distributors, or other key partners? Is it in the brand, or other intellectual property?

Once you are clear on this, you need to ensure that the value is being transferred effectively.

There are four ways to control the transfer of value in an acquisition:

- the structure of the sale
- due diligence
- operational approaches
- through the contract.

We will drill down into each of these approaches, but first a high-level discussion on how each of these value transfer control elements operate.

MANAGING THE STRUCTURE OF THE SALE

Considerations of the structure of the sale start with the choice between whether you will purchase the entity as a whole (a share sale, or unit sale), whether you will purchase the business, or whether you will purchase certain assets that you cherry-pick. Next is the choice of how the deal itself will be structured (whether the price is fixed, or contingent, and whether the price is fully paid when you take over the business, or if it will be deferred and paid over time). We discuss the relevance of these considerations for value transfer further below, because it is such an important topic to understand – but also see the **purchase structure** section later in this chapter where we dive into this area in much greater detail.

DUE DILIGENCE

Due diligence provides you the opportunity to dig deep into the business to understand how the value in the business is currently protected, and to map out a plan for how that value will transfer.

OPERATIONAL APPROACHES TO PROTECTING VALUE

As you develop a deeper understanding of the business through due diligence and the sale process, there will be a number of commercial

Due diligence provides you the opportunity to

DIG DEEP

into the business to understand how the value in the business is currently protected, and to map out a plan for how that value will transfer.

approaches to the transfer of value that you should be putting in place in tandem with each of these other control elements. As an example, this might include considering approaches such as:

- employee retention and how you will secure key staff through the transition (for example, through remuneration, leadership and communication)
- securing longevity in the location or premises where that is a component of the value, which might even involve considerations of trying to renegotiate the lease or extend its term
- the communication plan with clients.

PROTECTING VALUE THROUGH THE CONTRACT

Transfer of value is established in many ways through the contract – through the provisions that relate to the obligations of the seller, the conditions precedent (the conditions that need to be satisfied before completion), the warranties provided by the seller, the restraints on the seller after sale (which we dig into below), and sometimes also the engagement of the seller or key staff related to the seller, for a period post-sale.

CONSIDER THE STRUCTURE OF THE SALE

We discuss the decision points around deal structuring in the purchase structure section later in chapter 8, but it is useful to start with a snapshot here, to give some underpinnings of how your decision on sale structure can impact the transfer of value.

The first consideration here is whether to opt for a share sale or a business or asset sale. In simple summary, in a share sale, a buyer buys the shares but the business itself remains untouched. In a business sale, each element of the business is taken out of the selling entity, and transferred to either the buyer's existing business or to a new entity. In an asset sale, assets are cherry-picked and then moved over to the buyer's entity or a new entity. See chapter 18 for a detailed explanation of this topic.

For a business sale, depending on the specifics of each transaction, sometimes each key contract will need to be individually assigned or novated.[9] If novated, the process of moving this contract over will require the other party to the contract to sign a document to complete the transfer. This can be painful from a practical perspective, but also creates a risk of some key contracts not transferring.

However, as a positive, if you are opting for a business or asset purchase, it is easier to cherry-pick the elements you want and leave out the items you don't.

If you use a business or asset sale, you will need to specifically plan the approach for dealing with the customers, key suppliers and other key contracting parties to ensure you are able to transfer as many as possible without leakage. The less obvious the change is to other parties, the less likely it is that there will be leakage along the way.

You should also be considering what the process will be if contracts won't be fully transitioned at deal completion. You will need provisions in the sale contract for what the obligations of the seller will be until those remaining contracts are fully transitioned, and how revenue and risk under those contracts will be dealt with. For example, it can often be the case that these transitional arrangements are needed where there are government contracts being transitioned, where approval processes can often be long.

Alternatively, you can simply buy the shares, leaving the assets and contracts untouched. In many larger transactions, buyers will opt for a share sale due to the many benefits that it provides in terms of limiting the issues that can be caused in a business sale by the need to transition each client, each contract and each other component that forms the value of the business, and also by reducing that transitional work required.

Bear in mind however that even where the sale is a share sale – as opposed to a business or asset sale – there may still need to be

---

9   See the jargon busting chapter at the end of the book for the definition of 'assignment' and 'novation'. There is also detailed discussion about the differences in chapter 20.

express consent provided by certain customers and suppliers before you can take over control of the company if there are 'change of control' clauses in customer or key supplier agreements (or in many other contracts such as leases, licences, franchise agreements and distribution agreements).[10] It is imperative to pick this up through due diligence (including a review of the key contracts) to ensure you have identified where there may be change of control clauses and – as above with a business or asset sale process – nailed down the process for ensuring that these approvals are in place prior to deal completion.

While managing the practical elements here is absolutely critical, there should also be added protection in the contract. This added protection can take the form of warranties by the seller, specific provisions relating to the transition to you as the buyer, and financial considerations. Which leads me to . . .

CONSIDER STRUCTURING THE PAYMENT OF THE PURCHASE PRICE AROUND THE SUCCESSFUL TRANSFER OF THIS VALUE

Very often the concern about the transfer of value is what triggers buyers to consider using the payment of the purchase price as a lever in ensuring that each component of 'value' actually transfers. This can include withholding part of the payment at completion (when the business transfers to you as the buyer) until a later time. We refer to this as 'deferred payments'.

It might also include varying the purchase price itself based on the value that actually transfers, or the performance of the business for a period of time after sale (through utilising strategies such as earnouts and retentions, which we discuss in detail in chapter 18). But earnouts

---

10   A 'change of control' clause is a clause that allows one party to a contract to terminate the contract if control or ownership in the other party changes. For example, if a company being purchased has large customer contracts, we often find 'change of control' clauses sitting in these customer contracts, where the customer requires that their consent is sought prior to any significant change in the ownership of the business. If a customer isn't happy with their contract being serviced by the new owner, they may have a right to terminate the contract or to claim damages.

and retentions can act in a perverse way (which we will discuss later), so it's extremely important to be aware of the potential problems before you embark down this path, so that you are doing so with open eyes.

RESTRAINTS

In considering how to ensure value doesn't leak, it is usual to put in place restraints around the sellers and key personnel to ensure they don't continue or solicit relationships with any of the clients, key suppliers, personnel or other key contacts of the business. This can often also include a restraint on competition in general.

There are many considerations when setting up restraints. It's important to understand the distinction between 'solicitation restraints' and 'competition restraints', as this is something that is often misunderstood. In very simple terms, **solicitation restraints** relate to restraining someone from 'soliciting' (approaching) or sometimes even dealing with defined groups. For example, this is where there would be a specific reference to key people in the business (or their related parties) having a direct relationship outside of the business with the clients, staff, suppliers or other key contacts of the business.

Competition restraints relate to restraining any sort of competition with the business; this is usually bound by a certain distance and time.

Sale agreements may include both of these types of restraints, one – or none! So it's extremely important to ensure you have thought through where your exposure may be in the relationships between the sellers (or their shareholders or key personnel) and the customers, suppliers and staff.

Your legal team will need to set up these restraints balancing a fine line between protecting the value in the asset you are purchasing, and overreaching by creating a restraint that might be difficult to enforce. There are a lot of strategies that we employ from a legal standpoint to walk this fine line, including a consideration of the breadth of the restraint, who it applies to (as you will want to ensure that you have captured the right people and other businesses they may be involved with in the future), and an appropriate consideration of the area and the time in which the restraint will continue to apply.

Specifying an area and time may require clauses that are set out with alternatives, which we in legal land call 'cascading clauses'. I'm so often asked by clients why these clauses exist, because the clauses themselves don't make a lot of sense on the face of it. They are set out as options of time and area, often moving from the optimal position for the buyer (for example, a competition restraint of say two years) but then providing options of lesser periods of time, and varying areas.

The reason for the strange approach to the construction of these restraints is that if a court is to find that the broadest position set out in the restraints is unreasonable because it is too broad, then the restraint can be read down by the court taking into account another of its positions of time or area without invalidating the clause.

The other types of restraints you should be considering are the restraints for key personnel, as there might be significant risk of value leakage should any of the key personnel leave either during the transaction or soon after. As we will dig into later, due diligence investigations should include a review of the contracts in place to ensure there is protection against key personnel leaving and taking clients, staff or other key partners. And where the protection is not appropriate in the current agreements, you will need to ensure that there is a plan for how to deal with the contracts moving forward together with the risk should the personnel not transition.

WHAT IS THE VALUE IN A BUSINESS?

So, what is the value in a business? And how can each of these methods above be used by a buyer?

THE CUSTOMER OR CLIENT BASE

The client base is the obvious place to start because this is one of the key areas of value in most acquisitions. The value of the client base of a business is often, however, dependent on several other factors of key value; for example, branding, key staff that the clients are familiar and comfortable with, technology, location – and the list goes on. So, this element really intertwines with the other elements of value that we look at below.

The first question in assessing the value of the client base is to work out how the customers (and revenue) will transition over to the buyer and whether there is risk of leakage in this transition.

In some cases, a seller can show that the value in the customer base has been locked in by fixed-term customer contracts, positions on government or corporate panels, preferred supplier agreements, or technology. If this is the case, the contracts need to be reviewed from the perspective of understanding the steps that will be required to transition each of them.

But for many businesses, there is no guarantee of continued custom from the client base. In these cases, you will need to assess from prior performance and your own projections whether there are any risks in customers continuing to trade in the same way they had in the past after you take over. A job of the buyer and their deal team is to assess each of these elements and come to a conclusion on the likelihood of the current revenue base transitioning in full after sale, and whether there will be any disturbance to that revenue trajectory on the basis of a change of ownership.

This is not such a large issue for some types of business, for example some technology and retail businesses. Nor is it generally an issue for larger businesses where the owners are not key personnel. But it can be a particular issue for professional services businesses, smaller businesses where the owners are part of the key personnel, and any other business where the customer might have a concern about a change in ownership or where the process of requiring customers to specifically authorise a change might create some friction that could cause them to reassess their ongoing relationship.

To deal with this issue of transferring the value of the revenue base, you will need to consider: how the sale is structured (whether it is a share sale or a business sale), the structure of the payment (and whether the purchase price will be structured around the successful transfer), due diligence findings, operational approaches and the sale contract itself (including the use of restraints).

THE PEOPLE IN THE BUSINESS

Commonly the personnel of the business are a key component of the value you are looking to acquire. But additionally they can also be important to ensuring a smooth transition and the capture of value in so many other areas of the business; for example, they often have vital client relationships, and they often hold a significant part of the corporate history and knowledge that often is not properly codified in systems and documentation for the business.

There is much to do from a human resources perspective in a healthy transition of staff that is well outside the scope of this book. This is an exercise in change management, and I highly recommend devoting time and attention to how you will go about this process. I have seen some great examples though of this done really well, and in general the good news stories have involved strong leadership and communication, and sometimes also incentives for staff who hold particular value.

But from a legal perspective in the discussion of capturing and transitioning value, you need to understand what connection the team have to the inherent value of the asset you are buying.

We routinely review employment contracts for our buyer clients as part of the due diligence process, to ensure that there are suitable non-solicitation restraints to protect against staff leaving and taking clients, key partners or other staff. It might also be appropriate to have some staff committed to non-competition restraints. Where these are not in place, that risk will need to be dealt with, and care will need to be given to how to deal with the subject of transferring

From a legal perspective in the discussion of capturing and transitioning value, you need to **UNDERSTAND** what **CONNECTION** the team have to the inherent value of the asset you are buying.

employees (and their contracts) in the sale contract to ensure that you are able to engage the employees on more suitable terms.

If certain staff are particularly important and you want to ensure they transfer, you might also consider structuring the sale price around this, such as by making part of the purchase price contingent on the transfer of these key staff. For example, we worked on a sale in which there were more than 200 contractors that were of key value to the buyer. The buyer had structured the final payment based on the number of contractors that agreed to transfer across, and consequently the sellers worked incredibly hard up to completion to ensure that every contractor transitioned. This is a great example of both the buyer and seller getting fully aligned on ensuring the transfer of value. Ultimately the buyer achieved its aim of ensuring that the majority of the contractors transferred (on its terms), and the sellers achieved the ultimate price they had wanted.

You may also wish to put in place measures to keep staff engaged during the transition and engaged to help grow the business into the future. This is where you might start to consider incentive plans for staff, and potentially also the possibility of future employee shares which can be great for retention and mindset. (We talk about employee shares further in part II.)

THE INTELLECTUAL PROPERTY

Quite often there will be a significant component of value held in the intellectual property of the business, otherwise known as IP. This can take several forms.

BRAND IP

Brand IP refers to the value that sits in the name of the business and the name of the products. Where your target has a highly established and recognisable brand, ensuring your ongoing use of that brand will be very important.

There are a number of ways to do this, which come back to due diligence investigations of the business and how the contract is set up. During due diligence, your legal team will dig into whether the brands are protected by trademark registrations, and whether those registrations provide sufficient protection. This stage might also involve investigations into whether there are competitors using similar brands, or any other brand threats.

I have seen lots of cases of issues arising from these sorts of transactions. One example I remember clearly arose with two businesses in the education industry that had very similar names, but that had essentially co-existed for almost a decade. When new owners came on board to one of the businesses (who held a trademark registration), they took an aggressive stance to the similarity in the names. And while the other business had many arguments on its side, it didn't have a registered trademark. This was a fundamental issue, and when combined with lack of clarity about who had used the brand first, there were huge risks for the business that didn't hold a trademark registration. So that business subsequently took the view it was safest to change its name, resulting in it incurring significant cost after 14 years of growing its brand and goodwill in the market.

This was a very important lesson for the business about the importance of brand protection, because small issues one day can turn into very big issues in the future when there is a change of owners or managers at the helm. But this should also serve as an example to buyers about the importance of clearly understanding the intellectual property protection of the brands that form part of an acquisition, and ensuring that what you are buying is something that will last and withstand future attack.

In addition to due diligence investigations into branding, your legal team will need to use the sale contract to set up a number of protections for you in the acquisition, including ensuring there are appropriate warranties from the sellers about the ownership rights of any branding, and having the seller agree to provide background information about the creation of the brands just in case this is required for future protection.

You will also need to be provided with sufficient records to establish brand ownership back to the date of first creation and use of the brand, in case you need to bolster the IP protections or take action against a third party (or defend against an action by a third party) in relation to use of similar brands. This sometimes also requires the addition of contractual obligations to ensure that the seller will assist you in these actions in the future if it becomes necessary.

OTHER IP

But brand is only one component of intellectual property. There are many other types of intellectual property that might form part of the value of your acquisition. For example there might be lucrative rights in patents or designs held by the business, there might be copyright material, there might be significant value sitting in software code, or user manuals, or content used, sold or licenced by the business.

In all of these instances, as a buyer you will want to ensure you have clarity of where the IP value sits and how that value is protected, how the IP was created, who the IP owner is, and how to ensure that the value is properly transferred through the sale contract and also protected by the warranties and representations of the sellers.

Where components of this intellectual property sit in a range of areas, you might have to use separate IP assignments and other documentation in addition to the sale contract.

SUPPLIERS

Where supply is a key component of the value, it will be important for you to understand the supply relationships and how those relationships will transfer. You will of course need to dig into the contracts currently in force and understand the process for how they will transfer in a business sale, and for a share sale you will need to understand any authorisations that might be needed when there is a change in control of the company.

It will be important to then ensure you have established a clear strategy with the sellers for communication with the suppliers.

Where supply arrangements are critical to the business, you may also look at building into the contract provisions that the sale won't complete until all the contracts have transferred (or been approved), and you may also look at some of the value transfer concepts that we discussed earlier; for example, perhaps considering deferring part of the payment based on securing future supply.

OTHER KEY CONTRACTS

There are many other key contracts that may be important to the business that will need to be considered in assessing the value transfer. This might be

- franchise agreements
- licence agreements
- joint venture agreements
- referral agreements
- distribution agreements
- commission agreements.

And the list goes on!

The starting point is ensuring that it's fully understood what agreements are of value, digging into those contracts to understand how they work, and then using that knowledge to create the best strategy for how to most appropriately transfer those agreements or the value in them.

With franchise agreements and many licence agreements, for example, you will need approvals, and often this can take time and involve legal negotiations with those contracting parties. So, you will need to ensure that this is built into the process and timeline of the sale.

PREMISES AND LOCATIONS

In many instances there might be a component of value sitting in the actual premises of the business. Where this is the case, buyers will usually either take on a lease or take on the property purchase as part of the acquisition.

Leases can be seen both as a centre of value but also of risk. We discuss risk in the next part, where we will dive into the risks in leases, so for now we will just focus on the value component.

Where the value is in the current location, you need to evaluate how you will ensure you have the longevity in the premises that you require to maximise the value of the business after sale. This can be achieved either by taking on the lease (either through assignment of the current lease, or though entering into a new lease) or by acquiring the premises along with the sale (either at the same time, at an agreed future point, or by way of building in an option for the future acquisition).

Recently I spoke to a business that was acquiring a dental practice. They'd had a bad experience with their previous lawyer on the acquisition, who had charged a hefty sum for the review and negotiation of a lease assignment as part of the acquisition, but who had at no point identified for them that the options under the lease term had run out and that the current lease had less than one year to run.[11] The lawyer had been preoccupied with other lease terms and had just not thought about the impact of a short lease period. When the buyer tried to organise finance for the acquisition, the finance was blocked by the lender on the basis that the lease term was insufficient to support the value of the business that was being presented. Worse

---

11   Leases are generally set up as an initial period (term) plus additional 'option' periods. The option periods are additional 'terms' that the tenant can take up, and that a landlord must provide. For example, a lease might be structured as an initial term of three years, with two options each of additional three-year terms. This means that if a buyer purchases the business in the initial three years, they would then have the right to a further six-year period after the end of the initial term (two option periods of three years each).

still, the lender also found in the lease a demolition clause (which allowed the lease to be terminated at any time with three months' notice). Upon further enquiry the buyer found out the shocking reason – *the building was set to be demolished.*

This – of course – had a major impact on the value of the business, not simply because there was a real risk that changing the location would impact the ongoing value of the existing client base. But also because relocation costs (and the new fit out required in new premises) would be massive, and an expense that would have a major impact on what the value of the business should be in the acquisition.

This revelation was obviously a shock to the buyer, but it was also a shock to the seller of the business, who had only just purchased the business a few years prior – and was now seeing the value of their acquisition diminish in front of their eyes. Unfortunately for the seller, he had been completely unaware that he had bought a business in a location that was soon to be demolished.

Ultimately the buyer didn't go ahead with the acquisition, and the seller was left with a business that would be extremely difficult to sell, and undoubtedly a massively impacted sale price.

I hope it's clear from this example how important understanding lease terms can potentially be to ascertaining the underlying value of a business you are acquiring! Not only can it impact your ability to access finance, it can also underpin the entire value of the business for you as an asset moving forward, for your own future exit (if location is an important component of the value).

PLANT, EQUIPMENT, STOCK AND OTHER ASSETS

These other tangible assets of a business are often more straight-forward to deal with than the other areas we have discussed above, however there are still many steps to consider in the assessment of value in these other areas.

Firstly, it is important to confirm actual ownership. This might sound like an odd thing to say, however we have seen situations where buyers thought they were getting various assets in the sale only to find out as we dug into the detail that the sellers were not actually the rightful owners!

The sale contract will usually include an asset list – and it is important as a buyer to ensure you understand this list and that you have had someone physically inspect the assets. We have had enthusiastic buyers in the past decide physical inspections weren't required, and then discover post sale the error of their ways when the assets were not at the quality they had expected.

You will also want to take steps to ensure you understand if these assets are owned outright or leased or financed. This is particularly important if you are purchasing the business as a share sale as the liabilities will pass over on sale. But it's also important in a business sale environment to clarify actual ownership, and to understand it from a timing perspective, because assets that are financed can often take some time to pay out or reorganise if this hasn't been identified early enough in the process.

Chapter 6

PROTECTION: IDENTIFYING AND CONTROLLING RISK

The protection phase is about **identification** of risks, and then where possible, **control and minimisation**.

We **identify** the risks in a purchase through our understanding of:

- the headline risk areas that are common to most businesses (which we dig into in part II)
- the subset of risk that is specific to the industry and size of the target (which requires specific knowledge of the industry of your acquisition)
- the specific risk in the target business, which can be done through your due diligence process. (We dig into this in a lot of detail below!)

We **control and minimise** risk in three ways, which are similar to the approaches we use for value transfer:

- due diligence
- through the contract
- commercial and legal approaches post-acquisition.

There is also a fourth way of minimising risk – through insurance. As a buyer you should be considering both insurance for the business pre-sale and post-sale, and also potentially considering warranty and indemnity insurance. (More on that later.)

THE DIFFERENT TYPES OF RISK

Before we get started on looking at identification, control and minimisation – it's worth taking a step back to discuss the three general subsets of risk.

The first is **value risk**. This is the risk that the value you are looking for in the business either doesn't exist, or doesn't transfer in the way you require. And this is what we have just finished covering in our previous chapter on value.

The second is what I lovingly refer to as the **landmine risk**. This is the risk that something will blow up in the business and cause loss, or value leakage, relating to the business as it currently stands. We cover this below, and also in part II, Grow (the section of the book devoted to fortifying the business).

The third is **transaction risk** – risks that come from the transaction itself, which we delve into in detail in this chapter.

IDENTIFYING TRANSACTION RISKS THROUGH CAREFUL PLANNING

There are a number of risks arising out of the transaction itself – including employment transfer risks, tax risks (including tax outcomes, goods and services tax impacts, and elements that might trigger stamp duty), risks that the way the transaction is conducted creates a privacy breach or breach of confidentiality, and the risk that the transaction creates a breach of contracts that have provisions restricting assignment or change of control, or some other breach of contract.

There are also employment law risks that are worth discussing briefly. The sale of a business in Australia (or transfer of it in other ways) will generally trigger 'transmission of business' provisions set out in industrial relations and employment legislation and instruments, and thus needs to be approached with caution. There are obligations for sellers on termination of employment (including the risk of redundancy payments and employee claims), and there are issues for buyers relating to responsibility for accrued entitlements and service history which can trigger ongoing issues for buyers if they haven't been dealt with properly. Often this includes an election by the buyer to recognise, or not recognise, the service history of the staff. There have been lots of cases before the courts that have dealt with employment issues post-sale, and this is an example of an area where careful planning by your lawyers can provide protection for your engagement with staff after the deal is done.

Ultimately the transaction risks are the things you are engaging your lawyer to control, however it's important to understand that they exist, and to understand the importance of having a lawyer on your side who understands and controls them properly.

IDENTIFYING LANDMINE RISKS THROUGH DUE DILIGENCE

The bigger question, however, is *what risk is there in the business you are purchasing?* One of the key ways to identify the risk sitting in a specific target is through due diligence.

WHAT *IS* DUE DILIGENCE?

Due diligence is the term given to the investigation into a business before acquisition. It is a very important part of your acquisition process, because it is the step in which you dig into the strength and quality of the business and the risks that you might be taking on.

Ultimately due diligence is at its core about:

1. ensuring that the value you are looking to achieve in your acquisition is actually there, and protected
2. establishing how that value will transfer
3. identifying the key risks of the business
4. working out how you will deal with those risks through the deal process, and how you will manage them after the deal is done.

THE CORE OF DUE DILIGENCE

There are many different types of due diligence. Mostly we think of due diligence as primarily financial and legal. On the financial side, we are verifying the figures. From a legal side, we are verifying the legal backbone or foundation of the business, looking at many areas to ascertain the level of risk likely to be in a business that is being acquired. But aside from the legal and financial sides, due diligence investigations will (or should) also involve digging into many other areas such as operations, people, culture and technology.

With this information you can assess the business's current position and identify risks and future potential.

WHY CONDUCT DUE DILIGENCE?

I have already discussed in chapter 2 and elsewhere some of the massive risks that buyers run if they don't undertake proper due diligence. Due diligence gives you the opportunity to get to understand the business, identify issues in advance, and get a feel for how the business is run.

Many buyers are so eager to get the deal done that they don't want to devote the time and cost involved in proper due diligence, only to find out as they start to operate the business that problems appear. I know of a number of buyers who sold within their first two years of ownership (and a few within the first year) because the reality of the business didn't match their expectations.

However, on the flipside we have worked with many buyers who have understood the importance of due diligence and used this to their advantage. One instance of this was an international buyer we acted for that was buying into an Australian company to expand their operations into the Australian market. They were sophisticated buyers and had gone through acquisitions many times before, and so they understood the importance of proper legal due diligence.

In that due diligence process, we were able to identify risks that were sitting in the business from a legal perspective, but also a number of operational elements that were relevant for them in terms of understanding how the business would work moving forward. So when they decided to finally go ahead with the deal, they went ahead on the basis not just of the price and the commercial terms they had negotiated, but also based on the deeper understanding they gained from the due diligence process that helped them understand the business in a detailed way.

That deal happened a number of years ago, and subsequently the business here in Australia has been an absolutely roaring success. The reason for that success – the reason that the transition and integration worked so well – is in a very large part the amount of understanding they gained through the period of getting to know the business.

As you are buying a business, these questions that you are asking as part of the due diligence process aren't just to uncover risk but are also to help you understand the running of the business.

WHEN IN THE PROCESS IS DUE DILIGENCE DONE?
Depending on the specifics of the transaction, the timing of the commencement of due diligence can be different.

Generally buyers seriously commence due diligence once the price and general commercial terms have been agreed (or mostly

Many people are so eager to get the

DEAL DONE

that they don't want to devote the TIME and COST INVOLVED in proper due diligence, only to find out as they start to operate the business that problems appear.

agreed) and a terms sheet has been signed. Sometimes the bulk of due diligence might not be done until after the sale contract is signed, but in such instances, the contracts will preserve the right for the buyer to do (or finish) their due diligence investigations before they complete the acquisition. In these circumstances, the contracts will almost always provide a right for the buyer to pull out of the deal if the due diligence investigations identify previously unknown issues. As a buyer it can be useful to have exchanged contracts (and therefore locked in the seller) while you are finalising due diligence as a way to protect your financial and time investment in this due diligence process, to ensure that the seller doesn't jump for another offer that might come in.

But bear in mind that these investigations might raise information about the business that can impact the way you want to approach the structure of the sale, or the payment of the purchase price. Or it might impact the purchase price itself. So, generally the bulk of due diligence will be done before the contract is signed, but under the cover of an exclusivity period for the buyer during that process, to protect their investment in the deal.

In many smaller deals, however, the parties will not exchange (sign) contracts until due diligence has been fully completed – so that when the contracts are signed, both parties are committed to the deal, with no ability to get out. In fact, many small deals may not even move to the contract drafting and negotiation phase until due diligence has been mostly completed, and the buyer has agreed to move ahead.

Ultimately the decision about the timing of due diligence will depend heavily on the circumstances of your acquisition, including the size, the risk in the business, timing requirements and the experience of you and your advisers and the deal team of the seller.

HOW MUCH IS ENOUGH?

With any transaction, no matter what the size, there is complexity in deciding the appropriate level of due diligence. Every business is different. Every transaction is different. They all have their different value and risk points. So therefore with every acquisition the decision on what is an appropriate level will be different.

We have worked with sophisticated buyers who understand their industry deeply, and are so confident in their abilities to ascertain and deal with risk that they do very little formal due diligence in their acquisitions.

We have worked on multimillion-dollar sales of high-risk businesses out of listed entities where international consortiums of buyers have opted for a low-level due diligence, focusing only on some of the top issues.

But we have also acted in many small acquisitions of bread-and-butter businesses where risk would be presumed to be low, but buyers have spent months and months in due diligence.

Ultimately the determination of an appropriate level of due diligence really starts with standing back and asking that fundamental question of what it is you are looking to achieve in the acquisition, understanding where the value lies in the target, what the risk level is in the business, and determining your own risk appetite. And this is of course balanced against the size of the acquisition.

This then all feeds into an assessment of how much time, energy and money should be poured into the due diligence process for each individual acquisition.

We have on many occasions when acting for a seller seen due diligence checklists that were out of all proportion to the value and the level of risk in a business. And when you are dealing with a due diligence list like this, very often you risk losing the wood for the trees.

We have seen many examples of watching inexperienced buyers start with an overly comprehensive (and untailored) due diligence list, and halfway through decide that it is too difficult or time consuming to ultimately get all the information they had initially requested, and then move to the complete opposite. Their due diligence process goes out the window because there are timeline pressures that make them want to just get the deal done. On many occasions I have seen buyers just then throw in the towel, ditch further due diligence (that often should have been done) and just move on with the sale.

On the flipside, we have also witnessed inexperienced buyers become almost paralysed by the amount of information they are assessing in the due diligence process.

These are clear examples of the problems of not tailoring due diligence correctly to the size and risk value of the acquisition, and in not using advisers who can properly help guide this. But it also demonstrates that when deal fever hits, all sensible thought processes can go out the window to get the deal done in a quick time!

WHAT SHOULD I FOCUS ON?

The due diligence process itself must be reflective of the commercial realities of the transaction. You can't investigate *everything* in a business. You need to work out where to spend your time. This is particularly important with larger businesses and larger transactions, because when the business is larger sometimes there's the risk of not being able to see the wood for the trees if you don't have enough of a focus on what the commercial imperatives of the deal are, your risk profile and the risk profile of the target business itself.

Organisations of this size have a sea of documents and materials, and broad due diligence requests will result in a deluge of documents. Sellers will often then want to hide behind this sea of documents and use this to water down the warranties they provide about the business.

So, you need to be careful about what you ask for in the due diligence process, and how that is dealt with in the contract.

For example, if you're looking at employment contracts for a small business where there are 10 employees you might actually look at every contract to ensure you understand any variances. Whereas for a larger business with hundreds of employees or even thousands, you can't review every contract. You're going to have to ask for a sample, and have a process to locate and understand the outliers.

And this is where it's important to also tie the due diligence process in with the warranties and indemnities provided within the contract, so you can use both of those processes in tandem to achieve the required risk mitigation for you as the buyer. So, in the example above, for the larger business where you are reviewing samples rather than each individual contract, you may ask questions to confirm the samples are representative of all the other contracts, and you then may pair this with sensible warranties in the sale contract.

WHY A COOKIE-CUTTER APPROACH DOESN'T WORK

The cookie cutter-approach to due diligence (using templates without thinking about their applicability, and without tailoring to the specifics of your actual deal) is sometimes a crutch that people who haven't had a lot of acquisitions under their belt fall back on.

While templates for due diligence can be useful as a guide, what ultimately is most important is ensuring you have (or are surrounded by) experience with these types of transactions, and that you understand what the real issues are or where they may be lurking.

Ultimately it's about having an objective, thoughtful process. Because while it's important to have a template as a starting point, you also need to have the knowledge on hand that tells you where you need to look specifically on your deal. Don't let templates replace thinking.

THE KEY AREAS OF DUE DILIGENCE

So, what are the most important areas to examine as part of your due diligence? Even the most thorough process cannot consider *every* aspect of a business, so it's important that you know where to start and where problems most often occur.[12] Here are the key areas of due diligence you should cover:

- **Ownership structure and history.** One of the areas in which to commence your due diligence investigations is the ownership

---

12   To download some great due diligence resources, go to www.buygrowexit.com.au.

structure and ensuring it is properly reflected on the public records to make sure that who a seller says owns the business, actually owns the business. This sounds basic, but we have in many instances found very interesting results from doing basic searches in relation to the ownership behind the entities that are being purchased. This can include unveiling other entities that are running components of the business, or a mess of shareholdings, or simply getting clear on who the owners are to understand if there may be issues if all the shareholders aren't in agreement about the sale itself, or on potential components of the terms as you negotiate the sale.

For larger deals you might look closely at office holders, shareholders and shareholdings individually and together. If a business has a large controlling interest held by a particular individual, it may be appropriate to run some searches on the individual as well as the corporate structure to make sure you understand if there have been any issues in the past with the individual, for example with bankruptcy or litigation. You may also conduct historical searches to see previous directors and shareholders.

In this stage you can also consider looking back at the documents relating to the structure of the business, including the constitution and company register and any other documents that are relevant to the business, the corporate structure and the management structure.

- **Contracts with customers and suppliers.** Due diligence can help uncover three things with customers and suppliers:
  - The extent that the value with the customers and suppliers is locked in, and will transfer.
  - The risks (both from the past and into the future if you will continue under the same contracts), to enable you to include appropriate warranties and other provisions in the sale contract.

- The practical aspects of how you should best transition these contracts (and the extent of any requirement to obtain consent as part of the sale and transition).

As mentioned previously, your approach to this will be somewhat different depending on whether you are buying the shares, the business or just some assets. And indeed, your due diligence investigations might lead you to favour one type of deal structure over another.

- **Other commercial contracts.** In addition to key customer and supplier relationships, there may be other relationships that are key to the value of your acquisition. This can include partner agreements, distribution arrangements, JV agreements, commission agreements and many other types of contracts.

  As with the customer and supplier contracts, in this area you are digging once again into that three-part question:
  - How is this value locked in? Are the contracts really locked in, or do termination provisions undermine the contract term that has been promised?
  - What risk sits in the contract in the past, and into the future? You need to understand what is sitting in the risk clauses, what warranties and indemnities have been given (or provided by the other party), what obligations exist for past and future activity, and if there any known impediment to achieving these or risk existing from past activity (or inactivity!).
  - What do you need to do to transition the contracts?
- **Intellectual property.** Intellectual property will almost always form part of the value in a business. Sometimes it will be significant, other times it won't, so the investigations in relation to intellectual property will vary depending on how important the IP is to that business.

  In due diligence there are three main elements you are looking at in relation to intellectual property:

- *Ownership* – confirming that the seller is indeed the owner.
- *Infringement* – confirming that the seller isn't infringing on the rights of others.
- *Protection* – understanding what protection the seller has achieved for their IP, and what elements remain exposed.

As we have discussed, there will be warranties in the contract that will deal with each of these areas, but if an action is taken against the ongoing business for infringement into the future, the sale contract and warranties in it will only protect the business for a certain length of time. And of course, you will still be in the middle of the dispute, which will be an unwanted and time-consuming distraction.

If intellectual property is important or could create future risk or expense, it is important to be thorough in your due diligence process in this area.

- **Agreements with employees and contractors.** During your due diligence process you will want to understand the terms on which the personnel are engaged. This includes:
  - *How they are engaged.* It is important to start with understanding how they are engaged (such as being permanent employees, casuals, or contractors). This can often reveal a mountain of risk. I have been involved in many deals where due diligence has revealed incorrect classifications of personnel, and if a buyer was to carry this forward without review, it would create a massive body of risk into the future.
  - *The agreements that relate to their engagement.* Check for adequate protections relating to areas like confidential information, IP and restraints. Knowing about any restraints is particularly important for ensuring you understand if there is a risk that the staff might leave and take clients or other staff.

- *Awards, industrial instruments and enterprise agreements.* It is important to understand what specific terms and conditions are applicable to certain categories of personnel in the business. As a buyer, you will want to ensure you are across all of these in close detail.
- *Period of service and other entitlement considerations.* You will also want to clearly understand the period of service of employees and how this reflects in things like entitlements. This will usually be looked at closely in the financial due diligence, and also included in the sale contract where there is generally specific provision for adjustments for the entitlements. There are also intricacies involved in the treatment of employee entitlements, based on what components will be assumed by the buyer and which components will form part of adjustments.
- *Employment policies, manuals and handbooks.* Review any of these types of documents that are used in the business to understand the extent to which the business is compliant with (and how they have dealt with) relevant laws, and the organisational approach to dealing with issues such as recruitment, bullying and health and safety.
- *Share options or incentive or profit-sharing schemes or arrangements.* If in the sale contract you are agreeing to take on the employees on essentially the same terms as their current employment, you need to fully understand the extent of their current terms. You may not want to continue to provide certain elements of prior incentive or share option arrangements, in which case you will need to ensure you are clear on this from the start so that the sale contract and negotiations can be dealt with properly. Also, the details of the prior arrangements, like share options or phantom share schemes, might impact how you want the seller to allocate some of the sale proceeds.

— *Any complaints, actions or claims by employees that are current or have been made in the past.* A history of employment issues can be a huge red flag of potential future issues. You will want to understand these clearly to ensure you have appropriate warranties in place, and an understanding of the impact of any of this history on the future running of the business (for example, on the cost of insurance premiums).

- **Finance facilities and encumbrances.** This is another area where the level of focus will depend on the risk and transaction size. For smaller and lower risk acquisitions, the acquisition team will generally deal with most of the financing review.

  From a legal perspective, we undertake investigations into securities registered over the business on the Personal Property Securities Register (known as the PPSR), which can help to reveal if the business has borrowed money or if it has equipment that is leased or financed in some way. This is also an important step from a timing perspective because it is critical for a buyer to understand which of these will need to be removed before completion.

  You will also want to dig into what finance is in the business and whether these finance facilities will be continued. This can include understanding the terms of leasing and the financing agreements, and getting clear on any guarantees and letters of comfort that have been given on behalf of the business that might need to be replaced.

  Sometimes security clauses might also sit in customer contracts with large customers, or supplier agreements, so this also will form part of the review of the key customer and supplier agreements.

- **Real property.** A property can be a key component in the value of a business where the business is location dependent. The property in these instances will generally be either sold as a component of the sale, or leased. Where you are acquiring the property, there are also the obvious usual checks required that are part of the conveyancing process. If you are taking on a lease you will also need to assess future costs and risks (for example, if there are make-good clauses, you may want to understand the costs of compliance, and in some instances you may want to push this cost to the seller).[13]

- **Insurance.** What insurance is in place? Is it appropriate for the business and its risks? Will you require run-off insurance? This is particularly relevant for share purchases, or where there are products that could have product liability issues attached.
- **Litigation and disputes.** Is there any litigation or disputes currently active? Is there known potential for litigation or disputes at the time of the deal? This investigation is often done both through questions asked of the seller and, in larger transactions, through searching public court registers.
- **Licensing requirements.** Does the business require any licences, permits, accreditations or approvals to operate? It's important to get clear on this during the due diligence phase. I have at times seen this move what had initially been considered a business sale into a share sale when the difficulty of establishing the relevant accreditations or approvals in the new business became apparent.
- **Regulation and compliance.** Is there legislation or regulation that impacts the business, and if so, is the business compliant and will anything in the deal cause any risk of non-compliance? One example is the application of privacy legislation which does not apply to a large portion of businesses under a certain size threshold. If however after this acquisition the new combined business will come under the ambit of the privacy legislation, it might be that there is quite a bit of work required to bring the business into line with the legislation and you will need to consider how to deal with this during transition to ensure that you won't be in breach. Another common example of

---

13   We discuss the things a buyer should look out for in leases in quite a bit of detail in chapter 19 under the heading 'Lease Maximisation'.

important compliance considerations in a business trading with consumers is the extent to which their contracts and processes are compliant with the relevant consumer laws.

- **Other assets.** Where there is equipment or other assets of the business of value, the due diligence process will involve reviewing and identifying ownership, and the state of the assets. While this list is focused on the legal elements of due diligence, from a practical perspective you should ensure that you actually inspect the assets you are looking to purchase. This may seem like an odd statement, but as discussed earlier in this book we have seen many instances where buyers have neglected to physically inspect assets, and then later found out that they were not what they had thought them to be!

WHEN DUE DILIGENCE GOES WRONG

It is vital not to be flippant about the role of due diligence. The failure of buyers to properly understand the value transfer and risk in the target has in many instances led to very unhappy outcomes. There is a litany of cases of buyers taking legal action against sellers.

One recent case relating to the $10 million acquisition of a training business shows the problems that can occur with poor due diligence, and the way in which a business is valued.[14] The training business was valued at 5× the 'sustainable EBIT', based in part on financial forecasts provided by the seller during due diligence. What the buyer failed to pick up however was a condition imposed by the government relating to funding which was critically important to the ongoing operation and revenue of the business, which meant that the business could not have achieved the financial forecasts.

The business post-sale failed to achieve revenues anywhere near the financial forecasts, and the buyer subsequently sued the seller to recover the difference between what it had paid and what it

---

14   If you happen to be interested, that case was *Evolution Traffic Control v Skerratt.*

believed the business was actually worth, on the basis that the seller had not disclosed this important information that would impact the future performance of the business. Ultimately the court sided with the buyer, and ordered the seller to pay $3.5 million in damages.

This would seem to be a good news story for the buyer, however sometimes even wins like this end up as a hollow victory. By the time a matter gets to court, the buyer has already expended huge amounts of time, money and effort – with no guarantee that they would be victorious. Ultimately the buyer would probably have preferred that they had bought a business that performed in the way they expected – rather than spending years in litigation to try to make back some of the loss.

This is a great example of the importance of putting the required effort into due diligence investigations that dig into the ongoing elements of value of the business, and any risks in translating that to future revenue, rather than simply relying on warranties to hopefully save you if the business ultimately does not perform as expected. In this instance, prevention (the identification of the risk sitting in the government contracts and funding) would have been much cheaper and easier than the ultimate resolution (expensive and time-consuming litigation), even given that the buyers ultimately were successful in their claim.

It is also a great reminder that if you are valuing a business in part on its expected future performance, you need to take steps to protect your risk that the future performance does not end up as expected – either through deal structuring so the ultimate payment is tied to the business achieving that future performance, or through specific warranties relating to the accuracy of forecasts that have been provided during due diligence.

In the end, due diligence is your first line of defence in ensuring that you have adequate information to hand and that you have properly dug into that information to unearth the risks to you realising the future value. And it is also the last line of defence, by

If you are valuing a business in part on its expected future performance, you need to take steps to **PROTECT YOUR RISK** that the future performance does not end up as expected.

attaching that due diligence to appropriate warranties that will give you an action against the seller if information provided is found to be inaccurate.

Just remember that prevention is ultimately much cheaper and less time consuming than the cure! So, spending quality time in due diligence will always be the better approach, to find problems before they happen.

OTHER WAYS OF CONTROLLING AND MINIMISING RISK

None of your risk management tools operate in isolation. Each tool in this chapter should be used in an integrated way with the other mechanisms. Thorough due diligence is one of the most powerful risk management tools in your kit, but it's not the only tool at your disposal. You can also control and minimise risk through:

- the contract (warranties and indemnities)
- the structure of the deal
- commercial approaches.

Let's consider each of these.

PROTECTION THROUGH THE CONTRACT

Many people view the purchase contract as a tool that sits on its own, but the reality is that it is an integral part of your risk minimisation. The contract will enable you to control and minimise the risk of the acquisition through the interaction of:

- the obligations on the sellers relating to the transfer itself
- the restraints applicable to the sellers and their related entities
- the warranties and indemnities from the sellers (and any relevant guarantors).

WHAT ARE WARRANTIES AND INDEMNITIES?

Warranties are a series of statements made by the seller about the business and its assets. They are essentially promises by the seller about the ownership of the assets, the accuracy of the material they have provided in due diligence and about liabilities and risk in the business.

An indemnity is a promise by the seller to reimburse the buyer for any loss suffered for certain specified events (generally related to losses caused by a risk created in the business prior to the sale, or by one of the 'warranties' not being true).

Buying a business or shares is in many ways analogous to buying a house.

Like buying a house, you want to ensure that the value is there, that you understand the risks, that your i's are dotted and your t's are crossed. When you buy a house, you have a pest inspection report, you have a builder's report, you turn on the lights and taps, you look behind the doors, you check everything works. And in the sale contract for a house, you also have protections to ensure that the property is as it seems.

When you buy a business, you've got to do exactly the same thing. You need to test that all the metaphorical lights work. And this is where warranties also come into play. In the sale contract for the business, the warranties are essentially like a promise from a property seller that the lights work.

But this is also where due diligence comes into play, because in a business sale context the warranties will in many instances be linked to due diligence disclosures by the seller, where the seller will both promise that information disclosed through due diligence is true and accurate, but also on the flipside they will often also state that the warranties won't cover any specific risk that has been disclosed in that due diligence material.

This is why both the content of the warranties and the linking of them to due diligence material is so critically important for a buyer to protect against risks in the business. And also so important for a buyer to protect themselves against the risk that information provided by the seller (that the buyer has used to evaluate the business) is untrue or misleading in some way.

We discuss the operation of warranties and indemnities in much greater detail in part III, and I recommend reading further there to understand the types of decisions to be made in the drafting of these warranties in terms of the period of time of protection under them, and approaches that might be used by a seller to minimise their exposure to the buyer.

The other important item of note in discussion of the protection afforded by the sale contract is the subject of enforcement of that protection. *The warranties are only as good as the party giving them.* The selling entity that has provided the warranty might not have any funds, or even still be in existence, at the time of a loss that triggers a warranty claim.

This is why it's incredibly important to consider who is providing the warranty, and the ability to recover against them during the warranty period. Often it will be appropriate to include a guarantor for the warranties to ensure that if the selling entity has been stripped of cash post-sale, there is still someone for the buyer to turn to if a warranty claim becomes necessary. Thus security for the warranties is also an extremely important consideration.

There are many possible ways of dealing with the requirement of some sort of security, including:

- requiring that the warranties are guaranteed by others (for example, the individuals or parent companies behind the selling entities)
- by the buyer withholding part of the purchase price payment (or by having this retention held in escrow by the solicitors)
- through a security interest over the business assets.

An alternative may also be taking out buy-side warranty and indemnity insurance, or requiring the seller to take out sell-side insurance (which is likely to be more cost effective). This type of insurance allows a buyer to claim directly against the insurer for any breach of

An important item of note in discussion of the protection afforded by the sale contract is the

SUBJECT OF ENFORCEMENT

of that protection. The warranties are only as good as the party giving them.

warranties, and can provide a longer warranty period than a seller may otherwise have been prepared to provide.[15]

Ultimately, the take-home message is that the contract can provide important risk protection for a buyer, but it must be constructed carefully to ensure it does actually provide the protection that is intended!

PROTECTION THROUGH THE STRUCTURE OF THE DEAL

In addition to the protections afforded through the sale contract, the deal structure itself can also be used to help minimise risk. We cover this in detail in chapter 18. But briefly here, protection can be achieved through decisions made on how you structure the deal, for example:

- in your choice of share sale versus business sale (where a share sale may reduce the risk of value transfer leakage, but potentially increase the risk to the buyer in taking over the history of the business)
- how you structure the payment (where payments may be withheld until a period after completion to protect against various risks).

PROTECTION THROUGH COMMERCIAL APPROACHES

The final consideration in risk minimisation and control is the commercial approaches a buyer will employ. We have discussed many ideas for commercial approaches in each of the earlier sections identifying risks. The reality is that while the contract can be used to control some of the risk, this is not the full answer.

The information drawn through your investigations of the business in the acquisition and due diligence process should provide a good outline of the risks in the business, and you will then need to work through these risk by risk to assess the best way of controlling each one.

---

15   Make sure you check out the resources hub at www.buygrowexit.com.au to find out more about how this insurance could work in your transaction.

Outside of the sale contract itself, the control mechanisms will usually be as follows:

1. Setting up systems and processes to minimise the risk.
2. Setting up proper documentation to fill any gaps.
3. Putting in place appropriate insurance – which can be for the transaction risks, and also for the general risks in the business moving forward.

We dig into all these areas in more detail in part II.

Chapter 7

PROCESS: MAKING THE DEAL HAPPEN

WHAT HAPPENS WHEN THERE IS NO PRE-DEFINED CLEAR PROCESS

When businesses approach an acquisition or exit the focus is often on simply closing the deal, and they naively walk into the contract process feeling that given the high-level commercial terms have been reached, the hard work is done and the rest is just fine print that will be taken over by the lawyers.

However, the reality is that most deals will take considerably more time and energy in the contract phase than have been originally planned for, because of a lack of defined process once it hits this phase. And unfortunately, a slow deal costs time and money. It saps energy and dilutes your power.

There are so many examples that come to mind for me of this scenario, but one that sticks out clearly is a deal I worked on many years ago in the sale of a manufacturing business. Initially the deal was being worked on with another lawyer. The corporate adviser at the time had suggested that the sellers use a lawyer who specialised in business sales and acquisitions, but the client had a long-standing relationship with a legal firm that had managed all of the work for them over the lifetime of their business and they felt the better path was to stick with their known commercial lawyer. But what they didn't understand was that most commercial lawyers only have minimal dealings with business sales and acquisitions. Which makes sense if you realise that most business owners will generally only sell a business once in their life. That is, once in the whole lifecycle of that business.

So the sellers worked with this general commercial lawyer, who given his lack of expert knowledge spent months crafting the sale agreement (something that should have gone out to the buyer within days, not months), and who then spent a further six months in torrid negotiations with the legal team for the buyer. Unfortunately the buyer's solicitor was also unrelenting.

The emails were prolific! Backwards and forwards, forwards and backwards, as both lawyers tried to ensure their clients bore *no risk at all* – which is of course an impossible outcome.

The broker came to me absolutely exasperated. It had taken almost a year to find a buyer, and for the buyer to evaluate the business and agree on commercial terms. But now the lawyers were tearing the deal apart, failing to understand the commercial realities of how a deal is struck. And the further eight months now spent in legal negoti- ations and drafts and redrafts was killing the relationship between the buyer and seller, and was also about to kill the deal as a whole! And both buyer and seller were also racking up massive legal fees.

But the sellers absolutely needed to sell; they were desperate to retire and were done with the business (and even more done now that they had expended so much energy in dealing with this protracted negotiation).

And the buyer had an absolute imperative to buy. He saw the value in the business, he had at this point committed at least 12 months of his time to the deal, and had poured a ton of money into it.

They were both committed, but so worn down by the process, and scared because of the massively risk averse (rather than realistic) views of their lawyers.

And so it was at this point that the deal landed on my desk.

The seller had sacked their lawyers. The broker asked if I could see if there was any way to make the deal happen. I said I would give it a go. But as I reviewed the documents, it became very clear that the real issues in this sale had been lost for almost pointless legal wrangling. The lawyers had clearly lost sight of what actually mattered.

Focusing back on the primary goals of identifying the value in the business, ensuring the value transferred, and minimising the transaction risk, I was able to identify which issues in negotiations between the parties were red herrings (arguments that really had very little consequence for one or both of the parties). I could also see where there were issues that did have commercial or legal consequence. Out of this assessment, it became clear which points of contention could be agreed upon immediately and which needed to be *properly* negotiated.

Ultimately almost all of the points that had been in hot negotiation turned out to be red herrings. As we dug into each of them, it became obvious that there were commercial ways around the issues. By narrowing down the scope of what the parties were 'arguing' about to just a few remaining items, suddenly the task looked so much easier to both parties.

Next was to get all the parties in a room to talk, rather than redrafting the documents yet again. And ultimately, a deal that had spent eight months in legal wrangling to the point of almost absolute impasse, was resolved and happily exchanged within two weeks.

I keep in touch with those clients to this day. Even though I worked with them for only two weeks we forged a great relationship in this short time. And in good news, the sellers have gone on to enjoy a fabulous retirement, and the buyer has grown the business from strength to strength.

It ended up as a good news story all round, but it was so close to being the opposite – had the deal failed (which really would have been entirely due to the poor approach of the lawyers), both the seller and the buyer would have been incredibly negatively affected. The seller would have to spend at least a year in sourcing and completing another sale – and given they were so battle weary at the point I met them, I'm really not sure they could have withstood the process again (or maintained the value of the business during that period). The buyer also had at this point almost everything on the table, as he had turned so much attention to this negotiation that his other business had not been given the attention it needed for growth to sustain him for another search.

THE PROCESSES REQUIRED FOR A SMOOTH SALE

Let's break down what this example demonstrates about the processes required for a smooth sale.

YOU MUST HAVE A VISION FOR THE DEAL

Often buyers and sellers (and each of their advisers) become so consumed with the process along the way, they lose sight of what true success in the deal actually looks like. Understanding the end goal for both parties is a critical step in ensuring the outcome meets the actual end goal, and helps to clarify the motivations and levers of the other side, providing important ways to resolve speedbumps along the way.

At the outset of the process, you should be sitting down with your advisers and clarifying what your end goal is, what value you are seeking from the acquisition and what risks sit in the acquisition from your current perspective.

ALL PARTIES MUST BE ENGAGED IN THE DEAL

After clarifying the vision and end goal for each party, it is important that your legal advisers start the process with another very 'non-legal' step – which is the **engagement** of all of the stakeholders.

At best, there should be an initial meeting with all the parties to reconfirm the deal terms so that it is clear that everyone is on the same page.

But at worst there should be at least some connection made between the lawyers for both the buyer and seller, and ideally also with any other advisers involved (such as accountants or brokers) to ensure there is some sort of human connection.

The reason for this is twofold – firstly, it is to disarm the often initial reaction that lawyers will take of an adversarial relationship. Lawyers love to fight, and to be right! And by making an initial connection we can often connect to the people (and the personalities) in the deal. I'm not suggesting that we need to be great friends with everyone, but we do need to find the human component because M&A deals can be unlike most other areas of law, in that our job is to find a way to get a deal done well. We are unified by the outcome we are seeking. And of course we are all trying to minimise our client's risk. But we are looking to do that in the context of helping to get the deal done, not by being adversarial.

The concept of engagement of the parties is broader however than just engagement with the lawyers on the other side. The relationships with other key stakeholders in the sale process – such as the corporate advisers or business brokers, accountants and other key parties – are just as important.

Often lawyers work in silos, but this approach completely misses the opportunities provided by close relationships with these other stakeholders. For example, given their history of involvement with the seller, often the broker or corporate adviser can be a point of important communication between the parties if issues occur or the lawyers on the other side are slowing down the transaction.

Unfortunately many lawyers treat the brokers as just biased sales agents, rather than recognising that they can be an integral part of the process. While of course they usually act for the seller and will be biased towards them (as they should be), ultimately their mandate is to help get the deal done. When they are involved in the right way, they can play a powerful role in helping facilitate a smoother transaction and an effective outcome.

COMMUNICATION MUST BE PERSONAL AND REGULAR

Communication between the parties must at an early point become more personal than emails. Lawyers often love hiding behind emails, which is where the terrible results often come from – with redraft upon redraft, email upon email.

We have a two-draft rule in our legal practice. This means that we allow each party to have two drafts, then we do our absolute best to try to get all the parties together on the phone or in a meeting – this is to get cut through, and to drive the discussions to a head. This can be a great way to stop all the redrafts, force discussion about the critical issues and corral the parties to a final agreement.

THE DEAL MUST MAINTAIN MOMENTUM

Deal momentum is an excellent tool for getting deals done. When the parties are focused on timing, and the lawyers respond quickly, deals can be done in record time – and in these instances, the parties generally seem to have better outcomes and a happier experience.

But when a deal drags on and on and on, the parties often end up weary. This can cause one of two results. Either the parties become obstinate and more stuck, and the relationship between them deteriorates terribly. Or one of the parties suddenly gives away too much in the negotiations, because they have lost their energy. This can be a very dangerous outcome.

Ultimately it is far better to seize momentum and focus on finding ways to keep the deal moving quickly.

This requires, firstly, some idea of timing, ideally set out in a timetable between the parties.

Next, it requires advisers who are willing to act within that timeframe.

And finally, it requires experience in the advisers on both sides of the table to ensure they are able to review and turn over contracts quickly, are able to navigate and reassure clients who can be getting nervous at this pointy end, and have a process and a team behind them to ensure that all the wheels are continuing to turn effectively.

An acquisition involves a lot of moving parts, searches and documentation, and requires strong checklists and processes to ensure that the delivery of all of this documentation is done efficiently to save time in the deal and money for the buyer.

YOU MUST HAVE A DEFINED PROCESS

As alluded to in the point above, you need a clear process mapped out to take you from the beginning of the deal all the way to the very end – to combat the risk of deal fever taking over – together with a commitment by the deal team to go through the process step by step. This should include timeframes for each element of the process, starting with the expectations of the seller in the delivery of key information.

The ability of the seller to provide all the information that you as a buyer need, within reasonable timeframes, is imperative to your ability to move at the right speed through the deal (given you will often be relying on information from the seller to access and assess financing options, as well as to evaluate the business). The failure of a seller to meet those timeframes for the provision of information can also be an early indication of the way that the business is run.

Other elements in the process include the period of time you will have to conduct your due diligence investigations and, critically, how the contract phase will run.[16]

---

16   Check out our resources hub to get a copy of this process and an outline of how it works at www.buygrowexit.com.au. You can also download a copy of an example deal timeline.

But the most important point here is that you work with a deal team, including lawyers who have defined processes to keep deals on track. Because without a strong commitment to process and time-lines, deals can easily start to consume much more time, energy and expense than you had planned.[17]

YOU MUST OPERATE WITH EMOTIONAL INTELLIGENCE

Emotional intelligence is a critical skill to have in your deal team, but it is something that is almost never discussed. We discuss elsewhere in the book how emotion can have a huge (but generally unrecognised) impact on deals.

Understanding the emotion that is likely in a deal, and how to handle it, is such a critical skill for your deal team to have. Almost every deal will hit a roadblock at some point, and the ability of your deal team to understand what is really causing the block, and the motivations of each of the parties, will determine how the blocks will be dealt with. Either through argument and adversarial positions, which cause distrust between the parties. Or through sensible resolution using both commercial and legal approaches to find the win/win outcomes.

In the example at the beginning of this chapter, the sellers were nervous about ongoing risk but needed to get out. The buyer was of course, as all buyers are, concerned about his risk in the business moving forward. But while that emotion was playing in the background, his primary motivation was to complete the deal and get on with growing the business.

The original lawyer for the seller was motivated by his own ego, and by his fear of getting something wrong in an area he wasn't an

---

17 Check out our lawyer buying checklist at the resources hub www.buygrowexit.com.au for the things to look out for when choosing a lawyer. Bear in mind also that this phase will be much easier if both sides have the right lawyers on board, so you might want to suggest that your seller also uses this lawyer checklist before they 'lawyer up' so they understand the imperative of choosing the right lawyer for the deal.

expert in, and consequently he was so focused on 'winning' every argument, and picking up on every tiny hint of risk, that he didn't understand he was whipping his clients into a frenzy of unnecessary concern and creating an impasse.

But by looking at the deal from a perspective of respecting the emotion of both the seller and the buyer, and focusing clearly on what each of their ultimate motivations were, it became easy to identify how the impasses could be simply dealt with.

———

The ultimate take-away is this – your deals should be run with a strong emphasis on process. And as we have seen, process includes not just transaction timelines that all parties (and their lawyers and other advisers) are committed to, but also other elements like communication style and emotional intelligence that can be far less recognised and understood but can truly make the difference between transaction failure and success.

Chapter 8

PURCHASE STRUCTURE: MAKING THE TRANSFER WORK

When you are acquiring a business there are three key things to consider in structuring the purchase price and deal offer:

1. **The structure of the purchase** – is it a share sale, business sale or asset sale? Is it a full sale, partial sale or a sale over time (staged sale or sale in tranches)?

2. **The timing of payment** – will the full purchase price be paid at deal completion, or will payment be staggered over time?

3. **How the purchase price is paid** – is the purchase price set, or is it partly contingent on future performance or the achievement of predefined milestones?

Each of these components of the deal structure will relate back to the questions of value and risk that we looked at in previous chapters, because ultimately the structure of the deal can help to offset risks in the deal and in the business, and assist in value transfer.

Considering deal structure is really an opportunity to get creative – to work out how to shape the deal to meet your objectives, manage the nuances of the value and risk, and also factor in the objectives (and motivators) of the seller.

THE STRUCTURE OF THE PURCHASE

Many buyers I deal with (even the most sophisticated) and many advisers (even sometimes accountants who deal with structures regularly) don't fully understand the fundamental differences between share, business and asset sales.[18]

It's critical to get this clear as early as possible; I have seen many transactions end up in a complete mess when the parties change their approach late in the deal. One example I remember clearly was the sale of a professional services firm where the terms had included an 90% upfront payment and a further 10% payment one year after completion, on the basis that the clients of the business fully transferred over, and the revenue was maintained once the buyer was running it.

The buyer was of course attempting to protect itself against any leakage it might have suffered from clients transitioning from the old management to the new management (professional services businesses can have their value tied closely to the relationships with management, and in this instance the management was the seller, who was transitioning out as part of the sale).

The problem was that deferred payments can often create perverse outcomes. And in this instance, the seller was so focused

---

18   For a detailed discussion of the differences, see 'Share sale versus business sale' in chapter 18.

on achieving this final 10% payment that a number of problems arose. The sale was being run as a business sale, meaning each client needed to be transitioned. However, merely a day before completion, the seller realised there were issues in transitioning clients to the buyer (because in this instance each of the clients needed to agree in writing to transfer to the buyer). Fearing that this would cause a large loss of clients, the seller pushed for a last-minute change from a business sale to a share sale. Even though the seller was a seasoned professional, often involved in sale and acquisition trans-actions, he hadn't fully understood the ramifications of changing to a share sale so late in the deal. The financial accounts weren't in order, taxes hadn't been finalised, and money was sitting in bank accounts that hadn't been distributed. Also, the entire sale agreement needed to be changed from a business sale to a share sale agreement (which are two completely different types of agreements), creating massive pressure on both legal teams in the deal to rewrite and negotiate a 40-page contract in one day.

The massive time urgency created by the last-minute change created a mess, and caused tension between the parties.

But it got worse.

As soon as the buyer got into the business, he started making changes. The changes destabilised the staff, the clients, and in partic-ular the seller, who after 30 years at the helm of his own business was not used to having to deal with change or having his methods so publicly challenged. The relationship soured quickly and havoc ensued.

Ultimately clients started leaving, meaning not only did the seller not achieve his sale price, but also the buyer didn't achieve the value out of the acquisition that he had banked on. Unsurpris-ingly the parties ended up in a major dispute that went on for months and racked up massive fees.

This example demonstrates a lot of behaviours and outcomes that should be avoided:

- Changing decisions or approaches late in the deal.
- Perverse and unintended results from earnouts and keeping the seller in the business for too long, causing value leakage for both parties.
- Not understanding the emotion that a seller will go through during the sale, and not building in sensitivity around that.
- Not understanding how the process will run, or how value will practically transition to the seller.

As a buyer you need to be aware from an early stage of the differences between share and asset and business sales. The decision of which method to use will be impacted by the value that is transferring, the ease (or complexity) of that transfer, the timeline that you are working towards, and the risk sitting in the business. This decision can also impact stamp duty as in some states of Australia there are stamp duty differences between share sales and business or asset sales. And as demonstrated by the example above, changing approaches mid deal can have dire consequences!

FULL SALE, OR PARTIAL SALE?

Will you buy the whole business in one go (the most common approach), purchase only part of the business (which would generally be done by acquiring a portion of the shares in the company), or conduct a sale over time in stages (often referred to as tranches, or through options)?

Partial sales and sales over time would generally be done as share sales rather than business sales.

We cover partial sales and sales over time in part III, Exit, but here are two key considerations if you are considering a partial sale or a sale over time:

- **Value.** If you are looking to purchase further shares into the future – how will these be valued? They can either be valued now and the purchase can be set in stone, or you can create a purchase opportunity through the use of options. (We look at options in detail in the options section below.)

As a buyer you need
to be aware from
an early stage of the
differences between
SHARE and **ASSET**
and **BUSINESS SALES.**

- **Relationships.** For the period that you are a partial owner, you will need to carefully regulate the relationship between you and the other owners. One of the key requirements will be a shareholders' agreement. (Head over to part II for a detailed discussion of what to think about with your shareholders' agreement.)

THE TIMING OF PAYMENT

The next key consideration for a buyer in structuring the offer is when the purchase price will be paid.

You can opt to pay the full purchase price at deal completion, or you can stagger the payment of the purchase price in various ways. Later we dig deeper into whether that price is fixed or contingent on something happening; in this step you are simply considering timing of payment, and whether you intend to pay all at once at completion or to pay in stages over time.

There are several considerations that will impact this decision – including:

- **Funding.** How you are funding the deal will impact what you will be looking to offer in terms of payment timing.
- **Seller flexibility.** Deferred payments might be a more attractive option than third-party funding (often deferred payment can be negotiated into a deal without interest or any other uplift in price). This can be a great option if the seller is flexible enough to provide it. (This is sometimes also referred to as 'vendor financing', as the seller is effectively financing the buyer until the payments have been fully made.)

Deferred payments is where the purchase price has been agreed, a portion of the purchase price is paid at completion,[19] and the

---

19   Completion is that stage of the business or share sale where the business/shares transfer to the buyer. This is when you as the buyer take control and start operating the business.

remaining funds are paid later or in staged payments. Sometimes however the timing might be connected to hitting a milestone, and so this can be utilised to keep the pressure on the seller to meet those milestones (for example, this might be connected to a payment that is being withheld until various contracts are transferred after completion). From a buyer's perspective, even though deferred payments are payments that are due to be made and set in advance, because they are payments that are held back by the buyer, from a practical perspective they can still act as a bargaining chip.

Generally a vendor finance component will be provided on a much shorter timeframe than with a third-party lender – often this is a maximum of two or three years. And sellers will generally want security, for example over the business (which can sometimes restrict what you can do with the business until it is fully paid), and additionally or instead they may require personal guarantees.

You must also consider:

- **Control.** If there are elements that will still need to be delivered after deal completion, you might wish to hold back part of the payment to help provide you with some control to ensure those things are done.

- **The need for reconciliations.** Sometimes part of the payment will be held back to allow for account reconciliations after completion (this is used where there are payments and financial transactions that are constantly flowing into and out of the business which can't be reconciled completely at the day of completion).

- **Protection via retention sums.** A retention (sometimes also called a hold back) is a sum of money held back from the purchase price in order to secure value transfer or offset risk as collateral for the buyer's possible warranty and indemnification claims against the seller. We discuss this in detail in the chapter 18 – it is an important consideration for buyers in considering protection for risk and value transfer.

- **Sale in tranches (staged sales).** One final consideration is whether a staggered payment of the purchase price is actually a sale in tranches, where only part of the asset passes over for each payment that is made. This is most usually done with the sale of shares in a company, or the sale of units in a unit trust.

  For example, you might purchase 70% of the shares initially, and then over time purchase the other 30%.

  You can do this either by setting up the sale agreement at the beginning and setting out in advance the timing and price for each further sale.

  Or you can do this by way of **options**, where you as the buyer are given the option to purchase the remaining shares over time (at either a set value, or valued on an agreed basis at the time of sale), or in the alternative, the seller may have the option to force you to buy the shares over time. These are called 'put' and 'call' options, and there are a lot of considerations if you are looking to use options, which we discuss further below.

  The one thing to bear in mind if you adopt an approach of a sale in tranches is that you will now be in business with the sellers. This brings into play many questions you need to be asking yourself about how the management of the business and the relationship with the sellers will work. A strong shareholders' agreement will be critical!

HOW THE PURCHASE PRICE IS PAID

The last component to consider is how the purchase price is paid. Will it be paid in cash, or in shares, or a mixture of both? In some transactions, buyers will retain the seller in the business or in the new merged entity, and will use a share swap as part or all of the consideration. We look at this further in part III. Is the purchase price set, or is it partly contingent on the performance of the business post-sale or the achievement of certain milestones? This is where the discussion of 'earnouts' comes in.

EARNOUTS

We discuss earnouts in much more detail in part III, Exit.

Generally earnouts work on the basis that a payment is made at completion, and then further payments are made over time based on the performance of the business. This might come into play if you have a concern about whether all the customers or revenue will transition when new ownership or management comes in, or if there is other uncertainty about whether the value attributed to the business will actually be realised (for example, in a high-growth business with big future projections, where you as a buyer are uncertain about the validity of the projections).

It is also often used as a mechanism to keep the seller in the business and incentivised to keep focus on its performance.

A common approach to earnouts is the following type of breakdown:

- *At deal completion:* a payment of 80% or 90% of the agreed purchase price.
- *After completion:* a further payment of the remaining component over a period of one to two years if the revenue or profit of the business in the hands of the buyer has hit agreed milestones.

While this breakdown perhaps is the most common, there are many different approaches across different deal sizes. Earnouts might be a much larger component of the purchase price (we have seen almost every kind of earnout ranging from 5% to 100% of the price) and over varying timeframes. Earnouts can also be valued at either a set price on achieving a milestone or KPI, or on a sliding scale based on the future performance. When suggesting a payment structure that involves an earnout, bear in mind that a seller is likely to want control how that revenue, GP (gross profit) or EBITDA figure is calculated, and they are also likely to require several other controls in the business. We discuss this in part III.

It is also important to note that while earnouts for smaller (sub $5m) deals will often be calculated using a revenue or gross profit target, larger deals will commonly use EBITDA. But there are many possible ways to structure the triggers and calculations of the earnout payments, and there are no hard-and-fast rules. Just bear in mind that a seller is highly likely to want to be able to exercise control over the achievement of the metrics that are put in place, and sometimes these controls can seriously constrain how you operate the business while the earnouts are in progress.

So be careful about how you approach setting up earnouts, to ensure that you aren't creating more problems than you are solving!

And finally, bear in mind that earnouts are essentially a risk-sharing mechanism, where the buyer and seller are agreeing that they will share the risk of whether the future performance of the business meets the projections. Sellers are often very concerned about the likelihood that they will actually receive the earnout payments negotiated, given the business after the sale is under the control of the buyer. So it's not uncommon for sellers to want to participate in the upside, as well as the downside risk of the earnout not being paid in full, or not triggering at all! This can be reflected in the price that the seller negotiates in order to make the earnout component more palatable, or many other things. Consequently, if you are confident about the operation of the business and the value after completion under your new reign and you aren't motivated to keep the seller in the business, then you may be able to negotiate a much lower price as a full payment at completion rather than using an earnout.

There is a lot more information about earnouts in chapter 18, but before I leave this topic, I just want to provide a little warning. Using earnouts can seem like a great approach at the beginning, but they can be complex to work through, so be careful not to over-engineer the deal and create more complexity than is required!

Be careful about how you approach setting up earnouts, to ensure that you aren't **CREATING MORE PROBLEMS** than you are **SOLVING!**

OPTIONS

In the above sections I mentioned options as an approach to dealing with staged sales. Options provide contractual rights to buy or sell an asset at a set price on or before a certain date.

Options are different to straight staged sales in that with a staged sale the parties both are generally bound to the sale and purchase of shares, whereas the use of options means that obligations are generally one way (only one party has the obligation to buy or sell to the other party). The terminology given to these two different ways of setting out the rights under an option are 'put' options and 'call' options.

A put option is the right to force another party to buy. So, it is used by sellers.

Conversely, a call option is the right to force another party to sell. So, it is used by buyers.

WHEN ARE PUT AND CALL OPTIONS USED?

Put and call options are often used in the context of a sale and purchase of shares in situations where the buyer initially purchases only a portion of the total shares. The use of options may then be used to provide the future rights relating to the balance of the shares, to stagger the sale of those shares. It may be useful in situations where there is a tax or financial reason for the whole sale not to occur straight away, where a buyer is unable to obtain finance for the whole share purchase initially, or for many other reasons.

Options may also be used without any initial prior sale, where for example a buyer may be considering the purchase and may want to reserve the right to purchase the shares at some point in the future, but not have the obligation. Medical and veterinary practice buyers sometimes use this approach – to work in the business for a period of time to assess it before committing to a purchase (but who take out an option for the purchase to preserve that right).

Options are also often used when providing employees with ways to buy into the business. Often there will be an agreement for an option to be provided to the employee if they achieve a certain milestone or KPI (for example, if they hit a pre-defined revenue target, either individually or through a team that they manage), in which case they then have a future right to buy into the business (at a rate fixed at an earlier point, or at a discounted rate).

You can have an agreement that relates to a single option, or multiple options at multiple future dates.

Options can be a useful tool for a buyer to gradually enter into the business, or to reserve their rights while they get to know the business. For example, we have used this when acting for buyers who initially purchase a small parcel of shares and set up an option to purchase the remaining shares over time based on the business meeting set performance metrics, or simply based on our buyer's comfort in the business after a period of connection with it.

And in this sort of situation, while a buyer will still want to ensure they have done some initial due diligence before they purchase the shares and enter into the future option, because they are starting off with a smaller financial commitment and the right but not the obligation for the future purchases, due diligence doesn't necessarily need to be as thorough as if they were purchasing the whole company outright. It also gives a buyer time to get finance for the future parcel of shares; in many cases, financing a smaller component initially and then later a further component can be easier than financing the whole sum.

Here are some things to consider when dealing with options:

1. **The option fee.** This is the amount that is paid for the grant of the option. This may sometimes be a small figure, at other times it will be a significant part of the purchase price (for example, in the case of the buyer reserving the right to purchase shares in the future where they haven't purchased any shares initially).

2. **The exercise price.** The price paid to exercise the option (to actually purchase the shares). This can be a set price, or can reference a formula (for example, a multiple of the EBITDA).

3. **The exercise (or expiry) date.** Defines the period in which or set date when the options can be exercised.

4. **The trigger.** This is the criteria for triggering the right to exercise the option. This can be a date, the achievement of a certain milestone or KPI, or simply at the discretion of one of the parties.

5. **The documents needed.** There will need to be a number of documents governing the relationship of the parties while there is part ownership. For example, in addition to the option agreement you will need to have agreed in advance on a shareholders' agreement that sets out decision making and exit and all other important areas for the period in which you and the seller are holding shares at the same time.

THE POTENTIAL PROBLEMS CAUSED BY KEEPING THE SELLER IN THE BUSINESS

Earnouts, delayed payments, options, and other approaches to keeping the seller invested in the business or its performance after completion often seem like a very good idea to a buyer. For good reason. However, there is another side that I have seen play out on many occasions. That other side is the difficulties that can be caused by the seller's continued involvement.

I've heard the saying many times that once you have run a business for a significant period, you become effectively unemployable. When a seller has become so used to running their own ship, it can be incredibly difficult for them to run to a buyer's management tune. And this causes incredible stress for both parties in so many instances of business sales where the seller is retained either working in the business or with a vested financial interest in the business for a significant period post-sale (as we saw in the example earlier in this chapter).

One big caution for buyers is simply not to make changes too quickly in the business they have purchased (indeed I recommend generally allowing a business to continue to operate for at least a year before starting to bring in changes); another is to be very careful how they set up the ongoing relationship and interest of a seller. I have spoken with many buyers who have come to the realisation after a sale that having the seller make a swift exit can be a good thing.

So, make sure you consider in your approaches to deal structuring the level of involvement that really is necessary in your retention of the sellers. If you are going to buy only a portion of the business, or buy into the shares over time, or keep the seller otherwise engaged in the business performance, make sure you take steps to truly get to know them so you understand what that future period working together will be like. And build in ways to enable swift exits of the seller if things don't go to plan.

Chapter 9

YOU'VE BOUGHT THE BUSINESS, NOW WHAT?

FINAL BUYING TIPS

Here are a few final tips on the last stages of the business acquisition process, on transition and integration.

CREATE A COMMUNICATION PLAN

Carefully consider and construct your communication plan with clients, staff and other stakeholders. The communication plan is often left until the last minute, but it's important to consider how to orchestrate these discussions and communications carefully from day one.

KEEP STAFF ENGAGED

Consider how to keep staff engaged through the transition. Change can be difficult for people; you should acknowledge this and be providing leadership for the staff. Show them your vision for the future, and their role in it.

DON'T MAKE CHANGES TOO QUICKLY

Making changes too quickly is the number one mistake that many buyers make that can cause value erosion. Let the dust settle on the sale, let the stakeholders sink into the new ownership, and take your time to assess how the business is currently working before making any changes.

START WITH AN EXIT PLAN

It might sound weird, but you should ensure you have built your exit plan right at the beginning. Beginning with the end in mind helps to ensure you have a path for the future, and this clarity will help you build the right plan to achieve your goal.

PROTECT YOUR INVESTMENT

You have sunk a lot of money, time and effort into buying this asset, and will undoubtedly sink further time, money and effort into growing it – you now need to ensure that it is properly protected. Which brings us to our next chapter: Building the fortress to protect your business!

Part II

GROW

CHAPTER 10: BUILDING THE FORTRESS TO PROTECT YOUR GROWING BUSINESS 115

CHAPTER 11: IDENTIFY AND PROTECT: FINDING AND SECURING THE VALUE
IN YOUR BUSINESS 123

CHAPTER 12: PREDICT: ANTICIPATING THE LANDMINES BEFORE THEY
BLOW YOU UP 150

CHAPTER 13: PREVENT: ADDRESSING THE CORE SYSTEMS AND PROCESSES
FOR GROWING AND PRESERVING VALUE 157

CHAPTER 14: UNDERSTAND YOUR ENDGAME 197

Before you delve into this part, I recommend that you start by assessing how your business stacks up on value protection and risk minimisation by taking our short scorecard. Find the scorecard at our resources hub at www.buygrowexit.com.au.

Chapter 10

BUILDING THE FORTRESS TO PROTECT YOUR GROWING BUSINESS

Now you have your greatest asset, the next step is to grow it while also making sure you don't lose it.

In my decades of dealing with SMEs I have seen so many examples of the rollercoaster of business.

I've witnessed many businesses on incredible growth trajectories, where enthusiasm and motivation is high, at times almost manic as the owners and managers scramble to find enough seconds in the day to deal with all of the many competing demands on their time and attention in their fast growth machine. Deals are done left, right and centre.

But amid all this buoyant energy, I have also seen a lot more of the other side. The side where businesses have hit rock bottom and been completely wiped out by a legal landmine that has gone off when and where they least expected it. Or a series of fires drag down a once star business, ripping out the value that had been growing and leaving the owners tired and jaded. In so many instances, these have been the same businesses that were once growth stars.

In fact, my experience in dealing with these kinds of issues is what has driven me through my whole legal career to want to provide protection and relief for business owners. It's one of the reasons

Now you have your GREATEST ASSET,

the next step is to grow it while also making sure you don't lose it.

I wrote this book.[20] This takes me back to a story from almost 20 years ago, when I was a junior lawyer and met a business owner called James. James ran a construction company, and he had come to our legal firm because his growing business was in trouble. A lot of trouble.

His business had grown quickly, and having hit the point of exhaustion and being driven by the entrepreneurial dream of handing the business over to someone else to run, he decided to employ a general manager to take over the day-to-day duties.

Unfortunately, while the business seemed strong and on a massive upward trajectory, the legal foundations of the business didn't match the current size (which, I now realise looking back, is such a common issue). There were very few systems in place to manage risk of the size that the business was now running.

The new general manager took his eye off relentless follow up on slower-paying clients, cash started to slow down and then dry up, supplier terms and overdrafts started to be pushed to the limit, and then the largest client simply stopped paying.

James came to us in absolute desperation. The business needed cash. Quickly. All the overdrafts were now exhausted and there was nothing left in the financial reserve tank to deal with this out-of-left-field issue. Suppliers were threatening to stop supply, and there was no money left to pay staff and contractors.

There were legal avenues available to James to get his clients to make payments, and we quickly put these in action – but in the meantime the money simply ran out. James sought advice from his accountant and insolvency 'experts' who told him to pull the rip cord and sink the company. But it wasn't just the business that sank; his creditors chased him mercilessly and he went into bankruptcy.

He came to visit me one day, which I will never forget. He told me about the death threats to him and his family from creditors that his business had owed massive sums to (and that he appeared to

---

20　And also the reason for me launching the podcast show *Talking Law*. Check out *Talking Law* on your favourite podcast player.

have also signed personal guarantees for). He told me about his wife leaving him, overcome by the stress of it all. He told me about his employees and contractors who were left high and dry with no work and no money – a team who had been with him for years. And now of course all of his assets were also gone.

I was a junior lawyer, sitting with a man in tears who had lost everything, and I couldn't help. And I knew it may all have been avoided if he had taken proper advice years ago, if someone had been there to guide him in building up the legal infrastructure of the business at the same rate as its growth.

But of course, that thought bubble couldn't help him right now.

A year later James called me again, after he had been interviewed by the trustees in bankruptcy for the umpteenth time. He said he had spent hours and hours and hours being examined by the trustees, who were relentless – believing he had some assets hidden away. The latest trigger had been a record that had come to light that suggested he owned a boat, which had set off the trustees once again. Apparently the 'boat' was a rusted out old tinny that he had abandoned for scrap metal years ago. He told me he just didn't have the energy anymore.

I wasn't an insolvency expert and couldn't provide any helpful advice other than to just listen. And as I listened, I became angry. Angry that James hadn't gotten the right advice on his path to growth. Angry at some of the poor advice given to him during his saga. And then, just sad that it had come to this for him.

James was in my thoughts for decades afterwards, as I pondered at times my own career. Many times in those early years I wondered whether law was for me, whether it provided me with the meaning and depth that I wanted from my life's work. And whenever I had that inkling, I came back to James. Back to the memory of his pain in losing not just his business and his assets, but also his marriage. And it occurred to me that helping protect business owners from the pain that James had suffered was a goal that I could be proud of.

This point in the middle, the **PROTECTION** of a **GROWING BUSINESS,** is absolutely imperative to ensure that your story doesn't end in disaster.

You have already heard me discuss the joys of acquiring businesses, and later you will hear about the beauty of seeing a great exit that lives up to the dreams of business founders as they move onto the next phase after years of toil and growth. But this point in the middle, the protection of a growing business, is absolutely imperative to ensure that your story doesn't end like James's did.

And this is how I came up with the concept of 'Fortify' – a method of approaching the construction of a legal foundation that builds a strong wall around the business assets, locks in the value, and sets it up for growth. Fortify is the phase that should be revisited after every acquisition, during any period of fast growth, and before exit to maximise the value and provide longevity. It's the phase that protects the assets you have bought and built, and locks in that value. It's also the phase where you get to set the business up in a way that will maximise its value, and in the value you will be able to extract.

The decisions made in this growth phase impact your tax outcomes, and therefore the ultimate cash you will see out of a sale. But they also impact whether you will even make it to a sale. Because this is the critical phase for a business; testing the strength of the fortress that has been built around the business as it grows.

During the growth and consolidation phase every business faces repeated and often unexpected landmines along the way. Those landmines will threaten not just to erode the value in a business, but sometimes threaten its very existence. So in this phase, we lay the right foundations for maximising value, and we build the fortress around the business to fiercely protect that value.

This is a phase that is also critical to come back to before exit and investment and bringing on business partners.

The ultimate objective of Fortify – and of this chapter – is to help you understand how to grow your business so that you maximise its value, and so that value is protected along the way.

Let's look at how that can be achieved.

During the GROWTH and CONSOLIDATION phase every business faces repeated and often unexpected landmines along the way. Those landmines will threaten not just to erode the value in a business, but sometimes threaten its very existence.

THE FORTIFY METHODOLOGY

There are four very simple steps to Fortify:

1. **Identify:** Pinpoint the core underlying value in the business.
2. **Protect:** Lock in and protect that value.
3. **Predict:** Forecast the likely risks in the business that could drain value, and build in prediction systems to provide early warning.
4. **Prevent:** Build systems to minimise and where possible, prevent, the landmines.

We'll look at these in the following chapters.

THE FORTIFY PROCESS

Chapter 11

IDENTIFY AND PROTECT: FINDING AND SECURING THE VALUE IN YOUR BUSINESS

IDENTIFY (KEY VALUE ASSETS)

The first step in the Fortify process is to understand what forms the key value in the business.

In order to identify value you must step back from the business, from your everyday entanglement, and analyse what is the fundamental key value in this business you are in.

What are the fundamental underlying value drivers?

Look not only at what forms the key value in your business as it is today, but also assess the top players in your industry to understand what forms key value more broadly within your industry. It can be helpful to think about value from the perspective of a buyer. What you assess to be of high value in your business as it is today might be missing what the market thinks of value – so consider this concept of value broadly.

Building a business for a successful exit may or may not be in your plans now, but bear in mind that creating a business that has value at sale gives you choices and protection should you one day suddenly have a desire (or need) for a quick sale. Understanding the fundamental underlying value drivers in your business currently – and the opportunity for building value for the future – will help you to understand how to build this flexibility for yourself and drive up the value of your business.

Let's start working through where value generally sits in a business. This list is also the basis for the other components of Fortify (protect, predict and prevent).

Usually the fundamental underlying value drivers of a business fall into nine general areas. However, not all businesses draw value out of all of these nine areas. Every business is different! Your goal is to identify which are the particular value drivers for your business now, and also potentially what might be an opportunity for value drivers for the future that can be further developed. The drivers are:

- customers/clients
- team
- intellectual property
- business partner relationships, other key contracts
- systems and processes
- trade secrets
- supply chain
- premises
- equipment and other assets.

PROTECT (LOCK IN VALUE)

Once you have identified the value, the next question is how to lock that value in.

Bear in mind that there are of course many ways to protect the value in your organisation that fall way outside of the legal arena. Your marketing, your customer interactions and your HR approach are all examples of the very important areas that you should be focusing on organisationally to protect and enhance the value in the business.

But of course I'm a lawyer, so in this book I am focusing on the legal methods of protecting that value. Some of the value protection drivers I suggest may perhaps balance somewhat precariously between commercial and legal, but I just feel it important to make it clear that there are so many commercial measures that also need to be employed – the consideration of your legal protection is just one step in the right direction.

THE AREAS OF YOUR BUSINESS YOU MUST IDENTIFY AND PROTECT

Let's now consider the many areas you must identify and protect as you fortify and grow your business.

RETAINING YOUR CUSTOMERS

One of the most common areas of key value in a business is the customer base, given this is what drives revenue. The value of the customer base of a business is often intertwined with other elements of value, like the branding, the key staff that the clients are used to dealing with, technology and location.

The value of a customer base can vary depending on factors like the lifetime value of each customer, the length of time they stay and how often they repurchase. It will also be impacted by how dependable (or 'sticky') they are. And finally, from a practical viewpoint, the value of customers sits in the contracts they have with the business (whether that is one-off ad hoc, ongoing subscription or a locked-in contract), and in the actual customer database.

So how do you protect the value in your customer base from a legal perspective?

FIXED-TERM CONTRACTS AND OTHER CONTRACTUAL COMMITMENTS

One way to protect the value in the customer base is to have the value locked into fixed-term contracts. There are many instances where this can work exceedingly well for both the business and the customer.

Fixed-term contracts provide surety of the term of the relationship, as well as locked-in prices and other conditions. Sometimes prices, volume and other elements will also be locked in. This allows both parties to adequately plan – for the business this of course provides assured custom, for the customer they get assured supply.

An example of where considering this type of arrangement is critical is if the business is required to put a lot of time, money or effort into creating the infrastructure to service a particular client or contract, or if the business itself is taking on contractual risk to service the client (for example, if the business needs to lock in supply contracts over a set term to meet the client contract).

This perhaps sounds very obvious, but I have seen many instances of businesses failing to line up their risk level with locking in the client value to offset that risk.

Ultimately there are many contractual ways to lock in the value under a contract with the risk it generates. Here are some ideas:

- mirror contract terms (I discuss this more later on)
- get creative in how you negotiate deals and set up contracts
- insist on volume or time commitments in return for some other benefit you are providing (for example pricing, or extended payment terms)
- introduce a fee to cover costs expended under the contract if the volumes decrease, or the client wants to build in an early termination right
- hold back IP transfer until certain minimum contract volumes have been reached
- connect exclusivity that you provide the client with a guarantee from them as to volume or contract length
- tie higher performance levels or response times or lower pricing to volume

- build in rebates that only trigger after a certain volume or contract term has been reached.

And the list goes on . . .

RECURRING REVENUE CONTRACTS

In the point above we examined fixed-term contracts and the benefits of using the contract to lock in client value, but there are other ways to make clients sticky. One of the best that I see regularly contribute massively to the ultimate value of a business (and the profit multiple that a buyer will apply to how they value that business) is recurring revenue through subscriptions or other rolling contracts. These contracts can roll monthly, quarterly or annually – but the idea is that they continue to roll on, providing ongoing value for the client, and often automated payment, where it becomes easier for the customer to allow the relationship to continue to roll on than it is to stop.

I have seen many businesses increase substantially in value when they have found ways to implement subscription-type revenue by changing the way that they package their goods or services to their customers. An example is recruitment businesses that have moved from focusing entirely on permanent placements (one-off fees) to onhire labour (where they are paid smaller amounts but on a rolling basis for the period that the end customers engage the staff). Also coaching businesses that have moved from one-off programs to ongoing subscriptions. And IT consulting businesses moving from ad hoc to subscription maintenance programs. We have also seen this concept in goods – with subscription supply popping up all over the place. Toothbrush clubs where new toothbrushes are delivered monthly. Shaver clubs, wine clubs, gin clubs . . . the list is endless.

This strategy has perhaps most clearly played out in software businesses, which once upon a time were all based on a pricing model of an upfront payment plus ongoing annual maintenance fees, but now are predominantly monthly SAAS (software as a service) subscription models.

This can apply to almost any industry. For example, if you have a veterinary practice, you could introduce a low-priced monthly 'membership' that entitles your customers to annual checks and other services for their pets, to ensure they keep coming back to you (and to ensure you can be proactive with the health of the pets under your care, rather than your customers holding back until problems have gotten large). This can as easily be used in almost any industry where there is a benefit in ongoing supply: IT solutions, dental, physiotherapy, accounting, financial planning, coaching, and many more.

So if you're not utilising subscriptions, memberships or other approaches to recurring revenue contracts, take a step back and see if this is something you can implement.

ADDING PRODUCTS OR SERVICES

Having your customers using multiple products or services under the one brand is a great way to keep your clients sticky to your business. It provides a more holistic service for your clients that provides a fuller and generally better solution, and it also means it will be harder for them to find a competitor that provides the range of services you do than if they were simply comparing one service or product.

If you don't have complementary services or products right now, this is where acquisitions can be transformative for a business. We discuss the benefits of adding products and service lines more deeply in part I.

ASSIGNMENT AND CHANGE OF CONTROL CLAUSES

Check your contracts to understand if they have change of control clauses (clauses that restrict your ability to make changes in the underlying ownership of your business without getting prior consent from your clients) or other restrictions on your assignment of customer contracts. These types of clauses are very common in services and supply contracts with large organisations, government, or any high-value contract. And they can impact your flexibility in selling your business or bringing partners in and out of the business.

PROTECTING YOUR BRAND

Generally the brand of the business or its products will be the glue between a business and its customer base. Luckily protecting the value in a brand is relatively simple, and should be high on the agenda if customers recognise your business from its brand. Protecting the brand makes it far easier to limit the use of similar marks by competitors, which in turn provides strong protection for the customer base to the extent that their repeat custom is connected to the brand. We will dig into in this in later chapters.

RESTRICTING DEPARTING STAFF FROM DEALING WITH CLIENTS

In many businesses there is a risk that exiting staff might take clients. This is a real risk that plays out on a regular basis. This could be a staff member with strong client relationships moving to a new employer and encouraging clients to follow, or setting up on their own.

I have seen many instances of sales teams leaving with customer databases (which we will discuss below) which they then target in the future. I have also seen many instances of staff leaving and simply feeling it is their right to continue contact with clients that they had built up a relationship with over time.

This can be a massive drag on the value of a business, and I have seen it bring businesses to their knees.

There are numerous ways you can address this. Employment contracts should have strong (but suitable) non-solicitation restraints to protect against staff leaving and taking clients, key partners or other staff. It might also be appropriate to have some staff committed to non-competition restraints.

It's a widely accepted myth that restraints in employment contracts are unenforceable, but this is simply not true. The truth is that restraints can certainly be difficult to enforce if they haven't been set up properly, but if they are reasonable in the circumstances and have been set up carefully, they indeed can be entirely enforceable.

This requires that you have appropriate templates set up for different roles and seniority levels in your business, and that you have legal advice at hand to help guide you for each hire to understand what is appropriate. It also requires you to understand the difference between non-solicitation and non-competition restraints – because they are different, often with different approaches to enforceability – but they are so often lumped in the one basket.

A non-solicitation restraint is where you are seeking to stop the staff member dealing with clients, other staff, and perhaps key contacts of the business (such as key partners) for a set period after they cease their relationship with your business.

A non-competition restraint is a limitation on your ex–team member's ability to compete with the business – bound by a certain timeframe and area. This latter restraint is one of the more difficult restraints to enforce, and therefore must be set up very carefully if it is to be effective.

SECURING YOUR CUSTOMER DATABASES

In addition to contractual protections, it's also important to ensure you have put up technical or physical barriers to inappropriate dealings with your customer databases. We have worked on many matters where organisations have failed to do this – and the result has been that departing staff have been able to simply take a copy of the database to their new business or new employer, and use it for covert (and sometimes not so covert!) marketing to move the customers from their old employer to their new.

RETAINING AND PROTECTING YOUR TEAM

Personnel are often a key component of the value in a business. Not only are they what makes the business run, but they also generally hold important business intelligence and history that often is not properly documented in the business. And of course they often also hold client relationships, and relationships with other key value drivers of the business (for example, suppliers and partners).

So, in considering protecting the value of the team itself, you also need to consider how to protect the value that the team impacts on.

PROTECTING THE VALUE OF THE TEAM THROUGH CONTRACTS

One legal strategy to protect the value of the team itself is rigorous contractual protections against them being poached. The business should have strong employment and contracting agreements for all staff to ensure that if anyone was to leave the business, they would be restrained from taking other staff with them.

This is something that should also feature in other contracts – such as customer contracts (to ensure your customers don't poach from you the team members they are dealing with – this is more common than you might think!), supplier contracts and partner contracts. We have at times put this type of restriction into agreements that you may never have thought relevant, such as confidentiality agreements.

The most important thing is to be able to identify where there might be a risk of others poaching your team members, and then doing what you can in your contracts to specifically protect against that risk.

PROTECTING THE VALUE OF THE TEAM THROUGH BONUSES AND SHARE SCHEMES (AND 'PHANTOM' SHARE SCHEMES)

In the above section we were obviously focusing on how to stop others from making a move on your staff, but how do you stop your staff from wanting to move in the first place? Of course the topic of staff retention expands far beyond the scope of this book and involves so much more than just legal considerations, so in this chapter

One legal strategy to **PROTECT THE VALUE** of the team itself is rigorous contractual protections against them being poached . . . Ways to achieve this include: CONTRACTS, BONUSES and SHARE SCHEMES (and 'phantom' share schemes).

I just want to look at one particularly highly valuable staff retention strategy: employee shares.[21]

It is far more powerful and effective to have staff who are staying by choice. Providing a way for key staff to hold equity in the business can be a killer staff retention strategy, and therefore a killer protection strategy for your business. (See chapter 18 for a detailed discussion on this.) It gives them skin in the game (especially during a growth phase), it helps them to look at the business in a different light, it provides strong encouragement for loyalty to the business and dramatically reduces the risk of them leaving.

There are many things to understand when considering employees holding shares:

- Will this be a plan that you share across multiple staff, or even the entire staff pool, or will it be for only one or two key staff?
- Will staff have to buy in, or will they receive shares without having to incur costs?
- Will the shares be provided outright, or on the basis of hitting certain performance targets?
- Will they be shares or options? (Options are a method of providing a future right for a staff member to receive or buy shares, based on the achievement of certain milestones or performance criteria, without actually providing the shares until those agreed criteria have been hit.)
- What terms will govern their long-term holding; for example, can they participate in decision making, will you require that the shares are returned if they leave?
- What are the tax implications for you and them?
- How will this impact you at exit?
- What preparation do you need to be doing to set up the business in advance?

---

21 Head over to my podcasts *Talking Law* and *The Deal Room* for more discussion about this topic – or simply contact us at Aspect Legal to get further information or to book a free initial discussion with our legal eagles: www.aspectlegal.com.au.

- Will you be ready for and happy to share the full financial and profit details of the business?
- Are you structured correctly to allow for this?

Clearly there are a lot of questions to be answered, but this can be a great strategy for staff, and for the business as a whole.

If you are considering implementing this, I dig into the mechanics of this strategy in chapter 18 – you should read that section thoroughly to ensure you have a full grasp of the decisions to be made. I also in that section share a horror story of how it can all go wrong!

A good alternative to staff shares is a bonus scheme made up of either or both short- or long-term incentives tied to performance. This can be a far easier way to reward great performance and provide some sort of financial lock in for staff other than embarking on a plan for staff shareholding. And many staff might actually prefer this to holding equity. Long-term incentives (for example, where the payment of a portion of the bonus earned for performance in one year is deferred to one, two or three years later) can be a particularly effective way of disincentivising staff considering leaving, and can be a great alternative to sharing equity.

One other alternative to consider is 'phantom equity'. Phantom equity provides a bonus that effectively 'shadows' the performance of the company. This can provide incentives to employees similar to share ownership (by giving them a benefit based on the increasing value of the business) but without diluting the owners' voting and control of the company. This type of arrangement has grown in popularity over recent years. It can be an extremely effective mechanism, but a *warning*, **this type of scheme can have unintended consequences**. For example, in a recent matter I dealt with, a client at exit had one of these schemes in place that became very complicated to deal with. The trigger for the payment was the sale of the business. However, when the sale occurred, the business was now held by the buyer who didn't want their financials to be impacted by this payment. Consequently there were all sorts of practical issues that came into play, including the timing of the payment, who was going to make the payment (the business or the seller?), how the staff would deal with tax under the payment (which ultimately ended up being taxed at the higher income tax rate rather than being treated as a capital gain), and other various issues like payroll tax. Phantom share schemes aren't always triggered just by a sale event, however. They might be based around other calculation points, for example as annual payments based on growth of the business value over time. But in these situations, complexity can still arise from the process of objectively establishing what the business value at any point actually is. Bonuses and shares are often simpler.

Other legal strategies for protecting the value of the team include reviewing and creating company policies that protect staff and help you deal quickly with any issues that appear. This can include a code of conduct and policies on recruitment, anti-bullying, health and safety, anti-discrimination and harassment, and many more areas. While company policies are a risk protection mechanism, they are also useful in ensuring that the business has a defined procedure in place for common issues that come up in an organisation.

And finally, one last consideration to reduce your reliance on individual staff members holding key information is to ensure you have a rigorous process of creating and documenting systems and processes in the business to capture key knowledge, and create systems that allow for easy onboarding and training of new staff members.

PROTECTING THE VALUE THAT THE TEAM IMPACTS

In many businesses, staff members hold such value for an organisation because of their client relationships, and relationship to other key value drivers of the business (for example, suppliers and partners of the business). So any discussion about protecting the value in your team also needs to include consideration of how to protect the value that the team controls or impacts.

This should include a consideration of at least the following areas:

1. Non-solicitation restraints to ensure that departing staff can't leach the business of client, supplier or partner relationships, or take other staff with them.

2. Non-competition restraints. These restraints help provide protection against staff members – either during or after termination of their employment – acting in competition with the business. However, these should be used with caution and only where appropriate for the seniority of the staff (given the potential difficulties in enforcement of this type of restraint if not set up correctly).

3. Copyright assignment clauses to ensure that the value in the work created during the term of their employment or engagement with the business is owned by the business. While this is implied in employment situations, it is not in contracting arrangements – so it is important to deal with it carefully in all team contracts.

4. Moral rights waiver clauses are also an important inclusion in your contracts where staff are producing creative works for your business.

SECURING YOUR INTELLECTUAL PROPERTY

For many businesses, intellectual property (otherwise known as IP) can hold a significant component of value. Intellectual property refers to creations of the mind. Things that are intangible. It can be very clear if real property has been stolen (if you own a computer, you can tell if it has been stolen because it will no longer be on your desk). It can be much harder to detect infringement of intellectual property rights and to prove your ownership in order to enforce the rights you have over the property.

Over the past two decades, I have seen countless examples of businesses that have cost themselves massive amounts of money due to their inability to understand the value of their IP and failure to take the proper steps to protect it. Protection of IP can often be fairly straightforward and inexpensive. It is absolutely one example of an area where prevention is almost always significantly cheaper than the cure.

It is also an area where so much of the value of a business can sit. Many businesses don't realise this until either an issue occurs which threatens ownership of their IP, or someone else infringes it (whittling down the value to the business). Another common issue is businesses not realising the value of their IP until they get to the point of sale, then finding out that they haven't set the business up properly in terms of establishing and protecting the ownership of their IP.

Having the right protections in place can play a large role in helping a business achieve the highest value in a sale. Sophisticated buyers understand the value of IP.

THE COST OF FAILING TO UNDERSTAND THE VALUE OF IP AND PROPERLY PROTECTING IT

Neglecting IP can lead to a multitude of potentially expensive outcomes for businesses, such as:

- loss of client databases
- an inability to stop other people using your business's IP
- not owning the underlying rights to the IP or not being able to prove your business owns it
- not having sufficient protections built into your agreements with suppliers, customers, staff, partners, distributors and manufacturers.

We have dealt with so many organisations that have had an enormous leach of value through a failure to properly protect their IP that it is hard to come up with a single example, but I'll try!

I recall a few years ago dealing with a business that was ultimately forced to write off more than $60,000 it had spent on marketing costs for the development of a new brand. Unfortunately, the company

PROTECTION OF IP

can often be fairly straightforward and inexpensive. It is absolutely one example of an area where prevention is almost always significantly cheaper than the cure.

hadn't thought of trademark searching as part of the concept development process.

When we were approached to help in the last few days before the new brand went live, we had the unenviable task of breaking the news that not only could this new brand not ever be protected by our clients, but that if they used it they would be at risk of an infringement action by other organisations (some of them very sizeable) who had trademarks that were similar.

The company had a small understanding of trademarks and, in a classic example of when a little knowledge can be dangerous, had organised their own trademark search along the way. Unfortunately, trademark searching can be quite tricky. Whoever was searching missed a couple of hard to find but very important marks – resulting in them choosing a brand that would have delivered a massive amount of risk. While this was a terrible waste of the months of concept development and marketing fees, at least we were able to catch the issue before they went live and faced major consequences.

One of the worst stories I have seen in this area came from a business that had been around for 30 years with a brilliant and catchy name, who lost the right to stop competitors using the name simply because they had no understanding of the importance of a trademark registration (and had never considered it as part of their value protection)! The kicker was that this issue didn't come to light until the owner put the business on the market. When buyers of the business did their initial searches on the business as part of their due diligence at sale, they found out that a competitor had registered the trademark for the business name.

The competitor had only been in the market for a year, but had immediately recognised that the long-standing business owner had never registered the trademark. The competitor managed to register the mark, and unfortunately once that had happened, the 'rightful owner' faced a massive court battle to undo it. A court battle she couldn't afford and simply didn't have the energy for.

Unsurprisingly the sale fell through, leaving the business owner with an unsaleable business. Not the kind of news you want to hear about a business you have devoted three decades of your life to.

We also have lots of tales of IP woes outside of the area of trademarks.

The most regular IP issue we see outside of trademarks is the loss of important information by companies through a lack of proper contractual protections. We so often see ex-staff heading to competitors or setting up their own businesses and poaching clients and other staff members. This can be extremely difficult to prevent if the business doesn't have the right clauses in their agreements with their staff.

IDENTIFYING THE KEY AREAS OF IP
Common IP of value across most businesses includes:
- the brand sitting in the name of the business and the products
- the website and promotional material
- written material of the business (including manuals, articles, books, designs)
- software code where the business is a developer of software.

There are also many, many other types of intellectual property, so make sure you investigate what is relevant for your business.

HOW TO PROTECT YOUR IP
The value in IP is protected through IP rights. Some IP rights require a formal process of registration, while others do not need to be (and cannot be) registered.

There are seven types of IP protection:
- trademarks
- copyright
- patents
- registered designs

- confidentiality/trade secrets
- circuit layout rights
- plant breeders' rights.

For most businesses, the most relevant are:

- **Trademarks.** I have put trademarks first on this list because it is far and away the most common area of IP issues. Starting with the basics, a trademark is a 'mark' that distinguishes the goods or services of one business from those of another. This might be the business name, a product or service brand name, or a logo. It can also be letters, numbers, even colours, scents and aspects of branding and packaging.

   You can have unregistered trademarks, but generally speaking the best way to protect your trademark is by getting a trademark registration in each of the countries where you use it (or intend to use it). This can be one of the easiest and most useful types of IP protection in a business.

- **Copyright.** Copyright is an automatic protection in Australia for bodies of work, drawings, art, literature, music, film, broadcasts and computer programs. Many businesses don't understand the value of copyrighted works in their organisation, or the simple steps they can take to reduce the likelihood of infringement.

- **Patents.** Patents are less relevant to the majority of businesses, but if your business creates inventions or new processes, this is an important area for you to understand.

   A patent is a right granted in relation to a device, substance, method or process which is new, inventive and useful. The patent holder has the right to prevent others from making, using or selling the same device, substance, method or process for the period of the patent. Patents can be expensive to put in place and to enforce, but can be a lucrative asset of a business if done correctly.

- **Trade secrets.** This refers to confidential information in a business such as secret formulas, processes and methods used in production. Often, there are things in a business that may not be protectable by other intellectual property rights but that might be highly important and confidential to the business. It's important these are protected by limiting who has access to this information, and through contracts, confidentiality agreements, and appropriate clauses in agreements with people who might have access to the information.

There are several very simple things businesses can do to start to protect their IP:

- **Evaluate the IP in your business.** Understand what is there and what value it has.
- **Get brands registered as trademarks.** This is such a simple and inexpensive process, if done correctly and if done early enough. Don't forget to consider registrations in other countries if you trade now (or are looking to expand in the future) offshore.
- **Review contracts.** Go over legal agreements with anyone who is creating (or has created) IP for the business. Ensure IP ownership is clear, assignment is dealt with, responsibility for IP protection and infringement is set out, and moral rights have been waived (if relevant). There is a persistent myth that if you pay someone to create IP for you, you will own the underlying IP rights. The reality is if you have someone create IP for you who is not an employee, you must have an agreement with them that assigns you the IP. Otherwise they will most likely retain the underlying rights to what they have created and they might be able to go and use it with one of your competitors. They might also be able to prevent you from using it in certain ways.
- **Review agreements.** Go over your agreements with suppliers, customers and key personnel to ensure IP is properly dealt with.

- **Develop an IP register.** This gives you a simple process for recording the development of copyrighted works and other IP, in case you need to prove your ownership in the future.
- **Get the right insurance in place.** There is some great IP and trademark insurance on the market that can provide an extra layer of protection.
- **Seek advice.** This will ensure you understand what IP exists and is being created in your business, and how to protect it.

SECURING YOUR SUPPLIERS, BUSINESS PARTNER RELATIONSHIPS AND OTHER KEY CONTRACTS

In many instances there is key value in an organisation sitting in its relationships with third parties. That can include suppliers, franchisors, licensors, referral partners, distribution partners and sales agents.

The first step in securing these is to identify each of the relationships of value.

The second step is to consider how these relationships can be secured. From a legal perspective this is generally based on contractual arrangements. In most instances there will be some sort of contract in place. Where these relationships are of importance to the business, the terms of those contracts will become of greater importance. And where any of those relationships are critical to the business fulfilling its own contractual obligations (for example, with customers or other third parties) there needs to be a solid contract in place that mirrors these contractual commitments to enable you to meet your commitments. You should also have in place a contract register that contains the key information for each of these contracts, including renewal dates and any other important dates to ensure key dates are not missed, and to capture other terms that are important.

The other way of protecting your key third-party relationships is through non-solicitation clauses. Non-solicitation clauses can be built into employment contracts, to ensure departing employees don't take your third-party relationships with them. They can also be built into contractor and supplier agreements, to ensure those parties also don't take key third-party relationships.

And finally, you should be considering how to protect the value in work that is being created under these relationships. For example, if IP is being created under a third-party contract, you need to ensure that IP is clearly assigned to your organisation.

LOCKING IN YOUR PREMISES OR LOCATION

In many instances there will be a component of value sitting in the actual premises of the business. In chapter 5 we discussed how to protect the value connected to the premises from a buyer's perspective. We examined leases and the importance of locking in value through the lease terms, and in identifying and minimising clauses that could pose a risk. For example, demolition clauses that give the landlord the right to break the lease prior to the end date, often with little notice required.

Ultimately if your location is important, or relocation costs would be high (for example, because your type of business has high fit-out costs), you should do everything possible to lock in the future term of that lease. Ideally this should be done through multiple future options that provide you with a long lease term at your control.[22]

Another way of locking in the value in your premises is by buying it. We have many clients who use this approach to provide certainty and stability to the business. It can also provide massive personal financial benefit (for example, when they buy it through a self-managed superannuation fund). But that's another topic entirely!

THE VALUE IN YOUR BUSINESS STRUCTURE

The business structure is usually the place to start when looking at the legal underpinnings of a business, and it's an area that is important to include in a discussion of value protection in a business. However,

---

22   See chapter 5 for more on how lease options work.

this can be a poorly understood area – businesses often don't understand the structure options available to them, and the consequences of the type of approaches they have chosen.

The issue of 'structure' relates to lots of different considerations, including:

- what structure the business is operating out of right now
- how that structure will work in terms of the future plans of the organisation (for example, if you may bring on board staff or others to hold equity or if you are building for an ultimate sale)
- whether the business itself should have multiple entities (for example, asset holding entities and trading entities)
- the protections in place for the personal assets of the directors and other relevant stakeholders.

In focusing on value protection, we need to start with reviewing what is currently in place, and how well it protects the value in the business. Will it maximise your value if you ever exit?

The next step is to consider how your current structure protects the elements of value in the business. For example, where a business holds a large amount of value in certain assets (they may be equipment assets, or IP assets, or other types of assets), it may make sense to segregate that value in a separate entity, to protect it from risk sitting in the business. Many businesses have IP companies (or trusts) or holding companies (or trusts) that are separate to the trading entity or entities. The idea of this approach to structuring is to silo risk in one area and assets in another – to protect the value of those assets from the risks in the business.

But you should also consider simplicity. I have seen some horrendous examples of over-complexity of structure, and this can be a block for a future sale if done incorrectly.

Having the wrong business structure can cause a business to leak money, and can at worst mean that valuable assets are unnecessarily exposed to risk. On the flipside, getting a business's structure and structure documentation right can mean big financial gains and an easier business exit.

PERSONAL ASSET PROTECTION

And finally, but most importantly in this list of value recognition and value protection, we turn to the consideration of personal asset protection. This is critical, and is somewhat connected also to the questions in relation to the structure of a business.

What have you done to protect your personal assets? This includes not just your business ownership but also your assets outside of the business if you hold a position of directorship.

Personal asset protection is generally approached by looking at multiple areas.

THE WAY IN WHICH YOU HOLD YOUR INTERESTS IN YOUR BUSINESS

Do you hold your business interests in your own name? Or do you hold them through other structures like family trusts? For example, in many instances if you run your business as a company, having the shares in that company being held by a family discretionary trust is often a preferable approach to holding shares in your personal name because of the asset protection and tax distribution benefits.

THE AGREEMENTS THAT GOVERN YOUR BUSINESS OWNERSHIP

It is extremely important that you understand and regularly (at least every one to two years) review the agreements in place that relate to your equity holding if you have partners in the business. Depending on the structure of your business, that might be through a shareholders' agreement (if you run your business through a company) or unitholders' agreement (if you run your business through a trust).

It is critical that these documents protect the value of your equity in that business, by providing clarity around:

- how you can exit
- how you are protected if others are choosing to exit or need to be exited
- how decision making is dealt with
- what protections your estate might have if something happens to you
- what access you have to the information of the business (if you are not part of the day-to-day control or management)
- restraints on other equity holders taking staff, clients or suppliers, or competing with the business.

You also need to consider:

- **Your approach to signing personal guarantees (which should ideally entail that you don't ever sign any personal guarantees).** Where there are instances where you have not been able to avoid personal guarantees, it's important that you understand how these can be extinguished and that you have a clear record of these in one place that you can easily refer back to in the future.
- **How you structure the ownership of family assets.** In many instances family members who are the most exposed (for example, hold a director position in a business with risk) will not be the family asset holders. Instead, those asset holders will be either a family trust or a member of the family without exposure to business risk.

    I can't tell you the number of times we have had new clients come to us with risky businesses, and in our first review we identify that multiple family members are listed as directors. The issue with this is that a position of director comes with exposure (albeit the extent of that exposure differs between businesses, depending on the risk level of the business). Having multiple family members hold this role, where those family members are also asset holders in the family unit, means by extension that those assets are also exposed. Often the fix to this is simply refining the directorships to those who are really required.

One comment I feel compelled to add here however is to caution against the entire avoidance of holding a position of director in a business simply because of the potential risk. I have seen in many instances a client's reluctance to hold a position of director in a business they have financial interests in to avoid the risks of directorship – but in so doing, miss out on the benefits of control and information access. There are many ways to enable access to decision making and information outside of a directorship, in particular through the shareholders' agreement, but if the agreement does not provide that sort of access to shareholders, holding a position of director can be extremely useful. Given there are ways of protecting the value in assets for directors, it's important that you don't give up the benefits that a directorship might hold without weighing these benefits against the real residual risk after putting in place a proper asset protection plan.

- **Insurance for your personal exposure as a director or officer of the business.** This is generally provided under a director and officer insurance policy, or management liability policy.
- **What provisions you have put in place for wills, powers of attorney, and personal insurance.** Not a sexy topic perhaps, but one that is imperative to consider, and to have reviewed at any major milestones in your life (for example, the birth of children, entering or exiting a relationship, entering or exiting a business, or after large periods of business growth or change).

USING INSURANCE TO MANAGE RISK

One last area that should be discussed before leaving the topic of protection of value and risk management is insurance. The elements we have discussed above relate to the contractual, systems, training and commercial approaches to value protection and risk management. But no discussion about this topic is complete without diving into the relevance and importance of insurance, which is an important tool in risk minimisation for a business and for the individual owners.

There are certain types of insurance that are essential. For example, you are required by law to have workers compensation insurance, and you will be required by your lease or under certain customer contracts to have a certain level of public liability and sometimes also professional indemnity and product liability insurance. There are many other insurances, however, to also consider, such as general business insurance (like building, contents, theft and storm cover), business interruption insurance, management liability insurance, cyber liability insurance and tax audit insurance.[23]

Working with a good insurance broker in these areas can help to clarify which insurances your business should hold to add to the strength of protection provided by your contracts, systems and processes, and training that we have identified in this chapter. You may also wish to consider personal insurance; for example, director and officer (D&O) insurance, keyman insurance, and personal life, trauma, income protection and TPD insurance.

---

23   Make sure you check out the resources hub at www.buygrowexit.com.au for a free insurance health check.

Chapter 12

PREDICT: ANTICIPATING THE LANDMINES BEFORE THEY BLOW YOU UP

The next step after identifying and protecting the value in the business is to identify risks in the business that if they were to occur, would drain that value. These are the landmines that could go off that would take your eye off the ball of growth. Or simply the peppering of small issue after small issue that slowly but surely drains the energy you once had for the business.

In chapter 10 I shared the story of James, whose business had imploded because the legal infrastructure wasn't developed and strengthened in line with the growth. And this story of businesses imploding after a period of high growth is unfortunately far too common, because growing businesses are in their most vulnerable phase – the phase where they have something to protect, and also something to be attacked. Where they are doing lots of things that can involve risk, but with little framework to protect them. Because they often have so many balls in the air that it can take just one ball flying off course to set in motion a domino effect.

The first step in warding off problems is to identify what the risks are, and then put in place systems to prevent the risks from turning into problems. In this phase, you need to be reflecting on the common areas of risk and building a timeline for protection.

The second step is to have in place an early warning system, to ensure that you are alert to signs of problems developing before they develop into bigger issues. And to use that early warning prediction information as an impetus to develop new approaches to constantly refine and enhance the prevention systems you already have in place, because the risk-prevention systems must continue to evolve in a business as it grows and changes.

This system of prediction and prevention is like a constant feedback loop. Once you have put in place the prevention systems, you must conduct regular reviews to see what issues have occurred in the business (for example, disputes or slow-paying clients) and use this information as a guide as to which prevention systems to revisit. This should be done at least annually, but quarterly might be appropriate if you are growing quickly or if issues are starting to appear regularly.

AREAS OF CORE RISK IN A BUSINESS

The most common areas of core risk in a business include:

- cashflow
- client claims
- employment law issues
- IP
- supplier risks
- general contractual risk (problems in agreements you sign)
- marketing
- legislation and regulation (and keeping up with changes)
- business structure and relationships with partners
- personal risks as a director, and through personal guarantees.

This system of **PREDICTION** and **PREVENTION** is like a constant feedback loop. Once you have put in place the prevention systems, you must **CONDUCT REGULAR REVIEWS** to see what issues have occurred in the business.

EARLY WARNING SYSTEMS

Early warning prediction and management systems include:

- **Cashflow early warning signals:**
  - Look out for *slow-paying clients* – this is generally an indication of one or more of the following:
    - Your collection system needs a revamp (in many instances, simply changing the regularity of phone calls or what you are saying in your follow ups can make a massive difference).
    - There are solvency issues with individual clients (you need to jump onto this quickly to reduce your exposure, as we discuss below).
    - There is something going wrong in service quality, or price, or something else in which the business has not performed to your client's expectations. Slow payments can be an early warning signal that clients are not getting what they expect and are therefore hesitant to pay straight away.
  - Quickly identify if any clients are *paying late, in round numbers or making part payments*. This can be an early indication of client solvency issues, which you will want to jump onto quickly. Round number payments (or part payments) are a common approach of debtors who are in a position of needing to pay down a pool of suppliers from a cash pool that doesn't allow for full payment. So while complete non-payment of an invoice might be caused by many reasons (as set out in the point above), part payments in round numbers almost always indicates the debtor is having difficulty finding funds for full payment. If you identify this, you should be considering reducing the potential risk. You may decide to ease or slow your supply to these customers until they are up to date, or if you continue your supply then at least you will be doing this with your eyes wide open to the credit risk.

- Understand what *your average debtor days* are. Review that figure monthly to see if it is growing or decreasing. Increasing debtor days are an indication something needs to change. Decreasing debtor days are an indication you are doing something right. It's important to be able to identify both.

• **Complaints and customer feedback.** Customers might provide feedback outside of the client survey system you have established, and all customer feedback is massively useful to a business, whether positive or negative. You should have a system in place to collect the positive comments for use in future marketing (of course with permission provided by the customers), and both negative and positive comments can be great for providing feedback to the team and in helping to identify where changes might need to be made.

• **Disputes.** Disputes are an important identifier of things that need to change in a business. This might seem obvious, but there are so many occasions I have seen of businesses who come to us with a costly dispute, and when we dig into it we find that it was preceded by a number of smaller but similar disputes. These small disputes are often swept under the carpet when busy businesses are so focused on growth, and they 'don't have the time' to investigate the reason behind each little dispute and put in place a change to deal with the underlying cause (which is generally bubbling away, growing over time, getting ready to explode when the time is most inappropriate!). Even businesses who have ended up in large disputes can sometimes forget to go back and assess the root cause.

• **Regular reviews.** Businesses should have in place a system for ensuring that they review their whole business at least once a year, and in this review they should specifically assess what issues have come up in that past year, including problems, complaints, disputes, litigation, slow payment and any other indication that something might not be on track. Many businesses will perform this type of review far more regularly (and in some businesses, review meetings will be held as often as weekly to ensure that small issues are identified before they become big ones, and to shine a light on where gaps are forming that can be addressed by preventative measures).

- **Contract changes.** Ensure you have appropriate clauses in your customer contracts enabling you to charge interest for late payments, and to pass on debt recovery fees. Remind your customers of this right if they are late in paying.
- **Client surveys.** A system of regularly surveying the satisfaction of your customers is imperative for being able to quickly identify any issues that might be brewing. Poor client survey responses must be dealt with quickly by a personal phone call.

At Aspect Legal we use simple surveys based on the Net Promoter Score (NPS) that gives us a benchmarkable figure.[24] We use technology to automate the survey process so that it runs seamlessly and regularly in the background of our business, without waiting for someone to remember to run it. And finally, we pay attention to the results – segmenting results by solicitor and matter types – so that we can identify if there are any issues brewing.

We contact survey respondents if we ever have responses that aren't glowing, to identify why. We also use this approach with clients of new staff, to ensure we quickly get a handle on how happy their clients are. And to top it off, we also watch the percentage of NPS response completion, because a drop off

---

24   Net Promoter Score is a widely used method of tracking customer satisfaction and loyalty. It measures customer perception with a single survey question, asking customers to rate out of 10 the likelihood that they would recommend a company, product, or a service to a friend or colleague. The NPS of a business can be benchmarked against other businesses in the same industry, across all industries, and against their own business to enable tracking of any movement over time.

in the percentage of clients responding to the surveys can be another indication in itself.

It can be tricky getting clients to spend the time responding to a survey, so you should ensure you have someone in the team regularly considering how to increase the survey response rates. But from our time in using survey tools, I have gathered a few tips that might be of use in your implementation:

- tell clients about the process in their onboarding and explain the reason behind it
- make surveys short and very easy to complete (ideally one-touch answers, with a next step encouraging respondents to leave comments but not requiring it)
- consider adding incentives (we like to add a charitable giving connected to each survey returned, as a win–win–win for us all).

The client survey approach enables you to see quickly what is working well and what isn't. If there are issues identified, you need to address these quickly. This might be, for example, by changing how clients are onboarded, changing what is set out in the customer terms and conditions, or changing the way you charge.

But ultimately this approach gives you the opportunity to quickly identify issues and then to find and implement a contract, system or training approach to prevent them turning into major problems.

IDENTIFY ▷ PROTECT ▷ PREDICT ▷ PREVENT

Chapter 13

PREVENT: ADDRESSING THE CORE SYSTEMS AND PROCESSES FOR GROWING AND PRESERVING VALUE

In chapter 11 we dealt in detail with how to identify risks. The next and final step is, of course, preventing them from occurring. In many instances, it's very difficult to demonstrate the outcome of a great risk protection system, simply because risk protection is all about ensuring that the issues are prevented (and it can be hard to look back and identify the lack of problems occurring!).

But one of the best examples of the return for putting in serious time and effort into prevention is the story of a business I worked with very closely over many years in developing a suite of customer and supplier agreements.

DAVID AND GOLIATH

The business specialised in matching suppliers with customers. They had been in business for a number of years, and as is the case with so many small businesses, as their size increased, so did their need for the sophistication in their approach of how they dealt with their customers and suppliers, and their contracts. It had once been sufficient for them to use very simple contracts (in truth, often they used no contracts at all). But they realised that they had hit the point where their lack of structure around their contracts was leaving them more and more exposed as they grew.

So we set about putting in place an appropriate suite of contracts for their customers and suppliers, to protect the heavy investment of our client in each deal. My client – let's call him David – was a joy to work with because he was experienced and completely understood the benefit of taking time and consideration in building the contracts to ensure they were rigorous enough to withstand any issues that might arise. He was also very good at identifying where risk could lie, and in discussing with me ways that we could use the contract to prevent these issues.

One of the greatest risks highlighted in one of our discussions was the risk of early termination, with their suppliers all being very large corporates who would have deep pockets to fight if push came to shove in enforcing the contract. Ultimately the contract was implemented with many large businesses as suppliers to David's business. But of course, as happens with business, one day an issue occurred that meant that the contract had to be tested.

Quite simply, a large corporate supplier decided they had provided our client too good a deal and they wanted to pull out. The problem was that our client had invested tens of thousands of dollars, and hundreds and hundreds of hours, into putting this deal in place. Getting the deal together had taken months of focus for the team, and the prospect of losing it was disastrous.

However, because the areas of risk to our client had been so clearly identified and dealt with in the contracts, when this issue arose we were able to take immediate action. And so we went in hard. Unsurprisingly, the legal team of the business partner also rolled into gear to fight.

In any normal situation a small business like David's might consider backing down from a fight with a large organisation with very deep pockets who had signalled they were going to fight hard, and who had met every one of our advances with pages and pages of reasons why our client would never see a cent.

But we knew our contract was extremely tight, and so we held firm.

It was a David and Goliath battle of epic proportions – and ultimately our client walked away with a settlement to the tune of hundreds of thousands of dollars. All of this was able to be achieved without any litigation, and with minimal legal fees – simply because of the strength of the protection mechanisms that had been built into the contract from the beginning.

So while the risk-assessment exercise our client had gone through at the beginning didn't entirely stop issues from occurring, it minimised the likelihood and – more importantly – it gave David an incredible bargaining position when issues did occur. It gave him options, and ultimately it enabled the issues to be entirely resolved without needing to head into litigation.

And there, ladies and gentleman, you have it. This is the point entirely of a risk identification and prevention regime.

APPROACHES TO RISK PREVENTION

Let's kick off this last section of our Identify, Protect, Predict and Prevent framework with a quick outline of some examples of the three key options available for this last element – risk prevention:

- **Contracts**, for example:
  - Build solid contracts with customers, suppliers, key partners and staff to manage risk. These should be easy to understand and properly tailored to the relationship between the parties.
- **Systems and procedures**, for example:
  - Have a good system in place to manage those contracts, ensure key dates are met, and ensure that the obligations or other performance criteria are being met.

- – Build strong systems around cashflow.
- – Create an approach for dealing with disputes, so they take minimal time and energy and help you to sharpen the fortification of the business in a constant feedback loop.
- **Training**, for example:
  - – Train staff who deal with contracts in how to identify risks they are signing, or where to get legal help, training in systems such as cashflow and debt collection and training in areas of important legislation and compliance.

THE AREAS OF YOUR BUSINESS THAT PRESENT RISK DURING GROWTH

Let's look now one by one at each area of risk, and tips on how to minimise those risks during a growth phase.

CLIENT RELATIONSHIPS

Client relationships are one of the most important relationships for a business; however, they can also create a large source of risk for organisations if the right foundations aren't properly established from the outset.

One example springs to mind of a marketing company we worked with – let's call them Marketing Worx – who had landed a massive contract with an international customer, set to deliver hundreds of thousands of dollars in revenue per year over a five-year period. The contract required that Marketing Worx had capability to service the new customer across multiple states in Australia and to have personnel on the ground in one state where they currently didn't have a team. Marketing Worx was in party mode, as the win of this customer was not just a great boost in their revenue projections, but also a massive win for their brand.

And of course, suddenly this deal had to be finalised urgently. The new customer wanted Marketing Worx to get on the ground in a matter of weeks. Marketing Worx could only see dollar signs and huge press coverage about their win.

I, on the other hand, was worried.

Marketing Worx had rushed enthusiastically into the set up in the new state, lining up a flash new office and busily organising the interstate relocation of members of their team. And everything had to be done immediately. Of course.

I was concerned with the incredibly one-sided approach of the contract. The contract set out very clearly the new customer's expectations in terms of service, and their requirement that Marketing Worx have a presence on the ground in each state, however it didn't provide any sort of guarantee of the volume of work they would send to Marketing Worx. And to make it worse, the contract included restraints against Marketing Worx working with competing businesses (in a tight industry).

On the flipside, Marketing Worx was committing to numerous expenses, including a lease with a minimum fixed term.

I implored Marketing Worx to slow down – to work through the detail carefully and to ensure they weren't landed with commitments that could outlast the value in the client relationship.

While initially Marketing Worx seemed to heed my advice, after discussion with their new customer, they changed their mind. The new customer was a large international business, with all contracts issued from their offshore parent company. The new customer told my client they couldn't control the contracts – but convinced Marketing Worx not to worry because 'they had their back'. They assured Marketing Worx that their tight relationship meant they were sure they would deliver on the volume Marketing Worx had built its figures around. 'It is company policy that we can't provide volume guarantees – but don't worry, we need you and will look after you,' the Australian personnel of the customer had said.

And this is, after all, the type of risk you need to take to grow . . . *right?*

I totally understand that there is ongoing tension between the risk appetite needed to grow a business and the more conservative approach a lawyer needs to take to be able to both see and assess risk. But risk should never be pushed under the carpet.

I speak with authority on this not just because of the many times I have heard this kind of argument from businesses that don't want to hear about risks that they feel are very unlikely, and may be an impediment to their march towards growth. Or because of the many times I have seen these 'low-likelihood risks' eventuate, and cause catastrophe in their wake when they haven't been planned for. But also because at heart I am an entrepreneur. I feel the emotion of our clients when they are in the throes of growth. I have travelled the same heights myself of feeling that low-likelihood risk shouldn't stand in the path of incredible opportunity. I have felt that optimistic invincibility that risk can be avoided by a relentless focus on expansion, of feeling that we have the power to overcome anything with hard work.

But I have also felt the same lows that they feel when things go wrong, and felt the effects of landmines blowing up. And I have seen on so many occasions this repeat – ad nauseam – for businesses in growth phase.

So you can probably already tell what happened with Marketing Worx and the incredible customer deal they landed . . .

Of course it all started out brightly. Marketing Worx opened its new office with a bang – a huge party and much excitement. It announced the new client it had landed in exuberant emails and social posts. It quietly discarded the 'competitive clients' it had now agreed to no longer service, and it threw its full force behind this new client relationship.

However, just one year into the contract, the customer's business hit hard times they hadn't anticipated. And at a similar time, the Australian team that had the direct relationship with Marketing Worx changed. Marketing Worx lost its key contacts, and suddenly the relationship deteriorated. The customer went through a process of 'review' of all of its key Australian contracts in a bid to save money, and slashed the budget for Marketing Worx by 90%. Marketing Worx couldn't afford to keep staff in the new state office, but was left with an ongoing lease and other commitments, as well as a restraint that limited its ability to bring in other revenue in the same industry to partly recover some of the lost future revenue. We were able to deal with some components of this, but ultimately the loss of the projected future income from the client, together with the ongoing burden of the expenses they had taken on to win the client and comply with the onerous contract, took a huge toll on the business financially and emotionally. While getting into the contract happened in the blink of an eye, dealing with the fallout lasted years.

The story of Marketing Worx demonstrates the need to act with a cool head, to accept that unexpected risks do sometimes eventuate, and to dedicate the time needed to properly assess the risks and build clear risk mitigation and minimisation plans.

So the moral of the story is: if you are taking on substantial risk to deliver under a contract, you need to have protection. There are many ways to do this, and ultimately it is about being creative about what could work in each situation. Here's a few ideas of where to start:

1. Where possible, mirror the terms of the contract against any supply relationships or contractual commitments you have to fulfil that contract. Line up expiry dates, and line up other rights of termination. In supply relationships (and some service relationships as well) it may be appropriate to line up any warranties and exclusion of liability – so that risk is passed on down the chain of supply where it is reasonable. For Marketing Worx, given they had no volume commitment from the customer, they would have been far better to have opted for premises with lease term flexibility, and to have lined up their other commitments in a way that they could be exited at any point.

2. If you can't mirror all terms, consider what other avenues you have to minimise the risks commercially. This could include building in volume commitments, or providing pricing benefits

in return for a low-volume charge if the actual volume drops
from the predicted volume. You could alternatively provide
volume rebates, so the customers are incentivised while they are
purchasing in volumes that meet the risk you are taking under
the contract but paying an uplift in pricing when they aren't
meeting the volume.

3. You could also consider having other 'benefits' to the client
    phase out with declining volumes. In the Marketing Worx
    example, this could have been the competition restriction
    phasing out when the volume declined.

Ultimately the most important thing is that you have spent the time
understanding and assessing the risks and coming up with possible
approaches to minimise those risks – rather than simply running at
full speed into what ultimately becomes ongoing fires that sap your
time and attention and deplete the value of your business.

Here is a further list of regular issues that we see businesses
facing with their clients that should be an area of focus in building
your risk protection systems:

1. **Slow payment or non-payment.** As we discussed in the
    previous chapter, often the first area where legal issues arise
    in dealing with clients is slow payment or non-payment. The
    reality is that unless a business is getting all payments upfront
    it will likely hit a point at some stage in its growth cycle where
    slow payment (and non-payment) will become an issue and
    contribute to the cash crunch that is a reality that hits many
    fast-growing businesses at some point. So, one of the important
    things to consider is how to set up the legal foundations of
    the business from the point of view of avoiding or reducing
    non-payment and slow payment, and reporting that quickly
    identifies if troubles are brewing.

2. **Defining your obligations sufficiently.** The other main area of
    issue with clients is disputes about whether the goods or services

have been provided in accordance with the expectations of the client. These types of disputes can cost a lot of time and money, and fracture important client relationships. But having a tight approach to setting up your client relationships and contracts can go a long way to minimising these types of issues and reducing the time and complexity of dealing with problems that do arise.

3. **Inappropriate liability exposure through the contract.** Client agreements need to be carefully structured around this issue to ensure that the risk exposure under the contract is clearly defined and controlled. There are many tools available in a contract to help manage risk, however we have seen many contracts over the years where the risk taken on by an organisation with its clients far outweighs the value of the goods or services they are providing. Primarily this is because they have failed to understand what to look out for in their contracts and the vital importance of this step in assessing and managing risk under the contract.

One important thing to note here is that many of these issues can be dealt with by having a proper client agreement template or set of templates ready for use – which is an imperative for all businesses to have. The client agreement document can be called many different things: service agreements, supply agreements, terms and conditions of business, trading terms, sale terms, purchase order terms, and many other names. It really doesn't matter what it is called; it is effectively all the same thing – a document that sets out:

- how the goods or services will be provided
- payment information
- delivery timeframes
- the general obligations of each of the parties
- who owns the intellectual property (where IP is relevant)
- responsibility for risk under the contract (for example, through clauses relating to liability, indemnities and insurance).

It is extremely important to tailor your client agreements to maximise your legal protection. I have seen countless issues caused by businesses using client agreements that don't properly reflect their business and their business risks – often because they have been arrived at by downloading a generic template or were set up on 'borrowed' terms when the business was at a very different size and risk appetite. Your agreements must be appropriate for where you are today, must be thorough and considered, but must also be simple enough for your clients to be able to read and understand.

The other important thing with client agreements is that you and your team understand what is in these agreements. The agreement should be updated regularly as your business environment and approaches change.

Having your own carefully developed client agreement suite of templates however won't provide all the answers in situations where the business is required to sign onto the terms of the customer (rather than using their own standard customer terms). This is often the case where your customer is a large business. If your business will be required to enter into the contracts driven by your customers, you need to be particularly careful to ensure they have been properly reviewed, or if you are doing the review internally you need to ensure your contracts team is properly trained in how to pick up issues and in how to understand tricky and technical clauses like indemnities and warranties.

So in summary, the keys to prevention in this area are:

Contracts:
- Have a full suite of templates available for your clients (including a proposal and a client agreement – whether you call that terms of trade, client terms, service agreement, supply agreement or something else – and where relevant a confidentiality agreement).

Your agreements must be **APPROPRIATE** for where you are today, must be **THOROUGH** and **CONSIDERED**, but must also be **SIMPLE** enough for your clients to be able to read and understand.

- Ensure you have the right contracts in place for every single one of your clients (whether this is your contract, or your client's template), covering off all the elements we touched on above and incorporating any related documentation (such as proposals or confidentiality agreements).

Systems and procedures:
- Ensure that all new clients are onboarded with the client contract as an absolute first step.
- Monitor and track key dates and key obligations under each contract to ensure they don't slip. Consider creating a document that tracks contracts in progress, where there are key details that are important to keep on top of (such as review dates, expiry dates, special conditions or departures from your normal approach, milestones, and key terms).
- Put in place client satisfaction surveys to ensure you are regularly surveying your clients to identify any issues that might be brewing.
- Have a system in place to deal with problems adequately and quickly if they do occur, to shut them down before they do damage.

Training:
- Ensure that your staff who deal with customers at the sales, negotiation or sign-on phase are trained in your onboarding systems and processes, in understanding what your template customer agreements say, and in the basics of contract law.

CASHFLOW

As they say, cashflow is the lifeblood of a business. The story I shared earlier about James and his horrific business failure was a direct result of issues with cashflow. While he was in charge, and the business was growing slowly, he was able to keep cashflow in check. But when he hit his period of fast growth, and the focus on cashflow was reduced as everyone's focus was diverted to the other myriad things to think about during fast growth, small problems quickly snowballed into large problems and sunk the business, and took James's personal finances, livelihood and marriage too. James's story is depressing but not terribly uncommon. Speak to any business liquidator and you will get an understanding of the regularity with which failing cashflow kills a business.

Cashflow can be impacted by many things. It's not just the money coming in, it is of course also about the money going out. And the legal perspective of cashflow therefore does not cover everything you need to be thinking about in managing cash. As a business grows, you need to keep a hawk eye on expenses. You need to understand and allocate cash towards taxes. You need to understand the impact of supplier payment terms and your own immediate cash needs (like wages bills) pitted against the payment terms you are providing your customers. You need to understand your cashflow cycle.

But in this section we are focusing on the strategies, from a legal point of view, that you can use to reduce the risk of cashflow woes draining the business of its lifeblood, especially during a strong growth phase. As with the other sections in our risk-prevention chapters, there are three levers you can pull from a legal perspective: the contracts you use, the systems you have in place, and the training that you provide to your staff.

PAYMENT TERMS

A good cashflow management system requires you to start by setting up the payment terms with some forethought. Could you change the whole cashflow cycle around, and get customer payments upfront? Could you break your customers into different payment timing categories based on creditworthiness, value, type of goods or services you provide, or other criteria? Could you have your customers provide credit cards for automated payments at agreed periods? Could you convert ad hoc payments into subscriptions or memberships at set prices deducted automatically each month?

Many businesses have transitioned from being cashflow tight businesses with large average debtor days to businesses receiving payment from clients in advance of payments to their staff and suppliers simply by changing the overall approach to how they deal with their customers. This creates a massive benefit to a business from a cashflow perspective, and also from a valuation perspective. It will also simply make the business easier to run!

YOUR OWN CASH NEEDS

It is important that you understand your business's own payment obligations, and balance these against the payment terms you are requiring from your customers. In some instances, certain contracts may need to be dealt with differently to the norm. For example, if you have entered into a large contract where your supplier terms are particularly different to normal, you may need to adjust the corresponding arrangements with your customer. Or on the flipside if your customer requires an extended payment cycle, you may be able to negotiate a corresponding extended payment cycle with the suppliers relating to that customer contract.

There has been a recent theme of large businesses pushing payment terms out. In recent years this has seen many large businesses attempt to push payment terms out to 90 days; I have even seen payment terms pushed out to 120 days. Payment terms reporting legislation that commenced in 2021 requires large businesses to report on their payment terms and practices with small business suppliers in an attempt to reduce this practice. This is aimed at addressing the impact of delayed payments on small business cashflow, and while the regime does not require that small businesses be paid within a certain period, it does provide a framework for greater transparency over the payment practices being used by individual large businesses.

If you are at the receiving end of a push by your clients for long payment terms it is important that you don't simply agree without proper consideration. Can you push back? (In many instances, the answer is actually yes!). Can you add an uplift in the fee charged in return for the extended credit you are providing? Can you push your own suppliers out so that you are less exposed to a long payment cycle?

At the very least, ensure you understand the implications of extended payment cycles on the cashflow for the rest of your business.

CUSTOMER SET UP

There are several things you can do right at the point of customer set up and onboarding that can help to ward off cashflow issues from the beginning:

- **Provide clear client communication at onboarding.**
  Ensure it is clear in your initial client terms and onboarding communications what the expectations are in relation to payment. Many businesses include a section clarifying the points of invoicing and payment, and emphasising the importance of timely payments. In many instances, payment disputes can be avoided by ensuring that this initial communication is also clear on milestones and the expectations of you as a supplier. Providing clear metrics on what triggers the payment obligation for the customer can go a long way to reducing barriers to fast payment.

- **Check the credit of new clients.** When you establish your customer accounts during your customer set-up phase, it might make sense to require trade references or to use systems for credit reporting to check on the creditworthiness of your customer.

- **Create thorough and tight customer contracts.** Your customer contracts should include provisions for late payment interest and fees, and to enable you to pass on any debt collection fees. It should also include clear provisions for when the clients will be invoiced and be required to pay. The contract should provide clarity around these issues to ward off misunderstandings, and also to provide power to you if issues occur.

- **Consider director guarantees.** Consider whether you require director or parent company guarantees where payment may be at risk. While it is often difficult to get these types of guarantees signed, where your customers will be building up substantial credit accounts, or where you feel there is risk in payment, guarantees are an excellent way of not just ensuring you have another avenue to pursue if the customer doesn't pay, it also gives you more leverage for payment and increases the likelihood of quicker payment (given accounts with directors' guarantees are often the last accounts that directors will want to see left unpaid). In many industries directors' guarantees are standard, and we have seen this used many times by our clients very effectively.

- **Consider registration on the PPSR.** The PPSR (Personal Property Securities Register) is an official database of secured property in Australia. This can be particularly useful where you provide goods to your customers on credit terms (with the provision that you have the right to repossess the goods if they aren't paid for), or you hire or provide equipment that will be situated outside of your control. It's also used in many other financing situations. Registering your customers on the PPSR can be an important strategy for ensuring that you are able to take back possession in instances of insolvency of your customers, but there is a process that must be followed carefully to ensure that this is done properly.

SYSTEMS AND ESCALATION

It is imperative that you have a system in place that provides for customers to pass through different (ideally automated) cycles depending on their payment phase. For example, while a statement or payment reminder email might be sufficient for current accounts, when payments are late your system should be escalating the seriousness by including phone calls and strongly worded letters.

We have a system in place that we use for clients to help them set up:

- wording on invoices
- wording in statements
- automated regularity of statements (that increases as the overdue period increases)
- wording in follow-up letters as the overdue period increases
- escalation points for moving the follow-up into phone calls, letters of demand and third-party involvement.

We have found that simply changing some of the timing and wording in some of the initial stages of automated follow-ups can have a massive impact on speeding up payments and reducing debtor days.

CUSTOMER OVERSIGHT AND REVIEWS

You should also have a system in place for regular debtor reporting and review. This should happen at least monthly (but may need to happen more often if you have a business where cashflow is particularly tight).

In these reviews you need information showing the levels of debtors in staged sections of payment timings. For example, you might want to understand the value and proportion of customers in 0–30 days, 30–60 days and 60+. You should also be tracking any changes in the average debtor days. And finally, you need to be pinpointing any customers who have debts that are growing.

Tracking debtor changes can help identify when there might be issues brewing.

Where particular customers are identified as having growing overdue balances, it can be a sign to step in and escalate action. It's often the case that the 'squeaky wheel gets the oil'. This is so true for cash collection, because the longer a client goes not paying an invoice, the higher the likelihood that the invoice won't be paid. Chasing invoices can be uncomfortable. But I have seen so many instances of massive problems arising from delinquent customer accounts that could have been rectified with early intervention.

Having a system in place to create escalation points and actions doesn't restrict you from making variations for certain clients that you decide you want to allow further time for invoice payment. Compassion for your customers and the circumstances they go through in the ups and downs of their business can be an important component of building long-term loyalty, and is a normal part of the empathy that is required in business, and in life. But decisions like this must be made with clarity. You must not let discomfort at collecting debts or 'lack of time' cause sloppy cash collection to set in, because the result can be deadly to the business.

Regular reviews of customer satisfaction are an often-missed component of ensuring customers pay on time. Happy customers are generally much quicker payers. So no discussion on cashflow would be complete without also mentioning the importance of good products or services that meet (and ideally exceed) the expectations of your customers. Therefore as part of this review of cashflow you should also be considering your customer survey scores as well, to ascertain whether there is any correlation between customer satisfaction and payment timing.

And as a final comment on this section, you should at least annually reflect on your cashflow system as a whole to consider whether there have been changes over time – either positive or negative – that are useful to understand more deeply. While regular weekly and monthly reviews are important, sometimes the greatest insights come from tracking changes over time, which can also help identify seasonal and other movements that can help you then build in accurate future forecasting, to help arm you best for future growth and cash demands.

So in summary, the keys to prevention in this area are:

Contracts:
- Include key terms in your customer contracts about payment, interest for late payment, and the right to pass on enforcement costs.
- Be clear in your contracts when payment is due, and about performance (and payment) milestone triggers.

Systems and procedures:
- Consider payment timing with a bit of creativity (is there a better way than simply getting payments from clients in arrears?) and build in periods to review your system.
- Have a tight debt collection system in place, including automated follow up and clear points for escalation.
- Conduct regular debtor reviews to review individual debtors, and to look at the performance of the debt collection system as a whole.
- Regularly review customer satisfaction, and investigate whether there is a correlation with speed of payment.

Training:
Train staff in:
- identifying problems with payments, and when they should escalate debtor issues
- when and how to use letters, phone calls and other forms of customer collection strategies
- the concept of debtor days, and the business reasons for reducing this figure.

EMPLOYEES

Without staff a business can't scale, so staff are imperative to the growth and success of most businesses. But they also create one of the greatest areas of ongoing operational risk, and sometimes dealing with staffing issues can feel like a battleground.

Almost every fast-growing business that I've dealt with has at some stage had legal issues in the area of staffing. So, it is not really a case of *if*, it's really a case of *when*.

The nuances of the legal environment relating to dealing with employees and contractors are highly complicated. But there are lots of simple steps a business can take to protect itself; for example, things like avoiding unfair dismissal claims or protecting a business against employees taking clients or IP with them are a matter of just having the right understanding, and then putting the right contracts and systems in place.

Businesses also need to fully understand how to correctly hire and fire, how to manage staff, and the documentation required.

Whenever I think about employment law issues that derail businesses, I come back to the memory of a client we acted for a few years ago who had a small retail business that had been run by the family for almost 40 years. We were introduced to them at a time of great distress. Two days before Christmas they received a long letter from a legal firm representing a former staff member. The staff member had been with them for more than 15 years, but after a recent argument with one of the owners, he said he was quitting and walked out. So our client let him walk, organised his final payment and thought that was the end of the matter.

This letter they received came as an absolute shock. In the letter, the legal firm now representing the departed staff member accused our client of unfair dismissal and demanded a large termination payment sum. The letter also claimed that our client had underpaid the employee for their entire period of employment dating back 15 years because of a failure to allow a 10-minute break in the morning as was required under the award. While our client had provided a number of paid breaks that were over and above the provisions of the award, they had missed this one.

The upshot was a claim for a six-figure sum that – understandably – sent our client into hysterics and overshadowed their

Christmas with anxiety. While our clients could have chosen to fight all the claims made against them, this would have prolonged the problem and our clients were already emotionally drained from both their incredulousness that a staff member they had known for so long (and who they had treated as almost family) would take this approach, and by the impact the worry had caused to their family Christmas period.

So ultimately we negotiated a far lower settlement, but our clients still needed to seek external funding for the settlement given the business was run on a razor-thin margin without room for any unplanned expenses. The experience shook them, and so we then helped them prevent future issues occurring. But the lesson was clear for them; prevention of these issues would absolutely have been far cheaper, and less stressful, than the way it played out.

The most likely employee-related risks are:

- difficulties in terminating underperforming staff
- issues with behaviour or performance management (which can in some situations manifest as a reluctance to terminate underperforming staff)
- unfair dismissal claims arising from issues in your termination process
- underpayment claims
- incorrect classification of contractors or casuals, leading to a risk of audit or employee claims
- non-compliance with legislation or awards, leading to a risk of audit or employee claims
- workplace grievances
- health and safety issues
- failure to maintain proper documentation to help ward off disputes
- departing staff members poaching clients, staff or other key partners of the business
- departing staff taking confidential information of the business.

The lesson was clear;
PREVENTION of
these issues would
absolutely have
been far CHEAPER,
and LESS STRESSFUL,
than the way it
played out.

The keys to prevention in this area are:

- **Contracts.** You need robust contracts and other key documentation, including:
  - a strong, current contract template suite for each category of employee, with appropriate restraints built in
  - employee handbooks
  - company policies.
- **Systems and procedures.** You need systems, processes and documentation relating to:
  - onboarding
  - performance management
  - termination
  - work health and safety
  - good recording keeping
  - annual reviews of internal processes, employment templates and other documentation to ensure they are up to date.
- **Training.** You need training for key staff who are dealing with employees (including management, HR and accounts staff), including how to:
  - identify issues in the classification of contractors and casuals
  - deal with performance management and termination
  - understand key employment legislation and regulations, and how to ensure compliance.

INTELLECTUAL PROPERTY

As discussed previously in this book, for many businesses IP has a massive amount of value, but what we haven't discussed so far is the risk that it can also create. Aside from understanding how to protect the value in your IP, you also need to understand how to minimise the risks.

The largest risk arising out of IP in an organisation is the risk of an infringement action. The risk of IP infringement can come from many unexpected places; for example, allegations of misuse of licensed software (we have dealt with many instances of businesses facing infringement allegations arising from using software that they had not properly licensed), licensed images (stock photos on websites are another common area where letters of demand are received by unwitting businesses in relation to images on their website or social media posts, often accompanied by a demand for tens of thousands of dollars in damages), copied content (if content in articles or websites is claimed to be an infringement of someone else), and of course allegations of trademark infringement.

While trademark infringement allegations can come at any point for a business, there are two points where the risk is greatest. These are:

- when a brand is just being developed and is at the point of first use
- when a brand is being used in a new market.

This is also a great time to dispel a myth I often hear – the belief that if you are able to secure a business name registration, there is no risk in using this name for a business or product. This is a complete fallacy and can result in marketing companies, accountants, and businesses themselves choosing and registering business names and then later on down the track finding out they have a name that is not protectable or, worse still, a name that infringes someone else's IP rights.

The reality is that when you are starting out with a new brand, or using an established brand in a new market, you need to be very careful to ensure you are not at risk of an allegation of trademark infringement. One example of the infringement risks when entering a new market is an international professional services business I worked with a few years ago that was looking to expand to Australia. They opened in Australia under the mark they had been using in 10 other countries around the world. But as soon as they opened, they were pounced on by a small business that held the trademark right in Australia for that mark, who threatened taking action against our client for trademark infringement and demanded a payment of hundreds of thousands of dollars. Ultimately our clients were hamstrung. They either had to rebrand their

Australian division (which would cause a massive issue to the company globally) or they had to come to an agreement with this small business that was holding the brand hostage. Neither was a great option.

Ultimately they negotiated a deal with the small business and they ended up being able to trade in Australia under their global brand, but this goes to show just how important it is to establish trademark protections broadly across all countries in which your business might operate, to ensure you preserve the right to expand to those countries without ending up with litigation risk.

The above business fared much better than another client we dealt with who was forced to change their entire company brand after more than a decade of use because they had simply not thought of trademark registration earlier. They had operated during this time knowing there was a similar brand in the market, but both similar branded businesses had continued operating on the assumption that because issues had not arisen in the past, this would continue without issue into the future. What our clients didn't factor into their consideration was that the other business might one day be sold. And that's exactly what happened. New owners came in, took issue with a similar-branded business in the market and pursued our clients for infringement.

The sad part of this story was that if our clients had come to us just a year earlier, before they had been at the wrong end of an infringement action, we could have saved the brand for them.

Timing can be absolutely critical with trademarks, and this case was the perfect example of the risks in having an unregistered trademark, and the difference a few months can make.

In summary, the keys to prevention in this area are:

Contracts:
- Ensure you have IP assignment and moral rights release clauses in all staff contracts and contracts with anyone who is a creator of IP for the organisation. And, of course, make sure these are signed and easily accessible. (I can't tell you how many times

I am told by clients that they sent an agreement, but now 'can't put their hand on a signed copy' . . . This is very frustrating for everyone involved, and can often be a barrier to enforcement.)

- Ensure you understand the provisions of licences for any licenced material you are using such as software, images and other copyrighted materials, to ensure you are not in breach of those licences, and also to ensure that those licences can be assigned if they are of value to the organisation and it may one day be sold.

Systems and procedures:

- Have in place a process to ensure that for any new brands that are developed, or any new markets that are contemplated, you have proper legal searches conducted at the right time (before you have invested too much in the brand creation process).
- Ensure that trademarks are registered as early as possible.
- Create an IP register where all IP created in your organisation is stored together with evidence of its date of creation, to ensure that if you ever need to prove ownership you have on hand the evidence that may be required. Having a process that ensures a copy of all IP is saved to a central location upon creation is a much simpler and quicker way of having access to this information in the future, rather than being forced to collate it after the fact. It can also end up being a great resource for the business moving forward.

Training:

- Provide your staff with general training in the areas of IP, and how each type of IP is protected – so they can identify when protection is needed, and when further help might be needed.

BUSINESS STRUCTURE AND RELATIONSHIP WITH BUSINESS PARTNERS

Being in business with others can have massive benefits, and can create great leverage. It can be essential for bringing on different skillsets and points of view that can multiply the performance of a business. But it can also be a source of dispute and risk. While generally business partner relationships start out happily with a lot of energy and unity of vision, there is a massive incidence of issues we see as the reality of differing styles and motivations plays out. I've seen internal disputes between partners drag on for years, and watched businesses be brought to their knees because the owners were too absorbed with their internal fights.[25]

This is why it's extremely important to start every business relationship with clear guidelines that deal with the tough questions. It is much better to spell details out in advance before the relationship sours. Agreeing on important issues from the beginning often prevents trouble from brewing in the first place. And it is just as vitally important to regularly review your guidelines to ensure everyone stays on the same page.

In addition to questions about how to document the relationship between business partners, you need to have an appropriate approach to the structure of the business and how solid the structure is in protecting against risk.

As we discussed in the earlier section on value protection, the use of multiple entities within a business structure can help to segregate risk. If you have a business line that may hold a lot of risk or are embarking on a new business direction that holds new risk, one approach can be to move the business unit to its own segregated entity to quarantine that risk. In this way, the structure of a business can be something that may change over time. While the fundamentals of a business structure should be established initially with the future in mind and the protection of the business against risks as it grows, an approach considered appropriate for where the business is today might be very different to what is appropriate if the business

---

25   I have many stories about shareholder disputes, and I cover a great example in chapter 18 about a problematic sale to an employee.

doubles or triples in size (or risk!), or new business partners are brought on, or if new product or service lines are added.

So in summary, the keys to prevention in this area are:

Contract:
- Have a solid contract in place between the shareholders or owners that very clearly deals with decision making (including who has rights to appointment as a director, and the levels of decisions that will be made by directors versus the shareholders), dispute resolution and, perhaps most importantly, exit. The exit considerations should deal with how each equity holder can exit if they want to, whether there are situations in which some equity holders might be forced to sell their equity, and how value will be arrived at in those situations. It's also important to consider whether drag along[26] or tag along clauses[27] will be relevant.

Systems and procedures:
- There should be a system in place for regular review of the owners' agreement, and how well it reflects where the business and each of the equity holders are as time progresses. Having a system in place for this review will help keep the lines of communication open, which is a major factor in reducing disputes.
- There should also be a system in place for review of structure, particularly at key points in the business such as bringing on new partners, expanding the scope of the business, bringing on larger risk (for example, a large customer contract that might hold risk), acquiring a business, or after a period of major growth.

---

26 *Drag along clauses:* Drag along clauses enable one or more shareholders holding a major share of the company to force a minority shareholder to sell together with them – the majority shareholders get the right to 'drag along' the minority shareholders in a sale.

27 *Tag along clauses:* Tag along clauses enable a minority shareholder to sell their shares to a purchaser at the same price as any other selling shareholder – the minority shareholder gets the right to 'tag along' with the larger shareholders who are selling.

Training:

- Owners should be educated about what the structure alternatives are, how structure can be used to minimise risk, and how to make choices that will set them up best for an eventual exit.

SUPPLIERS AND OTHER KEY CONTRACTS

As we discussed in our section on value protection, there may be a large component of value in your business's relationships with third parties such as suppliers, franchisees and licensees, franchisors, licensors, referral partners, distribution partners, sales agents, and the list goes on. But there can also be a ton of risk sitting in these relationships as well.

Such risk can arise in three common ways:

1. From the impact created by these third parties not complying with the obligations you have set up in the contract.
2. By you simply not setting up the right obligations to protect your business.
3. By you taking on risk under these relationships (there being a risk transfer to you).

In supply relationships, you must assess the risk you need to offset in your agreements – for example:

- Timing of the delivery of the goods or services might be important, in which case this needs to be clear. And the remedy if timing is not met needs also to be specified (particularly bearing in mind any consequences the business may suffer).
- The quality of the supply might be important. Once again this needs to be clear and measurable so you can clearly ascertain if your supplier is in breach. You also need to be clear on what the remedy is for this type of breach.
- Liability and any limitations or exclusions on liability of your supplier need to be fully understood.

If you have a business line that may hold **A LOT OF RISK** or are embarking on a new business direction that holds new risk, one approach can be to **MOVE THE BUSINESS UNIT TO ITS OWN STRUCTURE** to quarantine that risk.

The considerations are similar for other third-party contracts. Ultimately in this prevention stage you need to assess the three risk areas set out above to evaluate what exposures you have under the contracts, and what risks are being transferred to you or that should be transferred by you to the other party. A mistake so often made is a failure to understand such risk clauses, as well as a failure to identify what risk transfer clauses you should have in place to protect your business. This is where proper staff training comes into play, and of course access to good ongoing legal advice.

The keys to prevention in this area are:

Contract:
- Ideally templates should be in place for key contracts the business engages in regularly. When these have been set up by your legal team, they can then easily be used again and again by the business with confidence.
- Involve your legal team in the review of key contracts the business is entering into, to ensure clarity in the rights and obligations of each party, timing, and risk allocation.

Systems and procedures:
- Have clear parameters for when to seek legal advice.
- Create identification and resolution systems, to ensure problems are identified and dealt with quickly before they cause greater damage.
- Carefully manage third-party contracts, including having a central place to record all key contracts for the business and any important review periods or milestone dates.

Training:
Train staff who deal with contracts in the following:
- how to conduct simple risk assessments
- simple contract law

- understanding indemnities and liability clauses
- knowing when to get legal assistance.

MARKETING

Marketing is an often-overlooked area of risk to keep on top of, but be careful because it is also easy to over-reach in this area. Some of the common areas of marketing risk are:

- contravention of spam laws through an overly ambitious email or text marketing campaign
- privacy law contravention through failing to have proper privacy policies and systems in place, failing to comply with privacy requirements under your customer contracts, or poorly written privacy policies unwittingly committing your business to privacy laws when it was not captured by the legislation
- claims of misleading or deceptive conduct in marketing materials that might over-stretch reality
- contravention of laws relating to promotions you may be running
- social media in general, which can cause numerous risks from not just what your staff are posting, but also what others might be posting on your social media accounts – requiring a consideration of risks of misleading or deceptive conduct and also of defamation if posts contain comments about others.

Ensure staff involved in marketing understand spam laws, and that the required permissions are in place before sending out marketing emails.

Make sure you understand privacy laws and that you have the proper privacy consents, policies and collection statements in place that are relevant for your business.

Read up on the laws relating to misleading and deceptive conduct to ensure that your staff aren't doing things that might risk being viewed as misleading or deceptive; for example, by overstating the results clients may achieve with your services, or the quality of your products. Also, be careful about promotions you are running, and that you have complied with trade promotion requirements.

You should be thinking about what risk sits in your business relating to social media marketing, and putting in place systems, procedures and company policies that regulate how your social media channels are used and monitored (bearing in mind that your business can be liable for things other people post on your social media channels, as well as for things that are posted by your business). Make sure you understand the area of defamation (particularly if you or others post anything about individuals or other businesses).

Have policies in place to restrict the way your staff deal with social media connections and how they can continue to engage (or not engage as the case may be) with connections after they're no longer employed with your business. So, for example, you might want to ensure that they don't stay connected to clients of the business after you have parted ways, even through social media.

So in summary, the keys to prevention in marketing are:

Contracts:
- Ensure you have the proper privacy consents, policies and collection statements in place that are relevant for your business.
- Ensure your staff contracts and company policies include provisions relating to use of social media in the name of the business.

Systems and procedures:
- Ensure the right systems are in place to collect marketing permission from all recipients on your promotional databases.
- Have in place a system for proper collection of privacy consents.
- Put in place systems, procedures and company policies to regulate how your social media channels are used and monitored.

Training:
- Ensure staff have access to training on:
  - spam laws
  - privacy laws and how they might impact your business
  - understanding misleading and deceptive conduct legislation
  - trade promotion requirements
  - defamation laws
  - the responsibility of a business for its social media pages (including what staff post, but also what third parties post on your pages) and best practice in minimising risks arising from social media usage for businesses.

COMPLIANCE WITH LEGISLATION

The last area we cover is legislation and compliance. The red tape of running a business might be an afterthought for some, but failure to have in place a process for understanding the breadth of legislation and regulation that impacts your business can result not only in costly audits and fines, but also reputational loss. A business will usually go through an audit or compliance-driven complaint only once before it suddenly makes this area of prime importance.

The most relevant legislation for many businesses are privacy laws, and the competition and consumer legislation (which includes the Australian Consumer Law – generally known by the abbreviation of 'ACL').

Privacy legislation in Australia is found in the Privacy Act.[28] Businesses who extend their reach offshore may also need to consider the EU GDPR.[29] The Privacy Act applies in Australia to businesses

---

28   *Privacy Act 1988* (Cth).

29   European Union General Data Protection Regulation 2016/679 – which is regulation in the European Union and the European Economic Area on data protection and privacy that impacts not just businesses within the EU but also businesses outside of the EU that have clients within the EU.

that are either over the threshold for annual turnover (at the time of writing, that is $3 million) or that are one of a class of businesses specifically listed, irrespective of annual turnover (for example, health service providers, businesses that trade in personal information or the sale of databases, contractors that provide services under a Commonwealth contract, operators of a residential tenancy database, and credit reporting bodies).

The *Competition and Consumer Act 2010* (which includes the Australian Consumer Law) is very involved, but here are the main highlights for most SMEs:

- *Unfair contract terms.* Unfair contract terms (between certain types of parties) are not enforceable. This provision relates to contracts between a business and a consumer, and it also relates to contracts with small businesses. This means you need to ensure that terms contained within any of your 'standard form' contracts (that is, contracts that are not negotiated, such as terms on the back of an invoice, in a PDF or on a website) are not 'unfair' as provided for in the legislation.

- *Automatic guarantees applying to consumers (which in some circumstances can also include businesses) when they buy goods or services.* The legislation provides a set of guarantees that you must be aware of in terms of the minimum standards relating to the goods or services you provide (this may also be useful for you to understand in relation to your rights connected to the goods and services that you buy from your suppliers).

- *The safety of products and services.* These provisions apply safety responsibilities on retailers, wholesalers and importers – and require identification and removal of unsafe products and product-related services from the market.

- *Misleading and deceptive conduct.* This part of the legislation provides that a business's advertising material, and any statements (including country of origin statements) made by it, must be clear, accurate and truthful. Allegations of misleading and deceptive conduct are a standard argument in many disputes. It is therefore important to take this seriously.

- *Anti-competitive behaviour.* These provisions are broad – they restrict anti-competitive behaviour (for example, price fixing and other specific types of collusion between competitors) and other behaviour that may have the effect of impacting competition. This is a broad topic and there are many provisions that businesses may not be aware of that can create risk for an organisation of a breach, so it's extremely important that businesses ensure that their staff have comprehensive training in this area and an understanding of the main provisions of this act.

What other legislation and regulation should a business be thinking about? I have set out a list here that is not exhaustive but provides a guide as to the areas you should be looking at (or have your lawyer look at!):

- employment laws, including work health and safety, provisions under the Fair Work Act, and other legislation relating to paying staff, insurance and so on
- industry codes of conduct, for example the Franchising Code of Conduct
- laws relating to importing and exporting
- laws relating to environmental protections
- fair trading laws
- taxation and record-keeping laws
- directors' duties and obligations under the Corporations Act and other legislation
- the Personal Property Securities Act relating to the registration of security interests (which might also limit your ability to deal with your assets).

So in summary, the keys to prevention in this area are:

Contracts:

- Ensure you understand any provisions in contracts that might create or pass on responsibility to your business under legislation that is greater than what your underlying obligations are.
- Ensure you have provisions in contracts with your own suppliers to pass on responsibility for compliance with legislation, to ensure that their actions don't cause you to be in breach.
- Ensure you have provisions in contracts with your clients and other relevant third parties to limit your responsibility and liability for their contraventions.
- Ensure contract terms you are using aren't at risk of being viewed as illegal, or unenforceable.

Systems and procedures:

- You need systems for proper review of contracts before the business signs them, to ensure that any provisions that create obligations relating to compliance are identified and understood (and that your business is capable of taking on board those provisions).
- You need systems for regular review (at least annually) of what legislation and regulation applies to the organisation, to ensure that the business is compliant.
- You need systems for ensuring compliance with lodgment requirements under various pieces of legislation.

Training:

- Implement training for staff in any legislation that applies to your business. In many instances, staff will simply not know of, or understand, many of the complex restrictions that are created by some of legislation outlined above.
- Provide training for staff in what to look out for in contracts that they might be signing. This is really important if your staff are

signing off on contracts without them going to legal review, to ensure that they aren't committing the business to something with high risk (that is often hidden).

PERSONAL RISKS

And finally, but perhaps most importantly, we come to a discussion on the personal risks that individuals hold through their involvement in a business. Generally speaking (assuming the business is not run in an individual capacity as a sole trader or as a partnership of individuals), the main risks to individuals behind a business will come through exposure either via their position as a director or through personal guarantees they may have signed.

It's amazing how many people sign personal guarantees and then simply forget what they have signed. You should be extremely careful about signing onto personal guarantees, as there are often many alternatives. You can start by pushing back on the requirement – this may be enough. You could also consider offering alternative types of security; for example, it is common in leases for landlords to start with a request for a personal guarantee, but for security deposits or bank guarantees to be sufficient once you have gone through the requisite level of negotiation.

But if you are in the position where a director guarantee is necessary, it's important that you document this and save a register of director guarantees in a place where you can easily find it. This is important for ensuring that you know what is in place in the future if you are looking to exit. And also so that as the business grows and potentially reduces the necessity of personal guarantees, you know which contracts will need to be renegotiated to remove the personal guarantees in place.

Other risk to individuals comes through their position as a director. A key exposure to personal liability as a director comes from the risk of allegations of insolvent trading if the company has traded while in major financial difficulty. If it is proven that the company incurred debts when it was unable to repay its existing debts, the directors can become personally liable. There is also potential director personal liability in certain circumstances relating to unpaid tax and superannuation. There are also many other areas of exposure through legislation in Australia; for example, taxation and workplace health and safety.

So what can you do to protect yourself and your assets? The keys to prevention in this area are:

Structure:
- Consider whether you really need to be a director. Are there other ways to achieve control (such as through a shareholders' agreement) without needing to hold a position of directorship?
- If you are a director, look to how you can put in place personal risk and wealth protection. Get the structure right to protect wealth; for example, by having a family trust in place (which removes you as the holder of assets in your own name, and can also often help to minimise tax at exit if your trust is used for holding the shares in the business).

Contracts:
- Have the right insurances in place (such as management liability, or director and officer insurance).
- Consider putting in place a deed of indemnity between the company and each director to provide a safeguard for the director.
- Be careful about personal guarantees in contracts the business is entering into.

Systems and procedures:
- Have in place good bookkeeping to ensure that you understand the financial position of the business, and that the directors have access to and regularly review the financial position.

- Put systems in place to ensure all your lodgement requirements are clear and diarised, and not missed.
- Have a central place for recording and keeping records of personal guarantees provided.

Training:
- Provide training for directors in director duties and considerations for them in running the business.
- Provide training for the business in key areas that can trigger personal liability for directors.

Chapter 14

UNDERSTAND YOUR ENDGAME

The last part of this section could also perhaps be positioned right at the beginning.

Understanding your growth endgame is a critical component to putting in place the rigor of the Fortify system around your business – in terms of helping you understand why it needs to be in place, and also because the process of fortifying is what will help you ensure you can achieve your endgame.

Your growth endgame might be to build a business that runs without you, that you are involved in only to the level of your choosing, while delivering you the returns that you dream of.

Or for many, the growth endgame is a total exit – leaving the business on a high and reaping the rewards from your years of toil, liquidating it and running for the hills with your bags of cash!

A STRONGLY FORTIFIED BUSINESS

Either way, whatever it is that you are aiming for, a strongly fortified business is the best way to get there. Because a fortified business run under a strong management team is the best way to achieve a top sale price, and competitive tension – a business that others want to buy. But ironically, it is also the best business to run with longevity yourself.

And now that you have a business that has value in the eyes of a buyer, and you have grown and protected that value by building a fortress around your business, the next step is to understand how to best liquidate that investment and maximise the pot of gold at the end of that business rainbow – either now or in the future – through Exit...

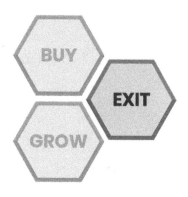

Part III

EXIT

CHAPTER 15: **EXITING IN STYLE**   201

CHAPTER 16: **THE FIVE ESSENTIAL DRIVERS OF A SUCCESSFUL SALE**   212

CHAPTER 17: **PREPARATION: THE MOST CRITICAL COMPONENT**   219

CHAPTER 18: **DEAL STRUCTURE: THE FOUNDATION OF A SUCCESSFUL SALE**   240

CHAPTER 19: **TRANSFERRING VALUE: MAXIMISING WHAT BUYERS WANT**   273

CHAPTER 20: **PROTECTION: MINIMISING YOUR RISK**   286

CHAPTER 21: **PROCESS: SEEING THE DEAL THROUGH**   304

CHAPTER 22: **THE END OF THE STORY**   316

CHAPTER 23: **JARGON BUSTER: TERMINOLOGY EXPLAINED**   321

Before you delve into this part, I recommend that you start by measuring your exit readiness by taking our very short scorecard. Find the scorecard at our resources hub at www.buygrowexit.com.au.

Chapter 15

EXITING IN STYLE

We have dissected how to acquire a business in the right way, and how to maximise that value during the transaction and after. We have also investigated how to grow a business understanding what creates value today and in the future, and how to protect that growing value by building the foundations of the business to enable it to weather the many inevitable storms along the way.

The next phase is the pinnacle of all of this planning and growth. It's where the rubber really hits the road. Where you can realise that long investment of time, money and energy in the business – and convert it to cold hard cash.

Exit is the final stage of value extraction. It is also the step where you least want things to blow up. It is imperative to understand the methodology of the sale process, and to understand the potential speedbumps along the way so that they don't throw you off course. It's also important to understand the levers you can pull, and ultimately how to control the deal and the risks, so that you can maximise the pot of gold at the end of that business rainbow.

For some, exit will be about the ultimate sale to transition to retirement. For others, exit is about moving onto the next business phase. Sometimes it's because the passion for the business has dwindled, sometimes life circumstances of the owners have changed (through divorce, sickness, or other changes), sometimes the business itself has gone through a large change (positive or negative) and needs new energy at the helm, sometimes it is as a path towards greater growth of the business (bringing on board new owners who will be able to supercharge growth), and sometimes it is just because the time feels right.

Whatever the reason for sale, the desire out of exit is universal: to achieve the best price and/or terms possible.

COMMON SALE PROBLEMS

There are however many things that can go wrong in this phase, and the issues can be summarised into three key areas:

- The sellers aren't able to extract the value out of the business that they had expected.
- The deal hits speedbumps and takes more of a seller's time, energy and money than they had expected.
- The sellers are exposed to risk during the transaction and into the future.

Let's consider each of these.

THE SELLERS AREN'T ABLE TO EXTRACT THE VALUE OUT OF THE BUSINESS THAT THEY HAD EXPECTED

For small businesses, and in particular lifestyle businesses (where the business revolves around the owners, who are key to the ongoing operation), the biggest surprise at exit is almost universally a complete mismatch between their impression of the value of their business versus the reality of what they will be able to achieve. This can be a culmination of their own 'research' as to indicators of value, their accountant's well-meaning valuation of their business based on generic valuation principles (rather than street-smart understanding of the reality of value at sale), or the experience of John down the

Whatever the reason for sale, the desire out of exit is universal: to achieve the

BEST PRICE
and TERMS
possible.

road who sold his business for a massive uplift and their extrapolation of this great result to their own business.

But then reality hits, and they find out the hard way that business value is not made up of what they want or 'need' from it – but what the market will pay.

This is a warning for business owners who are looking at their businesses to provide the pot of gold at the end of the working life-cycle rainbow, but without doing any work to understand what creates value at exit. Often they've built a business over many hard years and when they reach the point of 'cashing it all in', they assume it's going to provide a reward commensurate to that level of effort. And they're the ones who are most susceptible to a shock at the end of the day if their concept of value has been misplaced.

Exit price has nothing to do with the effort put in along the way, nor with the amount they personally feel they 'need' to extract from the business. Exit price is simply what a buyer will pay. End of story.

A failure of 'value extraction' however is not just about the sale price not meeting the 'dream'. It is also often also caused or exacerbated by the way the sale is structured, causing leakage along the way, or tax taking far more out than anticipated. Or by the price being eroded after due diligence if a buyer finds issues in the business. Or by earnouts not triggering in the way that had been expected.

This is not to say that vast, life-changing sums of money can't be achieved with a business exit. Indeed, they often are! But achieving a pot of gold from your sale is not simply a function of having a business that *you* perceive as valuable. It is instead a function of having created a business that the *market* perceives has value. And those are often two completely different things.

THE DEAL HITS SPEEDBUMPS AND TAKES MORE OF A SELLER'S TIME, ENERGY AND MONEY THAN THEY HAD EXPECTED

When the transaction proves longer or more onerous than sellers expected, they often make unnecessary concessions along the way and lose value in the deal, or take their eye off the ball in the business and risk losing it all if the deal doesn't proceed.

The sale process of a business is often far longer than business owners realise. By the time the parties are at the point where they have found a buyer, they often have already invested 6 to 12 months in the process. And when issues appear in the contract phase, and negotiations draw out further, this can be excruciating to a seller who is dreaming of their days post-sale sipping pina coladas on a white sandy beach.

Sometimes when they are so close to the finish line, and caught up in intense negotiations, or simply feeling the effects of 'deal fatigue', sellers make unnecessary concessions. Alternatively, there are some sellers who become caught up in the emotion of the sale and become belligerent, because they are having difficulty imagining what their life will look like, and what their identity will be, post-sale. Or they become paralysed by the fear that they are letting their pot of gold escape for a price that is too low or with terms that are too stringent, which they feel might be resolved if only they can wait for the 'perfect' buyer.

In both of these instances, poor sale and contract phase processes can leach time, energy and money, can cause deals to fall over, and can cause irreparable damage to the business in the meantime while these processes are playing out. I have met many business owners who have lamented about their period of sale causing the death of their business. In one case, an owner of an education business went to market, and found a buyer willing to pay more than $1.5m for the business. The buyer entered a due diligence process, and became incredibly demanding. The seller had become emotionally distant from the business, and during the period of due diligence poured his entire time and attention into answering every question from the overzealous buyer, and put very little time and attention into the direction of the business. Due diligence went on for months, and the seller got further and further removed from the operation of the business – focusing instead on finalising the sale, dealing with due diligence questions, and dreaming of his post-sale retirement plan.

However, after months of due diligence, the buyer had a change of heart and walked away from the deal. The seller took a few weeks off to deal with the disappointment, but by the time he came back, the business was a mess. After the months and months leading into the deal, and then the months and months in negotiations and due diligence, the business was in trouble. Staff had become disengaged, service had suffered and clients were moving away, cashflow had started to dry up. By the time the seller realised how dire the situation was, it was too late. The business was in rapid decline. And then COVID hit. The business owner simply couldn't bear the thought of the energy it would take to rebuild, and six months later the business closed down.

From a $1.5m potential sale, to $0. Clearly a disaster in anyone's books. And a sobering reminder of the absolute importance of taking the lessons in this chapter seriously.

THE SELLERS ARE EXPOSED TO RISK DURING THE TRANSACTION AND INTO THE FUTURE

This is perhaps one of the greatest concerns of sellers as they undertake the contract process and suddenly realise there are risks that might be triggered by the sale itself, and other risks that may continue past the day they hand over the keys to the business. Warranties and indemnities in the sale contract can seem daunting, and – for an uneducated seller without full trust in the deal team representing them – can create many sleepless nights as they balance the desire for an exit on their terms against the fear of post-sale risks coming back to bite them.

———

From a $1.5m potential sale, to $0. Clearly a disaster in anyone's books. And a sobering REMINDER of the ABSOLUTE IMPORTANCE of taking the lessons in this chapter seriously.

There are however a number of things sellers can do to minimise the risk of their deal suffering any of these issues, which I discuss in detail over the following chapters. The 5 Essential Drivers of Great Sales are:

- preparation
- deal structure
- value transfer
- protection
- process.

Unsurprisingly, these drivers are basically the same as the 5Ps Driving Great Purchases, but now you are on the other side of the fence.

When business owners properly understand and execute on these five essential drivers, they will set themselves up for a great financial outcome from the deal, a deal that is on their terms, and a deal that enables them to hand over the keys and sleep easy at night.

One last thing should be added into this discussion about exit: a sale isn't always about fully exiting. Often an owner might choose to sell down a portion of their holding to liquidate part of the assets in their business, to 'take some money off the table' as the saying goes, or to bring on board fresh enthusiasm, ideas and sometimes business smarts for the next phase of the business.

In such instances, the business still needs to be prepared for sale to maximise the value to be achieved from the part sale, and all of the elements that we are about to cover in part III are still equally as important as if you were selling the entire business. However, the additional important consideration will be the ongoing relationship between you and the other (new) owners in the business.

HOW BUSINESSES ARE SOLD

There are a multitude of ways to exit all or part of a business . . . and there's also a lot of jargon to match! Here are some examples of ways to exit in simple terms:

- **Sell to a third party.** The most obvious type of sale, and certainly the most common, is the sale to a third party. This can either be a full sale at one time, a staggered sale over a period of time, or a part sale. In some cases, this will be triggered by a buyer's interest rather than the owners' desire to exit.

- **Sell to existing shareholders.** Other owners of the business are often the best potential buyers, because they already know and understand the business.

- **Sell to management or key employees – either all at once, or slowly over time.** To achieve this you can sell shares, or you can use options that are triggered by the achievement of certain milestones or KPIs. Payment or part of the payment might be deferred over a time. The term MBO (management buyout) is often used to refer to this type of transaction, where the business or shares are being acquired by the management of the business.

- **Go public with an IPO (initial public offering).** This is where a private company lists (or 'floats') on the stock exchange and can then be traded publicly. It is a complicated and expensive route, but is where the headlines are made from business founders achieving eye-watering returns.

- **Transfer to family members.** A transfer to family members is generally done in a less formal way than a transfer to third parties, and may involve creative approaches to payment over time. It is also often done slowly with transition occurring over time.

- **Close the doors.** This is the last and generally least desirable exit type. But it is the final remaining approach when all else fails.

Whether you are selling or not, running a business in a sale-ready state is always the best way to run a business – because you never know when circumstances might change and a sale might be necessary, and you also never know when a potential buyer might come

Whether you are selling or not, running a business in a **SALE-READY STATE** is always the **BEST WAY** to run a business.

knocking on your door. Because in many instances sales are not triggered by the seller but by a buyer. And even if you don't sell in the near future, running a business this way makes it stronger, more efficient and – usually – more profitable.

We have had many instances of our clients being approached to sell their business out of the blue. These approaches generally come from strategic buyers, who have a particular use for the business in mind, generally as part of their expansion strategy.

But this can cause chaos in a business that is not run in a sale-ready state.

Firstly, business owners in this situation often simply have no idea what their business is worth – because this hasn't been a consideration. Next is the issue that the business generally doesn't look ready for sale, and isn't in the optimum position for extracting the best price. And often this is when it becomes painfully apparent that the structure of the business is not optimised for sale, and will trigger an excess of tax that would not have been required if the business had been well set up. And third, the approach out of the blue also means that there generally are no other buyers around, and therefore there is *no competitive tension.*

Understanding and preparing a business for sale should not just be the domain of business owners who are preparing for exit. It is an important step for all businesses, to ensure that they run in a sale-ready state, ready to take advantage of opportunities that might land on their doorstep.

Chapter 16

THE FIVE ESSENTIAL DRIVERS OF A SUCCESSFUL SALE

Over my decades of working with many hundreds of business sales and acquisitions, I have established the 5 Essential Drivers of Great Sales:

- **Preparation:** the work that you do prior to a sale, that will put you in the best position to maximise the sale.
- **Deal structure:** the different ways you can put the deal together, and the different impacts of each option.
- **Value transfer:** the way in which you have set the business up ready for a buyer to be able to recognise and extract the value in the business.
- **Protection:** the way for you to minimise the risks that exist in the sale, both during the transaction itself, and after the transaction.
- **Process:** the means by which the sale actually happens, a point in the transaction that is 'make or break'.

I have two stories to share with you that demonstrate the need for careful evaluation of each of these five drivers for selling a business.

A DEAL SALVAGED . . . BARELY

The first is a story about Rod and Jane, who had a distribution business with an 80-year history. And the second is a story about Ted, who had a consultancy business.[30]

In both stories, the way in which the sellers recognised and dealt with each of these five drivers had a massive impact on their sales. Both stories provide a cautionary tale, but also a glimpse of a lot of success. I could have chosen to tell you stories of utter disaster, and believe me, there are so many of those – where owners did almost no preparation and ended up with businesses that ultimately were unsellable. Or switched approaches during the transaction, such as starting down the path of a business sale and changing to a share sale right at the last second, with no preparation and disastrous consequences.

But while the disaster stories are voluminous, what they often don't show is the possibilities that proper preparation and engagement of these five steps provide. So I prefer to give you instead two stories that

---

30 Names have been changed to protect privacy.

help shed light on the benefits of recognising these five drivers, but also to provide a cautionary tale about what can happen when preparation is only half done.

Rod and Jane came to me when they were on the cusp of the sale of their business. They were selling the business to retire, having run it together for more than 40 years. Prior to that the business had been owned by Rod's parents and had been passed down to them, so there was a lot of history in the business. The sale was expected, and they had been planning for it for years.

They'd had the business reviewed by a lawyer years prior to the sale, with the intention that the business would be primed for sale. At the same time, they decided they would appoint a general manager to run the business, because they knew that a business that could be sold under management would be worth much more than a business that was still dependent on them to provide all the high-level knowledge transfer to the buyers.

They had prepared, they had recognised what would be required for proper knowledge transfer (value transfer) to the buyers. And they had in place a process that started them on this journey of change of their business well in advance of the sale.

So far, so good – their preparations were textbook to this point.

The problem however came from the advice they received. Firstly, the lawyers and accountants reviewing the business and readying it for sale were working in silos, without proper discussions between them.

Secondly, no-one was focusing clearly on what would be best for exit. Ironically, even though they had approached their lawyer early with exit on their mind, they became sidetracked looking at ways to deal with the general manager coming on board and how this might impact the business structure they were operating. No-one had focused on what the tax outcome at sale would be, or on how they would best prepare themselves for sale.

Unfortunately, structuring decisions were made at this point that created great issues for them later, and caused a massive slowing of the transaction and a much higher tax bill than would have occurred if the right tax planning, tied together with proper legal advice about exit, had been done at the outset.

But worse was about to come. They had built much of the value in the sale around the concept of value transfer sitting in the role of the general manager who was overseeing the running of the whole business. The plan had been that the general manager would transfer over with the business, providing the buyer with access to all that management knowledge and corporate history, to enable the business to transition seamlessly. But while value transfer had been on the minds of the sellers, what they hadn't considered was protection for them and the business if the plan with the general manager didn't work out.

It turned out that the general manager sensed an opportunity to extract value for himself out of the sale, and at the last minute, the general manager threatened to walk if he wasn't given a massive chunk of the sale price. Rod and Jane didn't submit to his demands, and in the dead of night just hours before the deal was to be settled, the general manager upped stumps and deserted them (taking client and supplier lists with him).

What ensued was a massive rush trying to save the deal, legal action against the general manager, rushed negotiations with the buyer, and finally a deal that was re-cut to save the day which then required more time and involvement of the sellers together with an earnout.

Ultimately it is still a positive story. The business was ultimately sold (using a creative approach to deal structuring). However, it ended up involving much more stress and more tax than it needed to.

It could very easily have been a very different story. The deal could have ended up with Rod and Jane in a much worse financial position. Or worse still, the buyers could have walked, leaving Rod and Jane to restart the process – it had taken almost a year to find the buyers and negotiate and finalise the deal. No-one at that point wants to simply start the whole process over again.

This is a great example of the benefits in preparing well for sale, understanding value transfer, and cleverly utilising deal structuring – because Rod and Jane only received the end outcome they did for the business because of some of the steps they took in the preparation, and the way in which the deal team ultimately came together to guide their sale to a positive end.

But it is also a cautionary tale – that simply following a checklist of things to do to prepare for sale and maximise price may go horribly wrong if you don't have a team around you that understands how best to maximise the value you can extract and minimise the risks in getting to a successful exit.

As we go through our 5Ps, we will dissect how these important areas of a deal impacted Rod and Jane, and the learnings for your business.

ALMOST A MILLION DOLLARS LOST

Ted had over 40 years built a fabulous consulting business, and as he neared the point of exit, he engaged a smart group of corporate advisers to put the business on the market.

He started his preparation for sale years in advance, ensuring that he understood what would create value in the eyes of a buyer and building that up in the business. When he finally decided to hit the market, he had multiple strong offers, which created competitive tension and ultimately landed him a great deal for the sale.

Unfortunately we were only brought in at this stage, when commercial terms were agreed, and the buyer was launching into due diligence. And unfortunately, this point of due diligence is where things started to unravel quickly.

Even though Ted thought he had prepared his business well for sale, at the time he had only been focusing on financial and operational preparations for sale – not legal. And there were legal landmines everywhere that the buyer was now uncovering.

The major part of the value in the business was in the workforce of hundreds of contractors. However the way the contractors were

Simply following a checklist of things to do to PREPARE FOR SALE and MAXIMISE PRICE may go horribly wrong if you don't have a TEAM around you that understands how to best maximise value and minimise risk.

engaged held a lot of risk from an employment law perspective, and the buyer (who was a large listed entity) was very quick to spot this risk, and it began to cause them alarm. We will dig into what happened later, but for now suffice to say that the revelation of these risks in the business, and risks in the value transfer of the contracting workforce, caused massive concern with the buyer, and risked the deal falling over altogether.

In the end, the deal was saved by some clever deal structuring approaches. However, this was not the only issue in the sale. The whole business was terribly structured for exit, which ultimately meant that half a million dollars more was paid in tax than would have been necessary had it been properly structured.

There had also been a large risk throughout the transaction that either the buyer would walk, or that the new way the deal was structured would mean that the seller only received a small portion of the expected sale price.

So once again, the story of Ted reminds us of some of the benefits of preparation for exit, but also of the massive risks that are caused by a failure to properly prepare, properly consider value (and how that is protected and transferred) and risk in the business, and to properly consider the opportunities provided in approaches to creative deal structuring.

———

Let's dig into these five essential drivers of a successful sale, in order that you can do it differently!

Chapter 17

PREPARATION: THE MOST CRITICAL COMPONENT

Proper preparation is the most critical component in maximising value at exit. Sellers who fail to prepare properly for exit will almost always suffer from issues along the way that can have a massive impact on the way the sale progresses.

On the flipside, businesses that are properly prepared generally will have:

- a larger pool of buyers (which brings with it not just the pricing benefit of competitive tension, but also inbuilt fallbacks if a buyer becomes too demanding)
- a higher multiple attributed by buyers (that is, a higher sale price)

- more attractive terms for the seller (businesses that are seen as less risky and more sale prepared will generally have offers with higher upfront payments, often full upfront payments, and less emphasis on at-risk payments like earnouts)
- a quicker and smoother sale, with fewer speedbumps along the way (because the last thing you want once you have kicked off the sale process is issues to then emerge that slow it down).

This is a reality that played out well initially for Ted, whose early engagement with specialist exit advisers meant he knew his potential buyer market well, and consequently at the point of sale had multiple buyers lined up – creating competitive tension that drove up the price and ultimately put Ted in the driving seat. He was then in the great position of being able to select the buyer for his business on the basis not only of price, but also terms of sale and the ongoing best fit for his staff and clients in the transition. However, as the sale progressed, a failure to properly prepare the business from a legal and accounting perspective undid some of his other great preparatory work as due diligence uncovered risks that threatened to undo the whole deal.

Similarly, Rod and Jane initially benefited from their advance planning for sale – and given they had built a business that was under management, they were able to find multiple buyers to create competitive tension and drive up the valuation multiple. But they too were nearly brought down by gaps in their legal protections that almost undid the whole deal, and in financial preparation that left them paying much more tax than could have been the case.

THE AREAS OF YOUR BUSINESS YOU MUST CONSIDER FOR YOUR EXIT

Let's examine some of the main elements that every business looking to exit at some point in the future should be thinking about. You must:

- understand tax, and the appropriateness of your business structure for sale
- understand the business from a buyer's perspective

- systemise the business
- become independent of the business
- understand the sale process, and the timelines
- be ready for DD (due diligence)
- get your deal team established
- have a post-exit plan
- run the business in a sale-ready state.

Let's look at each of these in detail.[31]

THE DIRTY THREE-LETTER WORD . . . TAX!

Tax preparation (or a failure of it!) is one of the biggest mistakes that I see made, again and again and again. It's one thing to negotiate a price for the sale of your business, but it can be a completely different thing when you find out what that looks like as dollars in your pocket, after tax. This perhaps sounds obvious, but around 80% of clients that come to us at the point of exit have very little idea of how this will play out for them.

I find when clients come in and we see tax issues on the horizon, and we then direct them back to their accountant to have them properly run through the cashflow of the sale proceeds to work out how much will end up in their pocket, versus how much they will pay in tax, they are absolutely blown away at the difference a change in the sale structure can make to the money that is left in their pockets. In the sales of small businesses, many owners leave the sale paying no tax whatsoever. But others, who have sold in a suboptimal way, can instead be paying millions. The differences can be staggering.

This can be seen in the story of Rod and Jane, who had done everything they could think of to build a long runway in preparing the business for sale, but had been let down by their advisers.

You may recall that when Rod and Jane came to us, they had spent years 'preparing' the business for sale. They had consulted

---

31 If you haven't already taken the exit ready scorecard, head over to the resources hub at www.buygrowexit.com.au to get a score now of how exit ready you are.

their accountant, who had sent them to a commercial lawyer, who had then restructured the business for sale. But when it came to the point of sale, no-one had told them that the way for him to achieve massive tax savings in the sale would be to sell the shares, not the business. In chapter 18 we discuss many of the differences between share and business sales, but for now it's enough to simply know that the tax difference can be huge.

Rod and Jane had then engaged a broker, who had spent a year negotiating a sale, and when they finally came to an outcome together – they found us to help with the sale. But in the first 10 minutes of our very first meeting together, I immediately realised there was a problem. The restructure had meant that our clients couldn't access some benefits of the old structure they had been in. And in the new structure they needed to be able to sell their shares to maximise the cash in their pockets out of the sale proceeds. But the year of negotiation with the buyer had all been around a business sale. Changing the deal at the last minute would cause massive problems – so I had to be sure that this was a real issue.

So Rod and Jane went back to their accountant to get advice on what the net proceeds (money in their pocket) would be if we switched to a share sale rather than a business sale. And the difference was staggering. In a share sale environment the tax would be zero. Nil. Nothing. Nada. They would keep the entire sale proceeds. But in a business sale they could end up paying $900,000 in tax. That's almost $1 million! Just in the difference in how the sale was conducted.

To say Rod and Jane were floored was an understatement. They thought they had done everything right, in approaching the sale well in advance and involving their accountant and lawyer. But what they didn't understand was that their advisers were acting in silos of advice. Because the lawyer they had seen didn't deal daily with business sales, they just didn't think about the implications of the restructure they were doing. And because they were busy on the day-to-day compliance, the accountant just didn't think to work through the tax consequences to ensure they were armed with understanding what the sale needed to look like.

Once we understood the significance of the structure in this deal, we tried to negotiate a change. But after a year of seeing the deal in a particular way, the buyer wasn't interested in changing the commercial terms of the deal. So Rod and Jane faced losing the deal altogether, or taking a massive tax hit. Bear in mind, this was all happening at the same time as the other difficulties with the sale.

They ultimately chose the tax hit, and we ended up being able to partly undo the restructure together with the accountants to get to a somewhat improved outcome. But they left the process still paying a large amount of tax (and of course much more than the zero outcome they could have had), and with the stress and time of working through what should have been done correctly at the beginning. (The reasons for the different tax outcomes are explained in chapter 18.)

Rod and Jane's story is so common it's scary, often driven by business owners who just don't think to involve their advisers early enough. But in many instances (as was the case in this instance, and also for Ted) it is driven by seeing the wrong advisers – by not involving advisers who do this regularly and deeply understand the complex issues at play.

This is of course not the only type of tax problem I have seen our clients grapple with at exit, or upon partial sell downs. There are myriad issues that can arise when businesses seek to use small business tax concessions. I've had clients tripped up by having multiple classes of shares within their structure (for example, where they have had A-class and B-class shares rather than all shareholders holding ordinary shares), and even by decisions they have made in relation to who in their family is the holder of personal investments such as investment properties.

Ted (the other story that we discussed earlier) also lost almost a million dollars in tax that could have been avoided had he been correctly structured for a sale in advance. His issues related to the complexity of structures that had been set up years in advance by overzealous advisers, but that had then been impacted by partners of the business slowly falling away over the years. So while ultimately he ended up being the only owner left, he had a business that was structured as though it had multiple owners.

This is a common problem – businesses are initially structured in a way that might make sense for where the business is at that time, but changes to ownership over time create the situation where the structure leading into sale is simply not the right structure for the business. This is something that can almost always be dealt with if it is approached well in advance of a sale. But in Ted's case, this was only identified at the point where the buyer had been found and the transaction was underway – and so it was far too late to do anything.

So perhaps it is sufficient to say that the tax considerations are complex and must be considered as early as possible. Because in many instances problems can be resolved if identified early enough, but once you are sitting at the point of sale it is usually too late to change, or very costly to do so.

Let's then boil down the preparation considerations in this area:

- Get advice early in relation to assessing how suitable your structure will be at exit. This might result in a need for a full or partial restructure. (But be careful that you have advisers who also understand the risks in a restructure, and are skilled in restructuring for optimal outcomes at exit.)
- Understand the tax outcomes of different ways that an exit could happen (for example, share sale versus business sale, part sale versus full sale, and all the other options set out in chapter 18 on deal structures).
- Get regular reviews and continue seeking advice from your legal and accounting/tax team working together (rather than in silos) each time your business goes through change, such as launching new entities and bringing on board new partners.

This is a common problem – businesses are initially structured in a way that might make sense for where the business is at that time, but **CHANGES IN OWNERSHIP** over time create the situation where where that historic structure is not the best structure for an optimised sale.

- When you are at the point of exit or partial sell down, make sure you understand any tax consequences of different deal structures, including share sale versus business sale, the impact of earnouts or deferred payments, and the sale timing of commercial property assets if they form part of the sale.

UNDERSTANDING THE BUSINESS FROM A BUYER'S PERSPECTIVE

In preparing for exit it is critical to understand what a buyer will value and what could scare them away. I approach this consideration by breaking the business into two areas: value and risk.

In its most simplistic form, you must assess what the key areas of value are in the business (and what they could be, even if they aren't there currently) – and lock those in.

You must also assess what risks lurk in the business, that could either destroy value before sale or reduce the value in the eyes of your buyer. You then need to take this insight and establish proper systems for reducing these risks.

I talk about both of these areas – identifying and protecting value, and predicting and preventing risk – in part II. If you haven't read those chapters yet, I highly recommend going back and reading them now. I also cover this further in the context of Exit as we progress through this chapter and investigate value and protection more deeply.

I cover these areas in a lot of detail because they are critical in helping you to achieve an optimal outcome at exit. In most cases the more preparation you do early in your exit process the easier you will find it – because often once you are in the exit process it is simply too late.

SYSTEMATISING THE BUSINESS

Buyers love businesses with good systems and processes firmly established. On the flipside, businesses where all the knowledge sits in the head of the owners or a limited number of key staff will likely have a smaller pool of buyers, and a reduced value at sale – and also pose an impediment for you if you want to get out of the business quickly at exit.

The reality is that once you have made the decision to exit, and then gone down the long path of finding a buyer and securing a deal, you will often simply want to get out as quickly as possible. If however the value in the business is tied at all to the knowledge you have inside your head, the likely outcome will be that the sale will be contingent on you staying involved for long enough to transfer that knowledge and value. Often it might also result in the sale price being contingent on that transfer.

So as part of your preparation for a successful exit you must systemise the business as much as possible, transferring knowledge and reliance on key staff into systems and processes that capture this critical business knowledge.

BECOMING INDEPENDENT OF THE BUSINESS

Businesses that are run under management, or that are otherwise independent of the owners, will almost always see a large uplift in their valuation multiple, and a quicker and easier transition. They are also often less susceptible to the sale price having a large component tied to an earnout (given earnouts are often a strategy used by a buyer to manage the risk of transfer of goodwill and corporate knowledge from the seller).

So if at all possible, in your preparation for exit, consider install-ing a good general manager, and start progressively stepping out of the business.

There is often an irony in this process. Once you start stepping out of your business, owning it can become more enjoyable and perhaps give you a different perspective on options other than full exit – where you may still have some involvement but without the day-to-day operational stress of actually running the business.

You might also consider giving the general manager or manage-ment team some skin in the game by selling them equity at a slightly reduced rate, or having them buy in over time. You might set up a 'phantom equity' plan, or some other incentive arrangement that provides them with a financial incentive for achieving a strong value at exit. You might also look at non-financial incentives. All of this must be considered carefully, and backed up by the right structure and agreements – to ensure you preserve enough flexibility for your future entire exit.

The sorts of approaches discussed above can also create the option of alternative pathways to exit, and the possibility of longer ongoing ownership with less stress.

The positives of these approaches include:

- potentially higher sale value
- an easier transition at exit
- an array of alternative ways to exit or reduce your time in the business.

There are however some risks that need to be considered seriously – in particular the key person risk that you effectively develop in that general manager or management team.

BEWARE OF KEY PERSON RISK IN A CEO OR GM

Rod and Jane are the perfect example of what can go wrong with this approach. As we discussed earlier, years in advance of their exit they had cleverly planned a new general manager role to reduce the reliance of the business on them. They hired a general manager and set about transferring their knowledge to him, and over time the new GM took over almost entire control of the business. However as you already know, this imploded at the point of sale, when he first held them to ransom on sharing the sale price, and then ultimately walked out of the business when they wouldn't meet his demands. This was catastrophic for several reasons. The GM was now a key figure in the transition of important business relationships and knowledge. Rod and Jane had done such a good job of transitioning their knowledge to him that they were now out of the loop, as the GM now held all of the close relationships and knowledge of suppliers and top clients. The buyers of the business of course were highly concerned about whether they would get the full value of these suppliers and top clients now that the GM was gone.

The GM also held a lot of business IP and confidential information, and there was a real risk that he was about to use it in competition with the business.

Ultimately the transaction was saved by a clever reorganisation of the deal, to protect against the risks that had come from the departure of the GM, and the buyer agreed to continue.

It was agreed that instead of being a full cash payment at completion, part of the sale funds would be retained by the buyer for one year and released if all suppliers and clients transferred over and the business maintained its pre-sale revenue. Rather than Rod and Jane taking the full sale price at completion and waltzing away into the sunset, they agreed to stay on working in the business to pass over the knowledge and relationships. Additional warranties were added to the sale contract. And a series of legal letters and demands were issued to the GM, to ensure that he didn't carry through with his plans of operating in competition, and to ensure he had no contact whatsoever with clients and suppliers of the business.

And so, with the ex-GM on notice about the severity of the matter, unsurprisingly he faded away without causing any further issues. Rod and Jane were able to transfer their knowledge and relationships to the buyer – and given that during the process of transition to the GM great systems and processes had been set up, this was a little easier and quicker than it had been feared initially. Ultimately the business went from strength to strength, and Rod and Jane got their full final payment.

But it wasn't the stress-free exit that they had hoped. And certainly on reflection they realised there were a few things they could have done differently, had they understood the risks and had a properly experienced deal team around them to support them in their preparation for exit.

The lesson here is that setting up your independence from the business must be done carefully.

There is one other story I want to add into this discussion. When considering installing a general manager into the business to enable you to reduce your involvement, you should also consider carefully the story of James in part II, who had a business that ended up decimated because of the failure to set up systems and processes to ensure that the general manager had his eyes on the right things.

Here is a shortlist of the sorts of things that could have been done differently in both the situations of Rod and Jane, and in the story of James:

- **Share knowledge around to reduce key person risk.**
  Rather than full knowledge passing to the GM, this knowledge and the relationships could be shared among a number of people – either on the management team or in senior positions.
- **Build strong systems and processes.** The transfer of knowledge and relationships should be done together with, or after, building the systems and processes to document them. The benefit of this approach is that if you need to replace key staff, there is already a process in place to make transition of that knowledge easier. The other benefit is that you create clarity in what the GM should be focusing on, and a way to minimise the risk of the business leaking value.
- **Build in incentivisation for key staff to help maximise the sale value and properly transition the business.** For example, this could be done in the form of a bonus. I have seen some incredibly successful deals where key staff bonuses had helped to drive the value at exit and provide a great transition for the buyer. In some of these instances, the sellers had also managed to get the buyers to agree to the payment

of all or part of those bonuses through the business when it was in the buyer's hands (so the payment did not impact the seller's return).

- **Consider staff ownership.** Depending on how far away you are from exit, you might consider having certain key staff hold shares, options or 'phantom' shares, so they feel some skin in the game in the preparation for exit and transition (but it's important that this is set up in a way that ensures they don't impact your control of, and flexibility in, the sale). We discussed this in part II, and discuss it further below.
- **Legal up.** Use very strong legal documents to ensure that key staff can't dilute or threaten the value of the business by taking clients, suppliers, staff, IP or critical confidential information.

UNDERSTANDING THE SALE PROCESS AND THE TIMELINES

One thing that sellers often don't fully comprehend is how long a sale can take. Once you have decided to sell and have finished all the necessary preparation (which as I have said more than once, can take years to do properly if you are going to extract maximum value), you need to engage help to find a buyer and secure a deal, and then go through the process of providing the information they need, negotiating the deal terms, waiting for them to complete due diligence, and then slowly transitioning across the business. At best, if you are in the fastest process possible, for example having been approached by a buyer out of the blue, it will still likely take many months (unless your business is very small or very simple). But if you need to find a buyer, and have the buyer go through the usual process of considering and then executing the sale, this can take a very long time. Some businesses report to me that they have spent years in the process (particularly if they have had the misfortune of having transactions fall through along the way).

I have included here a table showing a very simplified version of the process to provide a guide – you must ensure you have consulted your specialist deal team and understand what the process of preparation and sale will look like for your business, so that you are armed with knowledge well in advance of how long the process will take, and the important process steps that will need to be covered.

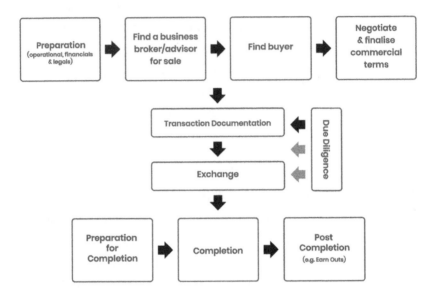

BEING READY FOR DD

Due diligence (referred to in the industry as 'DD') is the stage where the buyer investigates the value in your business and how that value will transfer, as well as the risk in the business. This will usually include an analysis of the financials of the business, the legal infrastructure and other operational areas critical to a buyer. It is the point of the transaction where the buyer lifts the hood of the business, and really gets to understand how organised the business is.

Generally a buyer will need to already know a lot about the business to make an offer. But after general commercial terms have been agreed, they will then start this process of deeply digging into the business. On a timing note, in many instances the sale contract negotiations do not commence until after due diligence is completed.

However, we also have seen many instances of the sale contract being in negotiation at the same time as due diligence is being undertaken, which is a great approach, particularly if timing in the deal is important. We have even seen some instances of the sale contract being negotiated and signed before proper due diligence starts. However, this is often not the best approach for a seller, given generally the buyer will want a right to pull out of the sale if the due diligence results aren't to their liking – in practice this can essentially mean that the seller is tied to the sale contract without a termination right but the buyer has this inbuilt ability to get out if they don't like the results of the due diligence findings. The timing of the due diligence and the contract negotiations varies from deal to deal depending on elements such as the size of the deal, complexity, and the experience level of the parties involved.

You want to give the buyer confidence that the business is well organised, you're well prepared, and that the buyer should not come across any issues after the acquisition.

Unfortunately we have often seen businesses enter into a sale process without proper preparation. This generally becomes painfully apparent when the buyer starts to identify risks in either the transfer of value or the running of the business. Unexpected issues identified at this point can cause major disruptions to the deal – including affecting the price – or indeed stop the transaction entirely.

In the later chapters on value and risk, we dig into each of the areas you should be working on well in advance. I also recommend reading the due diligence section in chapter 6, to ensure you also understand the buyer's perspective.

But as a general overview, getting ready for due diligence requires that you consider how your business would fare if it was on the market today, and what changes might need to be implemented now to improve that position. It's about understanding what you can do now to set yourself up so when you come to the point of exit, getting ready for due diligence is an easy rather than a hard process.

It's also about putting systems in place to ensure you're able to access documents and contracts and financials easily.

Proper preparation for legal due diligence involves putting in place systems to ensure:

- the business is legally compliant
- value has been captured, and can transfer
- risk has been minimised
- documents can be found easily
- critical contracts are properly signed, current (not expired) and complete
- the business looks well run and 'clean'.

Early preparation in each of these areas will help you maximise your pool of potential buyers and the potential sale price, reduce the issues that are likely to arise in the sale process, and ultimately speed up the transaction.

As we saw in the example of Ted's consulting business sale, due diligence was the turning point in this deal where the smooth initial progress gave way to a litany of issues that were identified by the prospective buyer, and a chain of events was set in place that meant the whole deal was at risk. While Ted had ensured the financials and operational elements of the business were squeaky clean, the strengthening of the legal foundations of the business prior to sale had been missed. This meant holes were found by the buyer that put the deal in jeopardy. Most of the problems raised by the buyers in the due diligence phase could have been avoided if Ted had conducted a legal review of the business in advance of the sale and these gaps were identified in time for them to be fixed.[32]

---

32   We have a free scorecard for you to undertake your own review of your exit readiness at our resources hub at www.buygrowexit.com.au or we also provide a professional service in providing a legal review of businesses in advance of a sale, which you can find out about at our resources hub, or through www.aspectlegal.com.au.

BUILDING YOUR DEAL TEAM EARLY

As the experience of Rod and Jane, and Ted, has shown, an important piece of the preparation puzzle is getting in place the right deal team early in your preparation, built from advisers who have done this many times before. You need to surround yourself with the right advisers – a good tax accountant, a good lawyer with solid experience with dealing with businesses at exit, and a good corporate adviser or business broker. The quality and specialist expertise of your deal team will be one of the most critical factors in ensuring that you understand and properly execute your preparations for exit, and that you choose the right path once you get there.

It is important to understand advising in business exits is not part of the day-to-day work for most commercial lawyers or accountants. General commercial advisers spend their days dealing with the regular issues that come up for businesses, while an exit is something that occurs only once in the entire business lifecycle for most businesses. So it can be a massive mistake for a business owner to assume that the advisers they use for their day-to-day legal and accounting needs are also the same advisers who will have the specialist knowledge they need to exit well, and to build the right preparation for exit.

Some common mistakes we see in our dealings with the deal teams of our clients and of the lawyers and accountants on the other side of our transactions are that advisers with a lack of experience and process can slow down deals, and are often less commercial in their approach, because they don't understand what is an acceptable level of risk from a commercial perspective.

When you are knee deep in these types of transactions day after day, you get a feel for what contains real risk and what are the things you really need to be aware of, and you learn how to not cloud the issue with a non-pragmatic attitude to areas where the risk in reality is extraordinarily minimal and highly unlikely to occur.

I've heard some horror stories (and indeed been called in to save deals almost entirely killed) where owners have appointed lawyers that they have worked with in other capacities, and where those lawyers (who ultimately had little to no experience in working with businesses at exit) tore the deal to shreds by taking overly conservative and uncommercial approaches. Or where lawyers most used to litigation came in with an adversarial approach, which left the deal in tatters and the buyer and seller at war with each other.

The story of Rod and Jane is a classic example. While Rod and Jane had been so sensible in understanding the need for early legal intervention in preparation for sale, the lawyer they involved didn't have sufficient knowledge of how to deal with businesses at exit, and therefore set them on the wrong path.[33]

It's also important that you build this advisory deal team early, because each of the professionals you will need for proper preparation will have different insights and different reach into the marketplace, so you want them all on board from day one. And finally, you will also want to ensure that you have a team that can work together, rather than in silos – so you have a united force in your deal team all pulling in the same direction at the same time, towards this common goal of helping you to achieve the best exit possible.

HAVING A POST-EXIT PLAN

This might seem like a strange preparation point to include, however I have put it here because the emotion of owners at sale can be pivotal in ensuring the success of an exit.

The process of a sale can trigger a lot of emotion that is often unexpected. In many instances the business has been created over many years. A business becomes such a large part of the lives of the owners as they build it. And quite often, a business also forms part of the owners' identity. So it makes sense that at the point of exit, there might suddenly appear one day a counter force. A reservation. A concern about the buyer or the process that sits well below

---

33   Get access to the lawyer buying guide and Rapid Contracting Process™ here: www.buygrowexit.com.au.

It's important that you build this advisory deal team early, because EACH OF THE PROFESSIONALS you will need for proper preparation will have DIFFERENT INSIGHTS and DIFFERENT REACH into the marketplace, so you want them all on board from day one.

the surface. Which is ultimately just an expression of the emotion that an exit brings.

If you are not clear on why you are exiting and what you want to do next, it can really create a problem in getting to that outcome and can be a major catalyst in a lack of satisfaction when the deal is done.

We have had many sellers get cold feet towards the end of a sale process and decide to hang on to the business. Who suddenly decide maybe they could hold on longer for a better price or better deal (partly because they simply can't see themselves in a life outside of the business). Or they go through with the sale only to suffer from vendor's remorse and kick around for months after, not knowing what to do with themselves.

Get clear on why you are exiting. And what you will do post-exit. Start to visualise that life.

RUNNING YOUR BUSINESS IN A SALE-READY STATE

While much of the focus in this chapter has been on the importance of preparation for sale, it is important to reflect on the reality that having a business that is properly groomed for sale is not just about having a mind towards exit. Because, ironically, having a business in a sale-ready state is ultimately the best way to run the business even if you never intend to exit. The goal of all business owners should be to run their business perpetually in a sale-ready state.

All of the areas of preparation we have discussed to this point – including locking in the elements of value in your business, minimising the risk, being aware of what creates value in the mind of a buyer – are fundamental drivers for running a good business. The bonus also happens to be that if there becomes a need or a desire to exit the business quickly, or to get finance or bring partners on board, the business is primed for that to happen. And the side effect of this planning is that in the meantime you will have a business that is ultimately smoother and more enjoyable to run, and most likely more profitable.

So I have put this as the last part of preparation, but it could very easily have gone in as the first. Because preparing a business for sale is not something to be done five minutes before exit. The best time for preparing a business for exit is on the very first day you own it. But if you missed that point, then as the saying goes, the second-best time is today!

Chapter 18

DEAL STRUCTURE: THE FOUNDATION OF A SUCCESSFUL SALE

When putting a deal together, one of the first key considerations once a buyer has been found is how the deal will be structured. This can be broken down into three main areas:

- Will the deal be a share sale, a business sale, or an asset sale?
- Will the purchase price be paid fully at completion, or will there be a component that is deferred (paid later)?
- If there is a deferred component, will this be contingent (based on the achievement of certain metrics) or guaranteed (paid irrespective of business performance)?

In this chapter we will also briefly look at two other areas:
* staged sales and partial sales
* sales that include a 'share swap' as part (or all) of the sale price.

SHARE SALE VERSUS BUSINESS SALE

The issue of share sale versus business sale is fundamental, but regularly misunderstood. Even many sophisticated buyers I deal with, and many advisers (even accountants who deal with structures regularly) sometimes don't have a clear understanding of the fundamental differences, and the different ways that each need to be approached. I touched on this in our chapters on acquisition, but have left the most detailed analysis here in the chapters on exit because it is at exit that the main differences can often be felt.

The discussion of share sale versus business (or asset) sale relates only to those businesses that are run through a corporate entity (or in some cases where the business is run out of a unit trust – in which case there might be a sale of the units, which is similar to a share sale). Where the selling business is run through a trust, partnership or even perhaps by a sole trader (which is unlikely, but still happens from time to time) rather than a company, there is likely to be no distinction between share sale and asset sale. The sale will usually simply be a business (asset) sale – so all the comments below in relation to how that happens will apply, but there will be no ability to choose any other path.

Also, if the sale is a staged sale or partial sale, it will generally be a share (or unit) sale. And so the discussion in the next few paragraphs is less relevant! (However, warranties and indemnities are likely to still apply, at least to some extent.)

WHAT THE HELL ARE THE DIFFERENCES BETWEEN A SHARE AND BUSINESS SALE?

As the following diagram illustrates, where a sale relates to a business run by a company:
* in a share sale, the shares are the assets that are being transferred
* in a business or asset sale, it is instead the individual assets that are transferred.

SHARE SALE

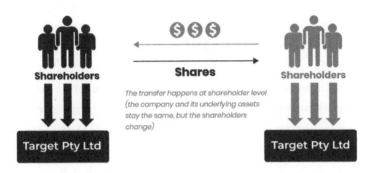

Shares

The transfer happens at shareholder level (the company and its underlying assets stay the same, but the shareholders change)

BUSINESS OR ASSET SALE

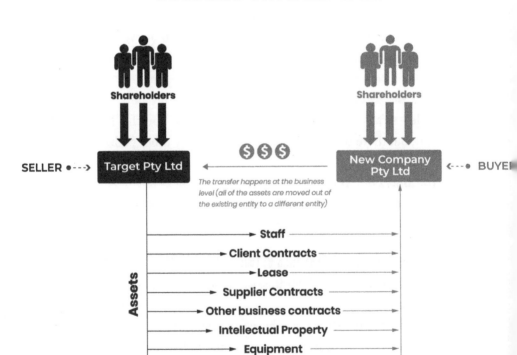

The transfer happens at the business level (all of the assets are moved out of the existing entity to a different entity)

Sounds simple, right? What many people fail to realise is that there are large differences between these approaches in:

- the tax treatment
- the level of work required in transferring ownership
- the level of potential leakage of value
- the risk level for the buyer and the seller post-completion.

THE TAX TREATMENT

Often one of the primary sell-side benefits of a share sale versus a business sale for businesses that qualify for the small business capital gains tax concessions (and even in larger deals where the small business concessions aren't relevant) is tax outcomes. Quite often a seller in a company structure environment will prefer to sell the shares rather than to sell the business or the assets because there can be far more favourable tax outcomes.

We touched on this when we discussed tax earlier in this chapter, and while I am certainly not an accountant or tax specialist and do not advise on this, I have seen so many transactions where this has become a major revelation for a seller, so I always focus on this as being the first area for review. I want to ensure that the seller has had proper, detailed advice on their tax outcomes, and on understanding which way of approaching the sale of their business will achieve the best tax outcome for them (and what the actual difference will be in their pocket at the end of the day in considering one approach versus the other). I want to be clear that the outcome is not always that share sale is the best. I have certainly seen situations in which business sales have delivered better tax outcomes. But the important thing is that you understand the difference, and that you have taken proper advice.

I've seen some sad examples of sellers who have gotten a great deal in a sale but ended up giving away a large amount of that in tax, because they had been incorrectly structured leading up to sale or because they then hadn't been able to negotiate the right type of

Often one of the primary sell-side benefits of a

SHARE SALE

versus a

BUSINESS SALE

is tax outcomes.

sale structure. This generally occurs where sellers have not properly worked through the cashflow prior to coming up with commercial terms with the buyer, before they had sought out specialist legal and tax advice. Often in these cases, where the deal is locked in before we have the opportunity to assist our sellers to understand some of the issues involved, sellers end up with an outcome they didn't expect and that could have been avoided if they had taken early advice.

However just because you decide that a share sale is better for you, doesn't necessarily mean that this is the way that a buyer will want to transact. But the first step is to understand what the differences will be for you, and then the next step is to bring the buyer along with you if possible.

THE WORK REQUIRED IN TRANSFERRING OWNERSHIP

There are other elements to consider in terms of the benefits of a share sale over and above simply taxation, and these can be fundamental in your discussions with a buyer to get them on the same page (if that indeed is needed – we act for many differing types of buyers and the most sophisticated are generally not concerned at all by a share sale, and often indeed prefer it – if, and this is a *big* if, they have confidence during their due diligence investigations in the way you have run the business, and that they aren't on notice of possible skeletons hiding in the company closet).

So let's examine in more detail some of the other benefits of a share sale.

In a share sale you are in the position where the business itself is essentially not touched. The ownership structure is where the change occurs, whereas the company and business itself continues. This is therefore a lot easier to transact in practice, as there can be more effort, cost and risk involved in transferring each of the contracts out of one entity and into another as part of a business or asset sale.

In a share sale, client agreements don't need to be re-executed, unless there are specific clauses within the client contracts requiring that the clients authorise in advance any change in ownership. These clauses are often referred to as 'change of control' clauses, and are not likely to be in your standard customer contracts, but may perhaps appear in large customer contracts that are driven by the customers (for example, if you transact with large corporations). Where you are transferring a business, all client contracts will need to be re-signed or assigned (or 'novated') in another way, and in addition, your clients will need to change the bank details they are using for payment. In many instances going through the process of getting clients to re-sign, and to change their payment practices, can disturb the client base as well as create a mass of work for both the seller and the buyer. And where the seller is required as part of completion to transfer all these contracts, or where payment is partly based on the full transition of all these clients, it can be a risk to the seller (as well as obviously to the buyer) in the potential leakage of client value if clients take the opportunity of all this change to reconsider their own supply arrangements.

In a share sale there can also be less time and effort involved in transferring suppliers because the supplier relationship with the organisation continues exactly as it was before – without the need for new agreements, new credit terms to be set up and so on (except of course for any contracts that have 'change of control' clauses, where the consent of the supplier may be needed before completing the sale if it is a key contract that the buyer has required consent for before completion can occur).

And of course employee contracts and other contracts are all the same, for all the same reasons. In a business sale each employee will need to be signed on to a new contract. Whereas in a share sale, the employees continue as they were, generally with nothing in their contractual arrangement disturbed.

Another relevant consideration is dealing with assets of the company, such as intellectual property assets. For trademark registrations, for example, the government bodies in each country in which each registration is held will need to be notified of a transfer of ownership in a business or asset sale environment, but not in a share sale environment.

THE LEVEL OF POTENTIAL LEAKAGE OF VALUE

It's important to bear in mind that because a business sale often involves the novation or assignment of individual contracts, often requiring the third-party suppliers and clients take some action (for example, in signing onto new contracts with the new buyer, or signing a contract that transfers the existing contracts), there is a risk of leakage of value in the transition. A buyer will sometimes try to protect against the like-lihood of losing some of the value during the transition process by requiring that some of the purchase price is contingent on this value properly transferring. We dig into deferred payments and earnouts later in this chapter. But for now, it is sufficient to bear in mind that where there is risk in the transfer of the value in the business, a buyer will sometimes want you to share in that risk.

THE RISK LEVEL FOR THE BUYER AND THE SELLER POST DEAL COMPLETION

The final difference between a share and business (or asset) sale that you must be acutely aware of is the risk level for the buyer (and therefore also for you as the seller) post-completion. There is gener-ally inherently less risk to a buyer in an asset sale or business sale environment post-completion. (We covered this in detail in part I, and that is important for you to read so you understand the perspec-tive that a buyer might be coming from.)

With a share sale, the buyer is purchasing the company as a whole with all of its trading history, and that also means any historical liability attached to the company – all the 'skeletons in the closet'. For example, this can include the risk of an action by a customer for services or goods supplied before the buyer takes ownership, or a tax audit that determines there has been incorrect treatment or payment of taxes in the period while the business was in the ownership and control of the seller.

To protect against these risks in a share sale, a buyer will want to use the sale contract to pass on liability to the seller for historical issues that may come up. They do this through:

- warranties in the contract (adding promises by the seller that there are no historical issues in the company that would cause the buyer any loss in the future)
- indemnities (where the seller agrees to pay if any issues come up that cause the buyer loss due to these 'promises' being incorrect).

It's important to realise that while on the one hand a share sale may seem like the best approach from a tax and practical transition perspective, you need to fully understand the risks that you will continue to run under the warranties and indemnities in the contract, and you will need to ensure that the sale contract properly manages those risks.

Ways to manage this include:

- minimising the timeframe that a buyer will have to take action for breach of warranty
- reducing the scope of what you agree to protect against
- negotiating the total value at risk under these clauses (which often is done through adding a maximum cap on your exposure)
- disclosing to the buyer any issues or liabilities in the business and reducing your exposure for these items you have disclosed.
- using appropriate insurance.

The purchase price, the risk involved in the business, the clauses relating to the warranties (protection to the buyer), and the clauses acting to control the risks to the seller and the way in which they work can take up a major proportion of the contract (and the negotiation time). But these are incredibly important issues, and deserve this level of time and attention.

The last element to bear in mind is that often a buyer will want to have some ongoing security to enforce the warranties and indemnities (alternatively they may take out insurance for this).

We cover this all in a lot more detail in chapter 20 on protection, but the relevance at this point is to understand that the consideration in share versus business sale should also include an understanding that the warranties and indemnities for you as the seller will almost certainly be different between the two approaches.

DEFERRED PAYMENTS, EARNOUTS AND RETENTIONS

There are three common alternatives to full payment of the purchase price at deal completion:

- An agreed amount to be paid at an agreed date or multiple dates after completion.
- An agreed amount to be paid upon hitting a milestone or target (or set of milestones) after completion.
- A future payment based on the performance of the business after completion (commonly called an 'earnout').

Let's consider each of these.

AN AGREED AMOUNT TO BE PAID AT AN AGREED DATE AFTER COMPLETION

This is also sometimes referred to as 'vendor finance', and is usually in place as a financing arrangement for the buyer. For example, the agreed purchase price for the shares or business is $3,000,000 and you have agreed that $2,500,000 will be paid at completion, and the remaining $500,000 will be paid 12 months after completion, or perhaps in equal instalments over the next 12 months.

I have found that this approach has become more common over the last few years, particularly for smaller businesses.

The most obvious risk for the seller with this approach is simply in securing the future payment.

More on that later.

AN AGREED AMOUNT TO BE PAID UPON HITTING A MILESTONE OR TARGET (OR SET OF MILESTONES) AFTER COMPLETION

This structure may be put in place so that the buyer and seller share the risk of the value in the business being fully transferred to the buyer.

We often use this approach where certain assets or contracts may not pass over fully at completion. For example, where part of the business assets includes large or lucrative government contracts, often these contracts will take months to get proper authorisation (for example to novate the contract in a business sale, or to get formal approval for change of control of the company in a share sale). So if we are looking to do a quick deal, we might complete the deal but hold back a component of the purchase price until the contracts in question have all transferred.

This is also the approach in some industries to ensure the full transfer of the client base. For example, in accounting practice sales it is common for 20% of the purchase price to be held back for one or two years with the milestone for payment being the maintenance of the client base. In this industry they call this a 'retention' or 'clawback', which I discuss later.

In addition to the risk for the seller in ensuring the buyer has funds to pay and does pay, there is the additional risk of ensuring that the target is met to trigger the payment. So in this instance the seller will need to think not just about security that they need to hold for payment, but also the mechanics of the clauses, which can sometimes be complicated.

A FUTURE PAYMENT CALCULATED BASED ON THE PERFORMANCE OF THE BUSINESS AFTER COMPLETION (COMMONLY CALLED AN 'EARNOUT')

This third alternative provides a mechanism for a buyer to ensure that the value in the business fully transfers, and is also often used where a seller has priced the business based on the performance potential. So this can be both a risk-sharing mechanism for the buyer, and also potentially a way for the seller to access a higher sale price if they are prepared to accept some risk. It's often also a way for a buyer to tie in the seller for a set period (which can sometimes be long, in some cases up to even five years) to continue to run or work for the business, or to provide a long period for appropriate transfer of their knowledge of the business.

Earnouts are a highly common approach, but are a serious source of concern for sellers based on the risk that they may not actually see any future payments once the business has changed hands, so let's dig into this in more detail.

RISKS RELATING TO EARNOUT ARRANGEMENTS

Earnout arrangements can be an opportunity for a seller to potentially achieve a higher value for the business at exit, and often also to increase the range of potential buyers. Many sophisticated buyers routinely use earnouts in their deals, so it can be very limiting for a seller to have too strong an aversion to at least considering an earnout arrangement.

But while there are certainly positives, there are also potential risks. Many potential risks, in fact.

I recall a discussion once with a guest on my podcast *The Deal Room* who had come onto the show to discuss her sale. When we were 'off air' we got into a discussion about her perspective on earnouts. She said that she and her mates who had sold their businesses had formed what they called the 'earnout survivors club', where they joined together once a month to share war stories about the progress of their own earnout periods and the pain they were enduring. She ended up walking out of the business before her own earnout period had ended, turning her back on hundreds of thousands of dollars because she simply couldn't bear walking to the buyer's tune anymore.

And therein can lie the difficulty of earnout arrangements – they are a mechanism of payment that kicks in once the business has changed hands. The control is now generally in the hands of the buyer, subject only to the protections set up in the sale contract for the sellers, and often they are contingent on the founders staying on board with the business to lead it and transition it for a substantial period of time. This can often see founders butting heads with the new owners on how best to run the business, and generally having a hard time adjusting to the new world order in which they have moved from being the one calling the shots to now being essentially an employee.

However, ultimately issues that many people have had aren't so much about the concept itself but in the way that the deal was structured, and sometimes also the personalities involved – bearing in mind that once you have run your own business for many years, it can be very difficult to effectively become an employee. But earnouts don't have to be structured in that way, so let's consider the many choices involved in structuring earnouts.

CONSIDERATIONS IN STRUCTURING EARNOUTS

PROPORTION OF PURCHASE PRICE

The first consideration is, what proportion of the purchase price will be paid upfront at deal completion versus the amount calculated based on the earnout. Often this will come down to the way in which the business is valued. If a business is valued to a large extent based on future potential, or there are risks in the buyer being able to fully transfer or sustain the value of the business, earnouts will usually form a larger proportion of the sale price than deals where the value is clearly related to recent sustained performance of the business where that performance is likely to continue.

As a rough guide, we have a lot of deals that have earnouts that comprise 10% to 20% of the purchase price (however we also have a lot of deals where the earnout component is a lot more). The calculation of this proportion will depend in a large part on the negotiation of the deal, the risks that are identified in the buyer getting the full value that they expect out of the acquisition, and the approach of the parties in how to appropriately share that risk.

CALCULATION

Earnouts are generally based on the performance of the business post-completion, but this performance can be defined in different ways. Some earnouts are based on top-line revenue over a period of time, others are based on gross profit, and others still are based on EBITDA.[34]

The other two key considerations in calculation of the earnout is whether it is a set figure or based on a sliding scale, and whether the seller will participate in a potential upside as well as downside.

For example, where there is:

- an earnout target as a set figure (for example, that the business achieves $10m in revenue in the year after the sale); and
- the earnout payment is a set sum (for example, $200,000 to be paid if the business achieves this revenue target)

the earnout will either trigger and pay the full sum, or not trigger and no sum at all is paid. In this way the seller is sharing in the risk of the buyer not achieving that revenue or profit figure post-completion. But there is no upside for the seller if the business outperforms. It is simply payment, or not, of the set earnout figure.

An alternative way of setting up the earnout is for the seller payment to be calculated as a percentage of the revenue or profit for set periods (and sometimes this will only trigger once revenue or profit hits a set level). In this way, once the minimum target is hit, the earnout is calculated based on the performance. In this way, the earnout can sometimes provide the seller the opportunity to get a higher earnout if the business after completion outperforms the financial targets upon which the initial sale price had been based (as well as of course risking loss of part of the sale price if the business doesn't hit the financial targets). This sliding scale approach is a way around the 'all or nothing' approach in my first example.

---

34   See the jargon buster chapter – in simple terms EBITDA is profit before interest, tax and depreciation.

TIMING

The first component of the consideration of timing is simply how long the earnout should last for, and the regularity of payments. Some earnouts will be short – for example one year. Some earnouts will go on for five years. As a seller, your decision as to what earnout timing you are prepared to accept will depend on the financial benefits being offered, the amount of control you have (or need) and the amount of participation required from you.

In some instances, earnouts are structured to ensure the sellers stay on in the business, fully involved, for a long period of time. This is the intention of them, and can be financially beneficial to the sellers but personally constraining – particularly if post-completion the reality of working for someone else turns out to be far different from what was imagined. This is the classic complaint that often comes from sellers in this type of earnout – that they ultimately just want to be free of the business, or they clash with the new owners, but they feel caught by the golden handcuffs that is their earnout.

In other instances, however, earnouts are not at all dependent on the continued involvement of the sellers.

One other consideration for timing of the earnout payments is whether there might be circumstances where the earnout payment should perhaps be triggered early. We often refer to this as an 'accelerated payment'. For example:

- the buyer is in breach of some of the agreed controls in the business (set out in the sale contract to protect the seller's achievement of the earnout)
- the ongoing involvement in the business and in decision making by the sellers is in the view of the seller an important protection for them and the employment of the sellers is terminated
- the sellers suffer a health event that means they cannot continue to work in the business.

These are all examples of circumstances in which it might be relevant to have an accelerated early payment clause that deals with the calculation and payment of the earnout in a different way. For example, the parties might agree that in these circumstances the full earnout amount that was on offer should be triggered early (irrespective of whether the earnout targets were met).

EARNOUT CONTROLS

In structuring an earnout, there is a fine balance between protecting you as the seller, and in impacting the buyer's ability to operate the business in the way they want.

As discussed above, earnouts can be based on top-line revenue over a period, gross profit, operating profit (EBITDA). As a seller, you need to carefully consider the level of control you will have over the business meeting these targets, and the level of control required will differ depending on what the earnout is calculated on.

For example, if the earnout is based on profit in the business (EBITDA) then you will need to have a way to control the actual costs, or the way the costs are calculated (what costs are taken into consideration in preparing the 'earnout accounts' – which are the accounts that are created to measure whether the earnout target has been met). But control of costs is not as relevant if you are measured only on revenue.

Let's look at some other areas of control that will be relevant for you to consider in working out the level of control you want imposed during the earnout period, to protect the likelihood of you achieving your full earnout potential:

- **Operational controls:** You will need to consider what type of operational controls will be relevant for you – this could include:
  - Who is going to be running the business? (Do you want to be around to run the business, or participate in management? If so – how much control do you want? And what if you

don't get that control because, for example, there is a parting of ways before the end of the earnout period?)
- What parameters are there going to be in running the business?
- Is there a business plan that will be followed?
- Will you want to limit the ability of the buyer to radically change the strategy of the existing business?

- **Financial contributions:**
  - What (if any) controls are needed to ensure that there will be sufficient resources and working capital provided by the buyer for the business to realise its potential?
  - If the earnout is connected to a revenue target, should the company commit to expenditure on costs (such as advertising and marketing) at least equivalent to a pre-completion period?
  - If the earnout is connected to a profit (EBITDA) target, should there be caps or other controls on expenditure? And particularly controls on buyer-imposed costs?

- **Staff controls:** Do you need certainty about the buyer retaining key staff in the business, or providing (or continuing to provide) certain financial incentives to those key staff? For example, in one of our deals, the seller felt it was important to incentivise the staff through bonuses to help achieve the revenue figures required to hit the earnout target. Consequently the buyer committed to providing an agreed bonus pool as part of the deal.

- **Retention of value in the business:** One last example of a control you may want to implement is a control against the buyer stripping value out of the business until after the earnout period. This might, for example, require controls against the buyer taking out any assets of the business, or trading with the clients of the business outside of the business, during this period.

FINAL TIPS ON EARNOUTS

Some final tips in relation to earnouts:

- Earnouts are particularly common where the valuation that has been used to arrive at the purchase price relates to future performance, or where there is some risk in the buyer being able to realise the full value of the business.
- It is often said that earnouts work best for sellers where the initial payment is something you would be prepared to accept as full payment (so the earnout is more of a bonus if it triggers). There are many instances where earnouts are however more substantial, and in those cases the contract must be extremely robust to properly protect those future payment rights.
- Ideally as a seller, if there is an earnout, it is often easier to control if the targets are based on revenue rather than profit (as it can be harder to control the costs that are used to establish a profit figure). However, earnouts in larger deals are regularly based on profit. So don't go into a negotiation with unreasonable expectations of this.
- Ideally try to share in the upside as well as downside risk.
- Consider including accelerated payment clauses.
- Ensure that you are working with a legal team experienced in earnouts so that your contracts are robust enough to protect these future payments.
- Ensure you have appropriate security over the business and/or the buyer to protect those future payments – which we discuss below.

CREDIT RISK FOR DEFERRED PAYMENTS – WHAT SECURITY SHOULD YOU TAKE?

The final important consideration for any payment to be made at some point after completion is how you will protect against the credit risk you have with the buyer: the risk that the buyer will not have the funds to pay, and indeed the ease with which you can force that payment. So a discussion about deferred payments should never be had without also having a discussion about the security that the sellers will hold for those payments.

There are myriad types of security available, however it's important to bear in mind that there can be a fine balance between protecting the seller and compromising or otherwise limiting the buyer's ability to operate the business in a way to maximise its value.

I have over the years seen many creative ways of achieving security, but here are the most common:

- A general security agreement or other secured interest, registered on the Personal Property Securities Register (PPSR) which is a public register. Depending on the type of security interest that is provided by the buyer, this may be used to restrict the ability of the new owners to sell or transfer out assets of the business. One potential issue that may sometimes cause reluctance of the buyer to provide this type of security interest is that it can restrict their ability to get other finance, so sometimes this may not be appropriate.
- A parent company guarantee from the buyer's head company.
- Personal guarantees from the directors of the buying entity.
- Money held in a trust account (for example, in the trust account of the solicitor of the seller) or in 'escrow' in a third-party account.[35] This can be a good option where there is a short timeframe for the deferred payment, but is generally less useful for longer-term payment arrangements or where the payment sum is uncertain. And of course, it requires that the buyer has the funds at completion.
- Bank guarantees. This is far less often used than any of the other options above, but is still a consideration for some deals.

---

35   An escrow is the use of a third party to hold assets on behalf of parties who are in the process of completing a transaction. It is essentially a contractual arrangement where the third party agrees to receive and disburse money on conditions agreed to by the transacting parties.

RETENTIONS

There is one other type of deferred payment to discuss – retention sums (often referred to as 'hold backs'). Retention sums are in practice generally just one of the above three options, depending on how the retention is set up – so it is essentially just a linguistic difference that occurs in certain industries.

For example, business sales in the accounting industry will almost always have a 'retention' component that is discussed as part of the structure of the purchase price. In this instance, it generally means an amount held back from the purchase price that will be paid out if the revenue of the business hits certain targets in a certain timeframe. By way of illustration, it is quite usual to see in these deals a retention of 20% of the purchase price, with half of the retention price paid at the end of the first year after completion, if the revenue of the business is at least the same as that prior to completion. And the final half of the retention paid at the end of the second year after completion, on the same basis.

This common retention arrangement is based on the reality that smaller accounting practices often have client bases that have a personal connection to the owners, so a retention is put in place to ensure that the seller does everything in its power to help the clients successfully transition and continue to work with the business post-completion, rather than taking the opportunity of change to move to a new accountant.

There is a similar approach in many other industries where there is a predominance of small businesses with close connections between the owners and the client bases.

Another example of when the term 'retention' may be used for deferred payments is if funds are withheld to enable post-completion calculations where adjustments are not able to be made at the time of completion. In this instance the purchase price is clear, but payments to staff, suppliers and others do not fit neatly into the completion date, therefore requiring adjustments to be made by the parties. In many instances those calculations can be made in advance and factored into the actual payment on the completion date. But in some instances the calculations will be too complex (and uncertain) to enable this to be done at the completion date, in which case a retention sum may be held back by the buyer (or held in trust or escrow) subject to these adjustments being finalised post-completion.

A final approach to retention is where this is operating as a sum withheld to protect against loss in the business in a defined period post-completion, as collateral for the buyer's possible warranty and indemnification claims against the seller.

SALES IN STAGES AND PARTIAL SALES

An alternative to a full sale is a partial sale or a sale in stages (sometimes referred to as tranches), to either existing staff or to third parties.

There is lots of jargon around sales in stages – check out the jargon buster chapter for what it all means. In this chapter we are going to stick with the basic concepts rather than jargon.

Partial sales and sales in stages will generally be in the form of a share sale (or unit sale) – or in some instances may require a restructure of the business out into a separate company, and a share sale out of the new company. There are other options available for the sale, however a share sale is the most common.

SALE OF SHARES TO EMPLOYEES

The sale of shares to management or key staff (sometimes referred to as an MBO – 'management buyout') can be a great way to move towards a full exit – either immediately, or over time. In some instances I have also seen it used very successfully as a way to move from being an involved owner of a business to being purely an investor in the business – as the management and running of the business is slowly taken over entirely by the staff who buy in. It can also be a powerful retention strategy for great staff.

The sale of shares to employees can be a

GREAT WAY

to move towards a full exit – either immediately, or over time.

There are numerous decisions and issues to consider if you are looking to bring employees on board in an ownership capacity. Let's examine the most important ones.

THE PRICE FOR THE SHARES

In some instances, owners will consider 'gifting' the equity in the business. Generally this approach is only adopted when equity is being used as a retention strategy – the idea being that once an employee has ownership they will have 'skin in the game' and be invested in the business, less likely to leave, and more incentivised to grow the business. The idea is often that having a cost attributed to the shares might act as a disincentive for the employee (who may not want to pay for the privilege). Equity is also sometimes given to 'reward' performance.

The problem with giving away equity is that it can often then be valued less by an employee than if they had purchased it. Or on the flipside, it can also create massive issues between the founder and the new employee shareholders down the track. I have seen many huge disputes caused by this approach.

I'll give you a snapshot of one example which is a classic case of how this can go wrong. I was acting for an advertising company. The founder had at some point many years earlier decided to gift 50% of the shares in the company to an employee to keep him on, to recognise his success, and to give him 'skin in the game' to incentivise him to grow the business with the same passion as the founder. For a few years things had gone well, but huge rifts began to appear, with the founder feeling like the contributions to the business were massively different and that the employee shareholder just didn't have the same dedication to the business and so therefore should not have the same right to profits of the business.

The problem was that when he gifted the shares, he didn't put in place any protections for himself, or to govern how decision making, exit and disputes would be handled. Ultimately he had completely hamstrung himself, and he was now in the position where he couldn't make any decision in the business unless the other shareholder agreed, and he was tied to an equal share of profits notwithstanding what was (in his mind) an unequal share of effort and contribution.

We tried to negotiate a resolution, but the relationship had soured to such a great extent that the only option that was palatable to either of them was to break the business apart, freeing them to go their separate ways, each taking half of the business.

The founder was beside himself because he felt like he had just lost half his business and received no payment for it whatsoever. The employee shareholder on the other hand felt terribly aggrieved by the founder's fury – he felt he had earned the shares with his loyalty to the business and his performance over the years in growing the business, and that his right to take half the business was justified.

Who was right?

Who knows … each had their own viewpoints that had never been discussed, much less documented. And neither of them was a winner out of the void that was created by the lack of formality and documentation in how the initial transfer of ownership equity was handled, because the dispute they ended up in had been bubbling away for years, damaging the business terribly. And when it became a full-blown argument, it then engulfed both of them as they both felt terribly aggrieved and battled out their own view of the 'principal' of the matter. They took their eye off running the business, and it then suffered terribly.

Ultimately the cause was a lack of structure and proper documentation at the point of the shares being transferred.

Often in the heat of the moment, when the plans of employees holding shares are hatched, the parties are in the full swing of a business romance. But of course as we all know, romance can fade! And in business partnerships it often does. When the fade starts, it's critical that the path is defined. This is why documentation in the form of a proper shareholders' agreement is so critical.

This example also demonstrates the very common issue that can be caused by gifting shares: the founder can often feel very aggrieved if they later find out that the rights they have given away contain far more value and loss of control than they initially realised.

The alternative to gifting shares is of course putting a price on them. And you will have to decide whether that price is the full value or a discounted value. (And you and the employee will need to also consider any tax implications of the price or of any discounts – more on that later.)

WHEN THE PRICE IS PAID

Where there is a price paid for the shares, the next consideration (aside from of course what the price will be) is when the price will be paid. Of course one option is to have the full purchase price paid as the employee takes the shares, but it is also common in this type of situation to have the purchase price paid over time, as a type of vendor finance, often 'paid' over time by the founder keeping the employee shareholder's component of the dividends to pay down the shares.

It is often forgotten that tax must be paid on dividends, even if the employee shareholder isn't receiving the cash in their pocket (because it is going directly to the founder to pay down the finance on the shares). It may seem obvious but sometimes it is a surprise for employees that they will pay tax even if they aren't receiving the cash in their pocket.

WHO THE SALE WILL APPLY TO

Will this be a plan that you share across multiple staff, or even the entire staff pool, or will it be for only one or two key staff?

THE STRUCTURE OF THE SALE

Will this be a share sale (either now, or at some set point in the future upon the achievement of milestones)?

Or will this be a sale in stages, with multiple transfers expected over time in order to fully sell out to the employee/s?

Or will this be by way of options? (Options are explained in chapter 8.)

If there are plans to fully sell down the business slowly over time, there are important decisions to consider in relation to the timing of those further sales, the value for those future sales, and who has the right to trigger the sale. This is so important because you do not want to be left in a long-term partnership that you feel you can't escape from if your intention had been to fully sell down over a set period.

THE TERMS GOVERNING THEIR LONG-TERM HOLDING

It is critical to have in place a shareholders' agreement that provides clarity on:

- what participation the employee shareholder has in decision making
- what obligations the employee shareholder has to ongoing participation in the business
- how the parties deal with disputes
- whether the founder has the right to buy back the shares if the employee shareholder leaves in set circumstances, and how the shares would be valued in that instance
- whether the founder has the right to force the employee shareholder to sell if they are looking to exit the business (bearing in mind it can often be very restrictive if you are only able to sell part of the shares in the business, rather than offer up the whole entity for sale – the pool of buyers willing to buy in with others they don't know is much smaller than the pool of buyers looking to buy a whole business).

This must be set up and agreed before you bring the employee/s on as shareholders, because once they are in it may be too late to achieve what you as the seller really want.

A SHAREHOLDERS' AGREEMENT must be set up and agreed before you bring the employee/s on as shareholders, because once they are in it may be too late to achieve what you as the seller really want.

THE BUSINESS STRUCTURE

Is your business structured in the right way to enable employee equity holdings? In many instances a restructure is required in advance to enable this, so this is something to take advice on early.

THE TAX IMPLICATIONS

The way you approach the sale or transfer will have tax implications, and this should be explored and fully understood as one of the first critical parts of the process, because while you might have grand ideas of the best way you feel this should all play out, once you get tax advice you might suddenly have a whole new feeling on the matter. So get this started early (and ideally before you have even raised the concept of ownership with any employees).

THE IMPACT AT EXIT

If you ultimately want to exit the business entirely, you need to ensure that the decisions that you are making in sharing equity with employees does not impact your flexibility to do that. Otherwise you could end up in a situation where you are effectively held hostage by the employee shareholders, even if they hold only a minority stake. We have unfortunately seen many instances of this, and the outcomes can be catastrophic for the business and the owners.

PREPARATION

Everything we covered in chapter 17 on preparation for exit is just as applicable when bringing employees in to hold equity. While your approach may be less rigorous if you are gifting or heavily discounting shares (on the assumption that the incoming employee shareholder will engage in less due diligence than a third-party buyer for full value), if employees start to see holes in the legal infrastructure in the business as they move into holding equity, this can fundamentally damage trust and the relationship.

They may come on board feeling you have a responsibility to have run the business in a clean and protected way. I have seen large disputes occur internally when some of these gaps have appeared over time, so – as you know by now – I strongly urge proper preparation of the business as an important step.

SALES OF SHARES TO THIRD PARTIES

Staged and partial sales are certainly not confined to employee shares. There are many instances in which it makes sense to look at these options with third parties. This might be triggered by a need for capital in the business, a need for fresh enthusiasm and ideas, or a need for a new management approach to deal with the new phase the business is moving into.

As with the above on selling down to employees, the devil is always in the detail. Many of the elements we covered in the sale to employees are also relevant here. You will need to ensure the business structure is appropriate for a partial or staged sale, you will need to have the right tax advice in advance, you will need to prepare the business for sale in the same way that you would prepare it for a 100% sale given your buyer will mostly likely do due diligence to understand the risk in their acquisition.

But the one thing that is of course very different from a 100% sale is that in a partial sale you will be in business with the buyer. So you need to be aware of, and plan for, the potential issues in having new business partners on board. It's critical that you understand the buyer very well. Indeed, you should be doing some of your own due diligence on the buyer (just as they will be doing on your business) to ensure you fully understand who you are getting into bed with.

You will also need to consider what portion of ownership you will sell. If you will end up with a minority interest, it's important to understand the difference in your position of power and control. This can be a huge adjustment for many business owners who are used to running their own ship.

And of course, you need to have a very strong shareholders' agreement that deals clearly with important issues such as decision making, how to exit, valuation on exit, whether any party can force the exit of another party, the obligations and expectations of the parties, and how to deal with disputes.

Often the idea of business partnership with a buyer can seem like a great idea, but if you are not properly prepared it can play out very differently.

But not all partnerships end badly of course.

If you are looking at a sale in stages, there are several additional elements you need to consider.

Is this a fixed sale in stages that is based on timing or milestones, or is it instead an option where there may be the right but not the obligation for the acquisition of future parcels of ownership? (Or on the flipside, the right but not the obligation for you to force the buyer to buy the rest of the shares.)

Is the price set now, or in the future? If in the future, have a valuation formula or approach agreed at the time of the deal to ensure there is clarity.

We covered a lot of the other considerations in chapter 8 where we considered this from the perspective of a buyer, but the one element I will emphasise here is that if the trigger of the sale of the future parcels of shares is not within your control, be aware of the risk of ending up permanently in business with the other party.

TAKING SHARES AS PART OF THE PURCHASE PRICE

The final addition to the discussion of structure of sale is where a seller takes shares in the buying entity as part (or in some cases, all) of the purchase price.

The benefit for the seller is the potential opportunity to share in the future growth of the business of the buyer. The benefit for the buyer is that they get to preserve cash, and they secure the ongoing involvement of the seller.

Often the idea of
BUSINESS PARTNERSHIP
with a buyer can seem
like a great idea,
but if you are not
PROPERLY PREPARED
it can play out very
differently.

This approach however raises several issues to be considered by the seller:

- **The value of the share swap.** If the buying entity is a new clean entity with no assets, liabilities or trading history, the question of value is straightforward. It can also be somewhat straightforward if the buying entity is listed, as the share price is publicly available (however, bear in mind that share prices change daily, so there may need to be consideration given to how to protect the seller if there could be significant variations in the share price between the date of exchange of the sale contract and the completion of the transaction). If, however, the buying entity is an existing privately held entity, the parties will need to agree on how to value the buying entity, which leads to the calculation of the share of the buying entity that will be held by the seller.

- **You are now a buyer.** The second consideration for the seller is all the elements that we have set out in part I – because you, the seller, are also now a buyer. You should be doing due diligence on the buyer, which of course will vary in degree depending on the value of the shares you are taking in proportion to the total purchase price.

- **Loss of control.** It is important that you fully understand the difference in your position of power and control. You as a seller will transition from being a full owner who has full control over your business to becoming a minority owner of the new or combined entity. Decisions affecting the value of the business will now be in the hands of the buyer. So it's important that you have built yourself an exit plan in case this transition in role and control doesn't suit you.

- **Your own exit.** Continuing the theme of the above point, you need a clear exit plan because you may ultimately want to fully exit the business. This may be simple for a listed entity, but for a private entity you will need to consider how you will exit.

It can be very difficult to sell parcels of shares of a privately held business to anyone but the existing shareholders, so if this is important to you, you might need to set up options that enable you to force a sale to those shareholders, or negotiate other mechanisms to enable you to exit. And of course, in this instance there are lots of other considerations to get clear, not the least of which will be valuation at that point.

- **Tax.** The final point is as always probably also a starting point – understand the tax impact.

Chapter 19

TRANSFERRING VALUE: MAXIMISING WHAT BUYERS WANT

One of the most fundamental elements in a sale is the transfer of key value in the business from the sellers to the buyers. As a seller there are three considerations:

- What is the primary value in the business to the buyer?
- How is that value protected?
- Are there any potential impediments to the full value passing over to the buyer as seamlessly as possible?

You need to be looking at this from the perspective of the buyer, as an assessment taken from a market view might be different to your own assessment of the value and the contributors to that value.

A buyer will start to identify these areas as they assess what they feel the value is in the business for them, and as they undertake their due diligence in assessing how that value will transfer. The more risk in the transfer of value that a buyer identifies in evaluating the business, the more likely it will be that the purchase price will be impacted (either in terms of the price offered, or the way that the price may be structured).

In parts I and II we have analysed the main areas of value in a lot of detail, so in this chapter we will simply revisit some of those core areas briefly from the perspective of the seller. But if you haven't done so already, I strongly encourage you to thoroughly read chapters 5 and 11 to get a full picture of both the preparation you should be doing in advance of a sale, and the perspective that a buyer will be bringing when assessing each of these areas.

THE CUSTOMER BASE

The customer base is often the most valuable asset of a business. There are varying approaches to the way in which the customer base is secured, and how much risk there is in the transfer of this to the buyer.

Prior to a sale you should consider how key customer relationships are secured, and the impact of any relevant contracts. You should also consider what steps you will need to take to transfer those relationships effectively to the buyer.

Fixed-term contracts and recurring revenue contracts generally provide the strongest value, but will still need to be effectively transferred if the sale structure is a business (rather than share) sale.

If you are selling the company (selling the shares) rather than the business, generally there won't need to be any changes to the contracts with the customers, unless the contracts contain a 'change of control' clause. Prior to a sale you should review your customer contracts to identify any of these clauses, and ideally in advance of a sale renegotiate the contracts to have these removed. Ideally you should begin this preparation years in advance of an exit so that the contract negotiations happen at an obvious point (such as a renewal date) or otherwise incorporate elements other than just the change of control clause (because if you are seeking only that change on its own and provide no reason, it will become apparent to the client that you are considering a sale – which may or may not be an issue). This is important so that when you come to the point of transition of the business and the due diligence phase you have minimised the risk that each of these clients might terminate when given notice of the change of control, and minimised the effort involved in having to notify each of the relevant contractual counterparties of the change of control wherever those clauses are relevant.

If you are undertaking a business sale rather than a share sale, you will need to assess whether the customer contracts will need to be individually novated (where the customer will need to sign the novation), or whether they can be more simply assigned. At a minimum, the customers will generally need to be advised of a new bank account for payment of invoices, and often there will be an agreed form of communication between the buyer and seller to go out to the customers to inform them of the transition.

There may also be other issues to consider in relation to compliance with legislation, such as the Privacy Act.

You should be aware of the process that will be needed for the transition of clients to ensure you understand any timeframes that may be impacted, the preparations you will need to make, and any possible reactions of clients, particularly if the sale price is structured around this transition.

KEY RELATIONSHIPS WITHIN THE BUSINESS

Where value in the business sits with key arrangements the business has (for example supply, distribution or licensing arrangements), ensure that prior to sale those key arrangements are contractually locked in.

I so often investigate businesses prior to sale (or in undertaking due diligence for a buyer) and find that many of these arrangements have been set up over time in a fairly relaxed manner. Relationships have started slowly and morphed over time into something that underpins the operation of the business, and yet these are so often overlooked in terms of having a contractual backing. While this may not have been an issue for the business in its early years as it grew, a buyer coming in will want assurances that these key relationships will continue, and they will value a business more highly if there is contractual assurance in place to protect the value in those relationships.

For example, if your supply arrangement is fundamental to the ongoing performance of the business, you should ensure there is a contract in place that will transfer with the business to provide that ongoing certainty of supply for the buyer. Or if the business has value flowing from its position as a distributor of single or multiple products or services or if you have value sitting in others acting as a distributor for your products or services, the value in these distribution rights should be contractually locked in. If you have exclusive distribution rights, this needs to be documented clearly to meet the scrutiny of a buyer who will want to be assured they will have those ongoing rights.

I met with a client recently who has a business that had gone through massive growth. During the period of fast growth he had added a number of product lines that he had managed to secure exclusive distribution rights for. He had trialled a number of these, and a few of them really started to take off in a big way. While he was setting up these relationships, supply and distributor contracts had not been top of mind – indeed they hadn't been on his mind at all. As he relayed to me, he was testing, and didn't even know if any of these lines would get traction, so the legals had not even come up.

When he poured his marketing nouse into building these brands, his sales of these products had exploded – and his business had gone through the roof. But as we discussed the value of the business and his plan for an upcoming exit, he suddenly clicked onto the realisation that if these distribution arrangements remained as casual as they were currently, he was building his business on a foundation of sand ... notwithstanding the millions he was making today, the suppliers could leave tomorrow and he would have no business. And a buyer coming in, fronting up cold hard cash, would flush that risk out in three seconds flat.

I've seen the same sort of scenario play out again and again and again. Businesses that have distributors of their products, but don't have strong contractual protections in place for those distribution arrangements. Businesses that rely on international licences to operate, without sufficient long-term protection in the ongoing right to the licences. Franchisees that are subject to contracts that limit their ability to transfer the business. Businesses with royalty arrangements and commission arrangements that are undocumented. Instances where these contracts *are* in place, but where change of control clauses and assignment clauses will cause issues in a sale, or where the contracts have expired or are close to the end of their term.

How many potential instances of that kind of unprotected relationship value sit in your business? Your job, leading into an exit, is to identify these pockets of value in relationships, and ensure that they are locked in with contract terms that will withstand the scrutiny of a buyer before your business hits the market.

INTELLECTUAL PROPERTY

Intellectual property is often an area of great value in a business, but it may not be fully recognised until the point of sale and consequently not be protected in the way a buyer would expect. We have dealt with this in detail in earlier chapters of this book, so now I want to demonstrate what can go terribly wrong at sale if you fail to understand the value in your IP and have this properly protected before sale.

How many
POTENTIAL INSTANCES
of that kind of
UNPROTECTED
RELATIONSHIP VALUE
sit in your business?

One of the standout examples here is a business owner I came across many years ago, who shared with me her horrific story of the sale of her business that was built around an absolutely fabulous brand.

Sally had started the business 30 years prior, initially as a hobby, and then as a serious business as it grew traction and international attention. Unfortunately, while the business and the brand had grown exponentially, the owner's understanding of the importance of IP protections hadn't. When it came time to sell and the buyer commenced its due diligence, a simple trademark search revealed something fundamental: the trademark to this incredible brand was owned by someone else.

A couple of years earlier, a competitor had filed (and subsequently had approved) the trademark registration simply because Sally had failed to get in first. While that didn't stop Sally's business from using the trademark, it did mean that her business didn't have the right to stop this other competitor using it. Of course this seems completely unfair, that a business that had been using a name for 30 years could have lost their rights against a competitor that had barely been in the market for two years. When this all became apparent (at the first attempted sale), Sally spent tens of thousands of dollars on legal advice that ultimately determined that she could fight it, but that the cost of that fight could end up as hundreds of thousands of dollars. And that was money she didn't have.

Unsurprisingly, the sale fell through.

She searched again for another year and finally found another buyer, and ultimately sold for a tiny percentage of the full sale value she could have had – simply because she hadn't realised the value in her brand, or protected it.

Brand protection is just one example of the IP that can have value in a sale. There are lots of other examples of potential IP value you need to be thinking about, to ensure you have the right protections locked in and that you have correctly identified (and protected) the

chain of title behind it.[36] Website code is often built on licensed plat-
forms; design and copyright elements of a business often have unclear
origins (and ownership); licence arrangements that are fundamental
to the operation of the business are often unclear and lack security of
tenure for the future.

This last issue played out recently with a client we dealt with,
who thankfully had come to us in advance of their sale to enable us
time to analyse the business and help them work through identifying the value and ensuring that value was protected. Their business
was based on a brand they had licensed from an American company.
The business had grown to be worth more than $10m by the point
of sale, but this valuation was in part based on the assumption that
the brand that had been grown so well in the Australian market
was the brand that could continue post-sale. The problem was that the
trademark licensing arrangement had been very relaxed over time,
and while there was a basic licence agreement in place, this licence
agreement didn't provide any fixed term. This meant that a buyer
coming in, paying an eight-figure price, couldn't even be certain how
long they would be permitted to continue using the brand for. And
there are very few buyers who would be happy with that.

Once our client understood the importance of the licensing
contract, and the deficiencies that were in place as the documents
stood at that point, they commenced negotiations with their international counterparts to secure this right – and given they weren't
on the market yet, they still had the time to get this in place. But
had this been revealed through due diligence by a buyer, it's likely
it would have either completely killed the deal or given the buyer
a strong negotiating position to start to make large reductions in
the price.

---

36   The term 'chain of title' refers to establishing and proving the ownership of the intellectual property, which can often have been generated through a chain of people/entities
(thus the reference to the 'chain' of title to the intellectual property). For a more detailed
explanation, check out jargon busting chapter 23.

Another area where IP issues regularly come up is technology- and software-based businesses, where often a significant component of the value (and sometimes all of the value) sits in the IP but where sometimes the actual creator and owner of the IP rights can be unclear. Prior to sale, it is important to ensure that a proper chain of title in relation to that intellectual property has been established, so you as the seller can clearly prove to a buyer that you are the rightful owner of that intellectual property.

LEASE MAXIMISATION

Where the value of a business and its customer base revolves around its physical positioning, or where the cost of fit out and moving is high, a buyer will place high value on your ability to have secured the premises. If you as the seller own the premises, quite often the buyer may also want to purchase the premises as part of the deal, or have some arrangement put in place for a future purchase (for example, through an option).

If the premises are leased, the terms of that lease will be particularly important for a buyer in determining the value of the business to them. Therefore, well in advance of a sale it's really important that all of the leases in relation to the business are reviewed to ensure that they have optimal conditions for a transfer to a buyer.

For example:

- How long is the lease term you have available? Ideally you will have a long potential lease term comprising multiple 'options' – which are rights for the tenant to decide whether to continue to lease the premises at the end of each set period. It is a less well known fact for sellers that for many buyers of smaller businesses the term of the lease will be critical in obtaining finance for an acquisition. For example, in the acquisition of a veterinary or dental practice, the major lenders will generally want to see that the property lease (including options) has a term of at least five to seven years, which is similar also in many other industries where location is important.

- Are there any impediments to the lease term? For example, are there demolition clauses that give the landlord the right to terminate the lease early?
- Is the rent being charged appropriate, or is it excessive for the market in its current state?
- Are the other lease terms particularly onerous for a buyer?
- Is the lease in the correct name of the selling entity? And properly registered? This might seem like an obvious one, but we have had several clients come to us to sell only for us to find out that the tenant on the lease was a completely different entity to the entity selling the business, or worse still, that the lease registration was still in the name of a previous owner (yes this really has happened – multiple times).

If your lease review identifies major issues, you may need to negotiate a new lease with more appropriate terms to ensure that the value in the premises is properly secured.

If you own the premises, it is often appropriate to ensure that the right lease terms are in place prior to the sale between the business and your entity that holds the lease, so that the lease is simply transferred as is rather than having to go through lease negotiations as well as sale negotiations.

KEY PEOPLE

In many business sales the transfer of key staff is critical to a buyer. I think it's probably fair to say that the retention of staff is often not the first thing that business owners think of when they are considering selling their business, however this can be critical to the buyer's perception of value in the business – particularly for an initial period after the sale, and even more particularly if you as the seller have gotten the business to a position in which it is operating under management without you being critical to that transition of value.

We have worked on lots of deals where the transition of key staff was critical for a buyer to the success of an acquisition, and where warranties and deal structuring were used to ensure that staff stayed on (and if they didn't, the purchase price would be massively impacted). It's a little bit scary for a seller at that point to realise they are exposed to the extent that their staff may not stay on board. In this sense, the buyer's issue also becomes the seller's issue.

This brings me back to the earlier story of Rod and Jane. You may recall that Rod and Jane had recognised the benefit prior to sale of getting the business to the position that it was fully managed, without requiring them to personally be in the business. They did this by installing a general manager, who over the years of their preparation for sale took over the full running of the business. When it came time to sell, this approach rewarded them with multiple great offers, and a high valuation supported by the fact that the business could be simply passed straight on to a buyer with the management and oper-ation not being disturbed by the owners' quick exit. However, what they failed to recognise was that they were setting up a concentrated reliance on that one key staff member – the general manager they had installed. They also did not anticipate that the general manager might turn on them.

As you may recall, the day before exchange the general manager orchestrated a showdown. He threatened to walk and leave the deal a wreck if Rod and Jane didn't agree to give him a proportion of the sale price. Rod and Jane didn't want to be held to ransom and didn't cave to this demand, and in the dead of night the general manager deserted them. Rod and Jane were absolutely distraught – they hadn't been 'in' the business now for at least a year, and they had been working on this sale for about the same time – a whole year of their lives that was about to go down the drain! The buyers were completely destabilised, and initially wanted to pull out of the deal.

Ultimately the deal was saved with an earnout negotiated for the buyer and Rod and Jane agreeing to come back into the business and help with the transition over the next year. While this was not the outcome they had worked so hard to achieve, it was far better than a lost deal.

What are the learnings out of cases like this?

Firstly, the importance of systems in a business that will outlive any staff turnover. The more systemised you can make a business and the less reliant on any particular key staff, the more value and less exposure your business is likely to have at exit.

Secondly, your employment agreements leading into a sale should be extremely tight, to ensure you have protected as much as possible against staff leaving and taking value (IP, clients, suppliers and other staff) with them.

And a final consideration coming from this example is the way in which you deal with the discussion of sale with staff prior to the sale (if at all). I've heard many people say that you should never let staff know about a sale until the latest minute possible. Sometimes this approach works, but sometimes it can be catastrophic. And sometimes it is just not possible to be silent (particularly in this example of Rod and Jane, where their general manger was required to be part of the deal team in organising for the transfer of the business). At some point staff are going to work out that the business is being sold, so you are going to need a good communication strategy, and in particular a good story for their future with the buyers.

I have seen some really successful strategies play out with clever sellers incentivising their key staff in preparing the business for exit, and transitioning the value in the business, with the use of financial incentives and bonuses tied to both the sale price and the successful transition. When the value or profitability of the business goes up, the employee gets to share the upside. I've also seen incentives for employees tied to them helping achieve performance targets that enable the seller to make the target for their earnout payments.

And in some instances, I've also seen clever sellers make it a condition of the sale that there is a payment of retention bonuses to staff for staying on for a minimum period after the sale. This is so clever because it can be a win–win–win outcome:

- a win for the buyer in having the staff stay interested in the business and invested in the business achieving its post-acquisition goals
- a win for the seller in having the staff incentivised to help support the business in achieving the earnout targets that will reward the seller
- a win for the staff in getting to share in the upside of the business performance and successful transition from seller to buyer.

Chapter 20

PROTECTION: MINIMISING YOUR RISK

Risk for a seller can be considered in three areas:
- One is the risks leading into the sale – arising when prospective buyers consider that the business presents inappropriate levels of risk or where loss of value or performance occurs in the business leading up to sale. This can lead to a reduction in value before the contract is signed, which can show up in many ways:
  - a smaller buyer pool
  - a lower perception of value by prospective buyers
  - the value of the business being driven down in due diligence
  - buyers offering contingent payments based on future performance

  – buyers requiring retentions of the sale price to protect
    them against risks converting into losses or value not
    transferring.
* The second area of risk comes from the transaction itself and
  the way in which the business is transitioned at completion
  of the sale.
* The third area of risk for a seller is post-sale – and in particular
  the risk in warranties that last for a period after the business
  passes out of their control, and the restraints that they will be
  subject to.

Let's look at these risk areas one by one.

PRE-SALE RISK

There are two main components to pre-sale risk (the loss of value in
the business before a sale contract is signed).

TAKING YOUR EYE OFF THE BALL

The first is that the attention of the owners and management team
are so consumed by a sale that they take their eye off the ball of the
business, and subsequently impact the business growth and performance. The reality is that deals do fall over from time to time. Buyers
can get nervous, sometimes they don't like due diligence findings,
they may have trouble locking in funding, and sometimes they simply
just change direction before signing on the dotted line.

A seller must always be ready to pick up the business and
continue running with it just in case their buyer falls away. But when
the owners and management team have been so focused on the sale
that they have taken their eye off the ball, a loss of a buyer can have
catastrophic consequences.

Taking your eye off the ball isn't just a potential issue in a loss
of a buyer, it can also have serious consequences if the sale terms
include an earnout. And even though initial sale discussions might

not be based on an earnout, if a buyer senses a change in the performance of the business during a transaction, they might make a last-minute demand to switch part of the payment price structure to an earnout. So, it is prudent, to say the least, for sellers to be careful that leading up to a sale they have put in place a process to ensure that the business continues to grow and thrive through the sale process while their attention is diverted into the mechanics of the deal.

When sellers are focused on a sale, this is often when fires start appearing in the business. This is why pre-sale 'fortification' of the business is such an important first step prior to engaging in a sale process, which I step out in detail in part II.

FAILING THE 'LIFT THE HOOD' TEST

The second pre-sale risk is risk that exists in the business that will be viewed negatively by a buyer when they 'lift the hood' during due diligence, and will subsequently impact the saleability of the business, the available pool of buyers, and the price, payment terms and retentions required by a buyer. The key risk areas have been discussed in detail in parts I and II, so I'll only add short notes here for sellers about risk and preparation that should be considered.

Buyers will generally scrutinise all key contracts in the business to understand the risk they pose for the future. Therefore, in the years leading into a sale, there should be a focus on ensuring existing contracts are reviewed with a particular focus on the risk and liability clauses, to ensure that the risk position under the contracts is appropriate – minimising risk that the business is taking on, and mirroring that risk position (where possible) in its supply contracts. Of course, personal guarantees should also be reviewed, and where possible removed, in the lead up to the sale.

Buyers will also scrutinise your employment practices. Are your employment contracts up to date? Do you have provisions in your employment agreements protecting the business from terminated employees taking clients and suppliers and other staff? Are you engaging your staff in the right way? Or are you using contractors and casuals in a way that might raise red flags for a buyer?

It's common to see outdated employment contracts being used, a lack of proper and well-documented systems, and red flags around staff classifications – but all of this can usually be fixed easily if it is addressed properly in advance of a sale. Templates can be reviewed and updated and employee manuals and policies put in place to address business risks and legislation changes.

One great example of employment issues jeopardising a sale is our client Ted, who we discussed earlier. As you may recall, Ted had a large workforce of contractors. These contractors underpinned the value in the business, but also posed a major concern to the buyer who had identified the large risk in the possibility that the workforce of contractors could one day be deemed to have been incorrectly classified as contractors – and as a result could expose the buyer to backpay for entitlements and other expensive issues that such a reclassification would trigger.

The buyer's assessment was that the only way they could adequately deal with this risk was to require that as part of the sale the seller organise the entire contractor workforce to agree to change their legal classification with the business, and sign on as employees of the buyer (rather than simply continuing as contractors as they had been for many years with the seller).

The buyer also put in place a sliding scale for the purchase price relating to the percentage of the workforce that signed on as employees. This was a huge risk to the seller, as he now had a large component of the sale price at risk if he was unable to get the workforce on board with the change. He had to find a way to convince all – or the vast majority – of the contractors to completely change the way they were engaged, and he had two weeks to do it in.

Of course, if he had understood this risk at an earlier point before sale, he would have had time to slowly educate and then transition the contractors. But because he had not done any proper legal preparation leading into the sale, this was a risk he had not contemplated and therefore he had done no prior work to lay the foundations for an easier transition for the team.

Ted and his deal team however worked furiously day and night for two weeks, visiting every single one of the 200 contractors, asking them to sign the new employment contracts with the buyer. And ultimately he got every single one signed, and triggered the full sale payment. But it wasn't without late-night stresses – for both him and me – for the two weeks as we worked furiously to ensure that the sign-on targets would be met.

While it ended happily (with Ted and I still in contact years later, as he updates me on his fabulous new life of retirement), it could so easily have been terribly different if he didn't have such a close relationships with the contractors that enabled him to get them all transitioned in such a major way and in such a small amount of time.

The far less stressful way of achieving this is always advance planning, when there is time at hand!

Due diligence investigations by a buyer will also flush out litigation that has happened in the business, so you should resolve any outstanding issues prior to the sale of the business. For example, ideally any major litigation should be resolved at least a year or two ahead of a sale. You should also be prepared to explain why litigation or disputes arose (if there have been any in the recent past), and what has been done in the business to ensure that they won't repeat.

Buyers will also scrutinise your dealings with IP, finance facilities and encumbrances, your property leases and your assets to understand the associated risks. There is a lot of information in parts I and II of this book that delve more deeply into all these areas. The most important thing for a seller is to ensure that you understand what a buyer will be looking for, and that you have taken action in advance to ensure that the business appears in its best light by the time due diligence comes around.

KNOW YOUR BUYER

I want to add a final note here in relation to pre-sale risk, to remind you that even though it is your business that is under examination during the sale, you should also approach buyers with healthy caution. I have seen many instances of sellers investing time and energy into a sale process only to find subsequently that the buyer was unlikely to ever complete the transaction. For example, buyers can come in without finance lined up, or waste incredible amounts of time due to their lack of experience and nervousness. Or they can be just plain dodgy. I have also seen a few of those!

In one instance in the sale of a $14m business, just before all the financials of the business were disclosed, the seller did some background research and found that the 'buyer' was a serial con artist, with a string of liquidated businesses to his name. The information hadn't been uncovered earlier as the buyer had been operating under a different name. When the seller pulled out of the deal, the buyer immediately threatened legal action, alleging breach of the commercial terms document that had been reached. The true colours came out very quickly.

This particular scenario is not common but it is possible, and buyers pulling out with cold feet or from lack of preparation or financial standing are certainly common events. So I suggest that sellers ensure they pay at least a little bit of attention to understanding their buyer, and getting an objective gauge on whether there is likely to be any impediment to the buyer following through with the sale. And of course, this is absolutely imperative if you will continue to stay involved with the business or the buyer post-sale, or if you have a significant or long-running earnout or deferred payment as part of the deal.

TRANSACTION RISK

Transaction risk relates to the risk created by the transaction itself. This has been covered in detail in part I, but there are a few items of specific note that I want to highlight for sellers.

The most important thing for a seller is to UNDERSTAND what a buyer will be looking for, and to have TAKEN ACTION IN ADVANCE to ensure that the business appears in its best light by the time due diligence comes around.

You need to ensure that the sale of the business or the transfer of contracts does not put you in breach of any other agreements. For example, if the sale is occurring through a share sale, it is important to identify in advance any contracts that contain 'change of control' clauses. This has been discussed previously, but in short it is a clause where a change in the ownership of the company might trigger a default under the contract. It is important that these clauses are identified well in advance, and either negotiated out (if there is time and necessity) or alternatively are factored into the process required for the transaction, to ensure that the process in each contract is properly met. Alternatively, if the sale occurs as a business or asset sale, you need to ensure that you aren't assigning contracts without the authority of the other party if the agreement specifically prohibits that. The difference between assignment and novation is an important consideration in choosing to deal with each contract, and we dig into the differences and the importance of that distinction in the next chapter.

If the sale is occurring as a business sale, there are a lot of specific employment law issues to be considered and properly dealt with. For example, there is a risk that employees might claim redundancy pay from the seller unless the buyer offers them employment on terms that are substantially similar to the terms they were employed under with the seller. Therefore it is important that the sale agreement and process leading into the sale requires that the buyer makes an offer to the employees on these terms, and ideally indemnifies the seller against any losses they might suffer if they don't make these complying offers. This may trigger a negotiation point between the seller and buyer if the buyer determines that the employment provisions are too generous, but it's important for sellers to understand the importance of these negotiations in the context of the redundancy exposure that they may be running and the potential resultant costs exposure.

There are also considerations in areas like privacy and confidentiality. You need to ensure that the way you deal with personal information and its transfer does not breach any privacy laws, and also ensure that the way you deal with confidential information and its transfer does not put you in breach of any confidentiality agreements or other obligations.

This is where it again becomes important that you have an experienced lawyer on your team to help guide you through these transaction risks.

POST-SALE RISK

Don't think your risk exposure is over just because the deal is done. No longer being involved in the business may not absolve you from responsibility for issues that occurred or began during your owner-ship. Let's investigate what you need to be aware of.

WARRANTIES

It is usual for a seller to be required to provide warranties for the business and for the due diligence material they have provided to the buyer. It is also usual for these warranties to trigger a large amount of haggling between the parties.

Warranties are statements of fact set out in the contract. They are in place to provide the buyer with comfort and protection that the business is just as it has been represented and that there aren't material issues in the business that haven't been disclosed. It's a method of risk sharing between the parties in an attempt to segregate risks created by the pre-sale operation.

Disclosures are (as they sound) information disclosed by the seller. This information is provided to give the buyer insight into the business but also, importantly, to qualify the warranties.

A simple example of a warranty and related disclosure is a warranty that the taxes of the business have been properly paid and that the business has complied with laws relating to it, except for one disclosed item of late payment. This is a basic explanation – ultimately the compilation of warranties is highly complex and must be approached with extreme caution and experience, because these warranties can often create ongoing exposure for the seller, and any other guarantor of the warranties, well past the date of sale.

There are a number of methods that can be used to limit the exposure of sellers under sale warranties:

- **Appropriate disclosure, and using the sale contract to specifically limit any warranties provided to the extent of any disclosure.** The contract will have a clause that says something to the effect that the buyer cannot claim against a warranty if the matter had been disclosed by the seller. It is therefore extremely important for the seller to ensure that it has made sufficient and proper disclosure about any items that might create an exposure, and that it is able to prove that it has made this disclosure. This brings with it a lot of complexity in itself – in ensuring that the seller is able to prove exactly what was disclosed to the buyer, particularly when warranty claims might be raised many years into the future when the disclosure material is no longer where it was when it was initially provided to the buyer.

- **Limitations.** For example, sometimes it will be appropriate for warranties to be limited to the extent of matters that the seller knows to be true and correct and can control (meaning that the seller provides the warranty and disclosures on the basis of what it knows at that time).

- **Liability caps.** This is a maximum amount set out in the contract for exposure under the warranties. For example, the warranty damages cap might be agreed to be set at a percentage of the sale price (such as 25%, 50% or 100%) or at a set dollar figure. Of course the lower this figure, the less the exposure of the seller. Caps can also apply to individual claims or an aggregated maximum figure. They can also be split up to provide different caps for different types of warranties.

- **Time limits.** This puts in place a maximum period in which the buyer can claim under the warranties. Sometimes there is a lot of haggling about time limits, and the warranties might be split up into two different types of warranties and be given different time periods for each type of warranty. For example, title warranties or tax warranties might be given a longer claim period than other warranties.
- **Minimum threshold.** This provides a minimum quantum of damages before a warranty claim can be made.
- **Step in rights.** This builds in the ability for a seller to step in to take over the conduct of a matter if a matter arises that triggers a warranty claim.
- **Mitigation.** This requires that the buyer takes steps to minimise the loss.
- **Adding specific exclusions.** For example, ensuring that damages aren't payable if the warranty breach has arisen from a change of a law, has been offset or provided for in the accounts, or is offset by a saving.
- **Being careful about the way in which warranties are provided.** Ideally the seller should never provide representations about the future performance of the business.
- **Insurance.** There are some great insurance products available that can protect you post-sale against exposures you have under sale warranties. This is an important area to get advice on, because it can be a simple and sometimes relatively inexpensive way of getting peace of mind.[37]

There is a great example that illustrates the problems with warranties, in a case that went to court a few years ago.[38] I have already

---

37   Make sure you check out the resources hub at www.buygrowexit.com.au to book in a free discussion about your insurance options.

38   *Evolution Traffic Control v Skerratt* [2018] NSWSC 49 (ETC).

discussed this case briefly in chapter 6, looking at it from the perspective of a buyer, but there are also some important points for sellers. The case related to a share sale for $10 million. The price was based on a multiple of five times EBIT. Importantly however, the multiple arrived at by the buyer was paid based on future financial forecasts provided by the seller, which the buyer relied on.

Those financial forecasts included a material sum that came from a government funding program, which as it turns out was not achievable in the future. This was something the sellers knew (or should have known) prior to the sale, but – surprise, surprise – they failed to disclose it to the buyer. When the buyer finally found out that the government funding was not able to be achieved after the sale, they sued the seller for misleading and deceptive conduct and for breach of the sale warranties.

The warranty in the sale agreement notably included that:

- all information disclosed in due diligence materials during the course of negotiations leading up to the sale were accurate and complete
- all information that would be material for disclosure to a prudent purchaser had been disclosed.

When the sellers were unable to convince the court that they had a reasonable basis for making the representations they had about the future financial performance of the business, the court awarded the buyer damages of around $3.5 million.

What's the lesson in this for you? Steer away from making representations about future performance if at all possible. And be very careful that if you are providing a warranty, you are sure it is correct. Working through warranties in a contract can be painful (as often they are extensive) but it is critically important in order to limit your future exposure.

And finally, to sum up this section, it is useful to note that buyers also give warranties to sellers, but there are far fewer. These warranties may for example include that the buyer has sought FIRB[39] approval if it is required to do so, that it has reviewed all the documents presented to it, that it has made its own enquiries into the business and is not relying on projections from the seller, or that it has the capacity and authority to enter into the transaction.

RESTRAINTS

As part of the deal, the sellers will generally be required to agree to restraints. These restraints will normally include a provision requiring that the sellers do not act in competition with the business, and do not take (or in legal terms 'solicit') the staff or clients.

These restraints sound simple on their surface, but can become more complex as you consider the following components:

- **Who the restraints will apply to.** Often the buyer will require that the restraints also apply to related parties of the seller – so where the selling entities are companies, this is likely to extend to the individuals who are connected to the business (who will generally also be required to sign a separate personal restraint) and to their direct family members, and any other businesses they are connected to.
- **Where the restraints will apply.** Generally the restraints against competing with the business will apply to a specific geographical area. This is particularly likely if the business being sold is a small business that services a defined area.
- **How long the restraints will last.** There will always be a length of time specified in the restraints. This is generally at least a year or two, but can often be much longer.

Think carefully about any restraints you may be inclined to agree to. I have had countless experiences with helping with the sale of

---

39   FIRB approval is approval by the Foreign Investment Review Board that is required for certain acquisitions made by foreign entities or individuals.

a business where sellers have been adamant that they are happy to provide any sort of restraint because they intend to never enter that industry again, only to find that after they have spent a bit of time recuperating and re-energising they suddenly have found a new enthusiasm and want to get back in.

It is of course extremely important for a buyer to feel that the investment they are making into the business acquisition will bring with it the clients and staff that they have paid for – and that you as the seller won't be opening up across the road in competition any time soon after the sale and leaching that value from them. However, on the flipside, it's important to make sure you aren't over-committing to restraints that aren't necessary. Ultimately you should aim to have some future flexibility to enable you the freedom to make decisions once the dust settles on the sale.

POST-SALE EXPOSURE THROUGH EXISTING CONTRACTUAL ARRANGEMENTS

Business contracts, such as customer and supplier agreements, can be transferred to a buyer as either an assignment or a novation. These are terms that I often find businesses don't understand well, and while they are a bit technical, it is important to understand the fundamental differences and the impact on the potential post-sale exposure of a seller:

- **Assignment.** An assignment of a contract creates the position where the buyer is entitled to all the benefits in the contract. This is generally the simplest way to transfer contracts as it can often be done without needing the express consent of the contracting party (the customer or the supplier, or whoever is on the other side of the contract being assigned) – depending on the wording under the contract in relation to assignments. However, the risk that is often completely missed by sellers in dealing with the transfer of contracts in this way is that the *obligations* of the seller under the contract cannot be properly transferred without the consent of the third party.

The sale contract or assignments might specify that the buyer is responsible for all the future obligations and risk under the contract, but if the other parties to the contract have not agreed to that change in responsibility (through a novation), that contracting party may still have rights against the seller if the buyer is in breach. This means that if contracts are simply assigned, the seller will continue to potentially have exposure to those clients and suppliers and other contracting parties – and while if they are pursued they might have recourse against the buyer under the sale contract, it is an argument that ideally they should never have to be a part of.

- **Novation.** A novation is a document signed by all three parties – being the seller, the buyer and the contracting party – where essentially the old agreement is terminated, and there is a new contract created between the buyer and the contracting party. This is generally more formal than an assignment, and more cumbersome to arrange because it requires the involvement and signature of each customer, supplier or other contracting party. However, where there are substantial future obligations to be performed, it's important to consider whether certain contracts should be individually novated to properly protect the seller from that future risk.

- **New contracts.** The final approach is for the buyer to simply execute new contracts with each party, and for the seller to terminate all their existing contracts at sale. This is often the approach for smaller businesses, and can be appropriate where there is little risk of losing clients or suppliers simply through the provision of new contracts, and where there is no risk for the seller in terminating the contracts (on the basis that none of the contracts have future or ongoing obligations). An example of where this can play out easily is where there are supplier contracts that simply relate to supplies as they are ordered, and don't create any future obligations for purchase.

In these instances, a buyer can simply set up a new account with the supplier, and the seller can terminate their account. As I mentioned earlier, this is often an appropriate approach for many (sometimes all) contracts of a small business – but the larger the business, the more complex their contractual arrangements become, and the less likely it will be that this is a viable approach to dealing with the potential post-sale risk for a seller. Even for smaller businesses, there may be certain contracts that can't be dealt with in this way – such as leases, finance, and customer contracts that have future obligations built into them.

One final note is a reminder that this approach to the transfer of contracts is only relevant where the sale is being dealt with as a business sale, rather than a share sale. In a share sale the contracts essentially remain untouched, unless there are change of control provisions (in which case express consent is generally required from the contracting parties) or where there are personal guarantees – which leads us neatly to our next section.

PERSONAL GUARANTEES

A personal guarantee is a guarantee provided by an individual to secure the obligations of another party. There are two main ways in which personal guarantees can feature as a potential risk post-sale:

- Personal guarantees **given in the sale contract**. Where the selling entities are companies, sometimes a buyer will want the individuals who sit behind those entities (who are often also the directors of the business) to provide a guarantee for the obligations of the sellers. Generally this specifically relates to the warranties, and comes from the buyer's risk that once the sale proceeds have passed over to the sellers, those funds will be dispersed to individuals, leaving the selling entities without any assets should the buyer need to pursue them for warranty claims. Sellers often are very nervous about putting their own names (and personal assets) on the line with personal guarantees. And the larger the business that is being sold, often the less likely it is that an individual will accept a personal guarantee. However, if sellers want to negotiate this requirement, they will generally need to have another option available to help reduce the risk to the buyer. This is often the reason behind the seller's acceptance of a portion of the sale price being retained for a set period to be available to account for any post-completion adjustments or warranty claims that may arise.[40] It is a balancing act between the timing of access to all of the funds from the sale, and personal exposure.

- Personal guarantees that have been **provided over the course of the business** and that can potentially continue to operate post sale unless they have been revoked. In many cases, directors of the business will have provided some sort of personal guarantees over the period of operation of the business. This is often for example a requirement of leases, and also of finance relating to the business – but also sometimes there may be supplier and other guarantees. Some of these guarantees will be easier than others to have removed, but it's imperative that these are all dealt with carefully in the sale because, while there should be protections in the sale contract, if the personal guarantees were to stay in place post-sale (not having been properly extinguished as part of the sale process) and the business were to default under the related contracts (for example, the buyer stopped paying the rent), the individual could find themselves being pursued personally for that default. And while they might have a right under the sale contract to take recovery action against the buyer it is far better to have not been caught up in the mess in the first place.

---

40   This is discussed in detail in chapter 18.

RISK PROTECTION

We have discussed the three types of risks that should be carefully considered in a sale, and interestingly the approach required to protect against all of these risks is pretty much the same:

- **Pre-sale preparation.** The business should be properly reviewed from a legal perspective well in advance of a sale, and an action plan put in place to remedy any legal deficiencies in the business. This type of process is sometimes called 'vendor due diligence', meaning a due diligence process conducted for the vendor (seller) in advance of a sale to identify the risks that would be identified by a buyer in the due diligence phase. Check out the scorecard at our Resources Hub to see how you fare: www.buygrowexit.com.au. It's never too early to assess your business for readiness for exit.
- **Disclosure.** Failing to disclose issues or risks that you are aware of to the buyer can create huge potential problems.
- **Tight contracts.** The approach to the contract for a sale of a business should never be viewed as a tick-a-box exercise. These are critical documents that will form the basis of your protection into the future – and should be approached with experience, and focus!
- **Proper processes.** Planning and attention to process and necessary timelines are required for dealing with the transfer of contracts, obligations and future risk.
- **Insurance.** Sellers should consider appropriate insurance to cover risks in the deal.

Chapter 21

PROCESS: SEEING THE DEAL THROUGH

In the contract phase of a business sale, deals are killed by **slow speed, poor communication between the deal teams,** or **poor control of the process** by the advisers.

Selling a business can take a lot of time. There is time needed for the preparation of the business for sale, time needed for preparing the information memorandum and getting the business to market, time needed to find a pool of potential buyers, and to narrow down the list to a final contender. By the time you get to agreeing on commercial terms you are generally more than a year through the process. The last thing you then want is a poor process in the contract phase that unnecessarily causes the deal to stall or fall over.

I have however seen many examples of just that. In chapter 7 I gave an example of a deal where both buyers and sellers had stuck with their usual lawyers, who were not experienced in dealing with business sales. The process went completely off the rails as the lawyers butted heads over what were essentially minor issues. The deal was only saved when we were brought in and quickly found solutions to the issues that had been holding the deal up.

THE TOP CAUSES OF SLOW DEALS

Several times in the book we have discussed the issues caused by having the wrong legal team and by not having processes or by having faulty processes. But there are so many other reasons that deals slow down or hit roadblocks:

- **Lack of preparation by the seller for the sale and for due diligence that slows down the delivery of key business information to the buyer.** Sometimes sellers completely fail to understand just how time consuming due diligence can be in terms of how long it takes to dig out the information required by the buyer to assess the business. Due diligence checklists and requirements differ from deal to deal depending on how big the sale is and the buyer and their approach, but generally a buyer of a business will want a lot of good quality information for them to feel comfortable about the purchase. Being slow to produce this information is likely to raise red flags for a buyer.
- **Unexpected things come up during due diligence.** When the seller is not prepared before they put the business on the market, unexpected issues are often uncovered during the due diligence process. We see many examples where sellers either lose their buyers or have a massive hit on the sale price or terms when a buyer identifies issues through their due diligence investigations that were previously undisclosed. In these instances the buyers may pull out because they are

concerned about the implications for how the business is run and the level of risk, use it as a way to negotiate down the sale price, or require far more stringent warranties and indemnities.

- **Lack of preparation by the buyer that slows down the timeline.** For example, this might be delays caused by not having finance properly lined up, or not understanding what they are looking for in due diligence. Sometimes if they are a first-time buyer, they might have a lack understanding of what will make a deal work for them.

- **Slow lawyers who don't have templates and checklists ready to go.** This usually results in the lawyers being slow to initially issue contracts, and then working at a snail's pace turning around reviews and amendments. And then – horror of all horrors – engaging in long, protracted emails forwards and backwards, nit-picking over every tiny word in the contract and every single risk they can possibly come up with.

- **Poor communication between the parties.** Emails forwards and backwards for an eternity overtake sensible engagement through a more personal (and fast-paced) negotiation process.

- **The emotion of the deal taking over, causing roadblocks along the way.** Emotion is such a huge component of this process – and is mostly completely missed by lawyers as the underlying root cause of issues. I talk about emotion in a deal in much more detail below, because it is of huge importance to how the deal will run.

- **Practical issues not being dealt with in advance.** Often sellers will have pages of registrations sitting on the Personal Property Securities Register (which is like a public noticeboard of security interests over a business) that haven't been cleaned up in advance, and that ultimately slow down completion where some may take time to remove. Contracts in the business may need consent prior to their transfer. Leases will need consent from the landlord prior to their assignment. If these types of practical processes aren't identified and put in a timeline well in advance of completion, they can cause delays.

- **Deal fatigue.** If a sale starts to drag out, often caused by unnecessary ongoing negotiations over the sale contract and deal terms where legal advisers are wanting to point score rather than help facilitate a good deal, the parties can start to lose momentum and slip into what is often referred to as 'deal fatigue' – that space where a party on one side (or both sides) gets so worn down by the deal that they either completely dig their heels in and risk the transaction slipping away or start to make unnecessary concessions that dilute their outcome in the deal.

The answer to all of these issues is speed and tight processes. But how do you achieve that?

HOW TO ACHIEVE THE NIRVANA OF SPEED AND TIGHT PROCESSES

Over the years I have considered this issue constantly. Almost obsessively. Trying to work out how to form the best processes to drive deals. This is constantly in refinement as I work out new ways with our team at Aspect Legal to keep improving the process. Here is the list of elements in our processes we have in place currently to combat the regular issues that come up during the contract phase of business sales:

- **Preparation.** We ensure the parties are properly prepared and primed for the sale, which starts with a legal review of where they are now, and what they need to do or change leading into a sale. This means ensuring they are educated (indeed the very reason for this book, and for my podcast *The Deal Room*), and have taken the necessary steps to prepare in advance. They are ready for due diligence with the information and documentation required at hand, they understand any gaps and risks in the business and have dealt with or minimised them, they understand the tax implications, they understand what consents will be required for each of their contracts to be transferred, they have cleared out old registrations on the PPSR and know what will need to be dealt with at sale, they have cleaned up issues in the business, and most importantly their business looks clean and tidy and ready for sale.[41]

- **Timelines.** Keep the deal moving by using target timetables, and by using processes (such as the 'two draft then meeting' process I talk about below).

- **Stakeholder engagement.** Engage all the stakeholders that can impact timing and deal success. This includes the legal team on the other side of the deal, the accountants, the financiers and the business broker or corporate adviser (who can be a great asset in keeping communication flowing if there are blocks created by the legal team on the other side).

- **Communication.** Keeping communication flowing is critical. Left to their own devices, most lawyers spend far too much time (and their clients' money) in time-consuming redrafts that are passed between the parties for what feels like an eternity – and consequently lose perspective on getting the best deal. At Aspect Legal, we combat this with our approach of limiting amendments to two rounds each, then getting on the phone or in a meeting to get to a commercial outcome on the sticking points. We intentionally design the communication flow between all parties in a way to increase the speed in the deal, and reduce speedbumps. We also use a project manager to ensure that all of the stakeholders are kept constantly in the communication loop.

- **Commercial focus.** It's imperative that the commercial realities are not lost in legal wrangling, and that the legal process maintains a strong connection to the commercial landscape of the deal. We train our lawyers in thinking about

---

41   If you would like to assess how ready your business is for exit, check out our simple scorecard on our resources hub at www.buygrowexit.com.au.

the commercial issues at play, and in how to balance those against the legal issues – to find win–win solutions, rather than simply digging for risk without thinking about how that risk can be dealt with.

- **Driving the parties.** There are many parties to wrangle in a sale, and as we discussed above, each of these parties can sometimes move at a snail's pace. So we use a project manager whose main role is to find ways to keep chasing each of the parties to move them forwards as quickly as possible. We have also developed a Rapid Contracting Process™ (check it out on the next page) which has been designed to reduce time and confusion by getting the parties and their lawyers to the table together to finalise issues quickly – in order to ensure a quick and smooth deal. The idea behind the Rapid Contracting Process™ is ensuring that the parties agree to come together quickly in a joint meeting if there are issues in the contract negotiation phase, rather than allowing the matter to wallow in multiple drafts and redrafts passing between the legal teams, causing delays.
- **Internal processes.** We aim for 24 hours to turn around the first-draft sale contracts for small (sub $1m) sales, and are modifying our systems constantly to enable our team to push out drafts and deal with any issues evolving quickly. We also have developed over our decades in this area countless templates and checklists that we use to ensure that our approaches are thorough, but also fast.
- **Constant refinement.** Ultimately the best approaches come from processes that have been refined and consistently improved over time. We use monthly debriefs across all our lawyers on our M&A deals to brainstorm how we can improve our systems and processes, and how we can keep evolving our approaches to getting to fast, smooth deals.

The reality is that while we can control our approach and our timing, we can't easily control other parties. While we have employed many tactics over the years to try to combat this problem – like our project manager role (which was designed to enable us to keep pushing the parties to keep them moving quickly) and our Rapid Contracting Process™ (which is an attempt to get the parties on the same page in relation to timelines and an agreed process) – ultimately better outcomes come from having advisers on both sides of the deal that subscribe to a commercial and systems-based approach. So you might want to suggest to your buyer to read this section or direct them to our 'lawyer buying guide' before you both 'lawyer up', so they also understand the imperative of choosing the right lawyer for the deal.[42]

UNDERSTANDING THE HIDDEN ELEMENT: EMOTION

I have already mentioned the role of emotion in a deal, but I think it is so important, and often completely unrecognised, so I want to spend a little time explaining my perspective on this in a deeper way.

In my experience, most business owners who sell to retire really don't completely understand what life looks like without the business that had been so linked to their self-identity for many years.

This dawning can hit at different times.

Sometimes this doesn't hit until some point after the sale is done and dusted, and the joy of endless pina coladas and white-sanded beach holidays starts to dim.

But sometimes it hits much earlier in the process, when getting close to the point that they are about to fully commit to the deal, or when exchange is imminent. This can often fuel either concern that the deal that has been struck is not the right deal, or resistance to elements of the deal. The reason you need to be tapped into this as an issue is because it can impact the sale process and certainly

---

42   Get access to the lawyer buying guide and Rapid Contracting Process™ here: www.buygrowexit.com.au.

The reality is that while we can CONTROL OUR APPROACH and our timing, we can't easily control other parties.

can make negotiations harder when there is unrecognised emotion at play below the surface. So if you are a seller, think about this aspect of your emotion, and go into the deal with your eyes wide open as to the changing thought processes that might start to occur for you throughout the deal.

So what are the emotional challenges particularly for a seller?

One of the biggest likely emotional challenges for a seller (particularly a seller who is retiring) is a crisis of meaning and identity. The point where they suddenly wonder what it might mean not to have this business that has probably taken massive chunks of their time prior to the sale. The point where they start to wonder what they are going to do, and who they are going to be if they are no longer the captain of their business ship. What are they going to now do with their life?

This is unlikely to ever be a topic that a seller consciously considers. But it can show up in their behaviour in the form of obstinacy, of stubbornness and resistance to the process.

So I strongly recommend that all business sellers have a clear plan in place for what post-sale life looks like, some new goals and aspirations, and just a little bit of education about the warning signs of emotion in a deal. Think in advance about what you are going to do to fill your time after you've left your business and how that's going to affect the people closest to you. Start to consider creating purpose for life after business.

It is also important to understand the potential emotional rollercoaster for a buyer. Sophisticated, experienced buyers will be unlikely to be impacted by emotion in a deal, but inexperienced buyers are often caught up in an emotional journey at some point. The trick is to be able to identify the warning signs that emotion has crept into the decision-making process, and to work with it; for example, by keeping up strong momentum in the deal.

The reality is however that most advisers, and most sellers and buyers themselves, don't understand that there is this emotional

I STRONGLY recommend that all business sellers have a CLEAR PLAN in place for what post-sale life looks like, some NEW GOALS and ASPIRATIONS, and just a little bit of education about the warning signs of emotion in a deal.

undercurrent at play. And that this ultimately manifests in many instances in problems along the way. I have watched with interest as this has recurred so many times in so many transactions I've been involved in. And ultimately, I began talking to psychologists to understand the mental process more, so that we could adapt strategies in our processes to combat these issues, and to help our clients in successfully navigating this somewhat emotional journey.

To sum things up, here are three tips for business owners who are considering selling their business in the future:

- **Prepare yourself emotionally.** I know it sounds a bit touchy-feely, but the important thing is to recognise that the process can be exhausting at times and it can evoke emotions that are unlike most business transactions you engage in. Just be aware that the emotions might come up.

- **Be very clear about your end goal.** This is what we like to call your WHY-power. Before going to market, you must deeply understand your reason for selling and work out the kind of life you envisage yourself having after the sale. Identify your motivations – these motivations will help carry you through the emotional ups and downs of the deal.

- **Get the right advisers on board.** Make sure you find people to surround yourself with that you can trust and who share the same values as you. Surrounding yourself with the right kind of people throughout this transaction can make all the difference.

As an aside to the M&A advisers who are reading this book, I absolutely believe that you hold an indispensable role in caring for the emotional wellbeing of the business owners throughout the sale process. Here's some tips for you in dealing with the emotions that pop up during a transaction.

- **Don't be surprised.** Emotions are inevitable when you're dealing with human beings. By having realistic expectations of the process, half the battle has already been won. This also means that you have a duty to prepare your client for the emotional hurdles that are waiting up ahead.

- **Very importantly, show empathy.** It's important to remember that a business sale is not just another commercial transaction. By this I mean that we must acknowledge the emotional undercurrents behind every decision made at every step in the process. You need to be sensitive to the emotional needs of your clients and understand that if they dig in or appear to overreact to certain events, it might actually be that something deeper is going on, that can be resolved with an empathic approach.

- **Get educated and learn from other people's best practices.** Never stop learning. If you want to see better results, you must constantly work on improving yourself, and one of the ways to do that is from learning from other people's mistakes and successes. That's one of the reasons I produced this book and *The Deal Room Podcast* – to help all those businesses out there at the M&A coalface to get great insights from other advisers and professionals, and also to hear the stories of the business owners who are involved in sales and acquisitions.

Chapter 22

THE END OF THE STORY

A COMING FLOOD OF COMPETITION ON EXIT?

There has been a lot of media in the past 10 years about the impending likely flood of SME business sales resulting from the exodus of baby boomer owners. The theory goes that given the large number of businesses in Australia (and indeed internationally) owned by baby boomers, as they reach retirement age we will see a glut of these businesses on the market, with the peak expected in Australia in around 2028. While there is a lack of data in Australia to clearly indicate whether this demographic trend will cause the tsunami we have been warned of, it is clear that we have a wave of baby boomers approaching retirement. It is also clear that a large proportion of SMEs in Australia are owned by baby boomers. So therefore, it isn't a stretch of the imagination to think that the scale of exodus of baby boomer owners will lead to an increasing number of businesses for sale in coming years.

It is yet to be seen whether a glut of businesses on the market is on its way to deluge us all. Or whether this is the cycle of sales, transitions and other exits that will continue in an orderly fashion as it is now, with a new wave of buyers meeting the upsurge in business sales. Irrespective of whether a business will be 'harder' to sell in the future or not, the reality right now is that good businesses sell well, and can provide their owners with the opportunity of a choice between a sale and an ongoing operation in an investment capacity. Whereas businesses that are not primed for market, are not run in a sale-ready state, are not an attractive option for buyers, are right now and will continue to be in the future, hard (and some cases impossible) business to sell.

So this discussion should lead each business owner to consider what their plans are for the future of their business. And this includes *you*.

ONE FINAL NOTE

We have discussed buying, growing and selling a business, but there is one last thought I want to leave you with.

Business ownership provides an incredible opportunity for control over your own life. While many people start out in business attracted by this concept, the reality is that they often end up controlled by their businesses.

I've seen this so often. I've also lived it. I understand what it takes to work hard to build something of value.

Hopefully the learnings in this book will help you ensure that the asset you have created through all this effort is not destroyed by either landmines that blow up along the way, or by small choices you make every day that whittle down (rather than accelerate) the ultimate value.

But in addition to implementing all the elements in this book to increase value and protect the asset you are creating, be aware that there might be something deeper about your business that will give you the strength, the passion and the purpose for the journey.

I had a moment about six years ago, when I wondered about my own business. I had been in law for almost 15 years at that point, and was feeling somewhat jaded. I was juggling growing a business with also growing a family. I was struggling with growth, and staff and all of the things business owners struggle with day in and day out. I took work along with me on holidays. I worked hard day and night. And I was having difficulty seeing the point of it all. I remember spending hours reflecting on what I wanted out of my business, and indeed out of my life. I wasn't a doctor or nurse who saved lives, or a teacher who helped shaped the future through our children.

What did I do that made a difference?

But as I reflected, I started to remember the pivotal moments of my career. I remembered the story of James, whose life at the point I met him was in tatters because he didn't have guidance about how to protect his business as he grew. I remembered the many stories of the business owners I had worked with who had blown themselves up along the way by legal mis-steps, or simply the failure to grow their business in a way that provided them with an asset that they could sell for a reasonable price.

I also remembered Ted who was living a fabulous retirement after a solid sale (notwithstanding a few issues appearing on the way to it!) and the many other clients who had found their nirvana at exit. And I realised that there was a pattern.

And in this reflection I accidentally discovered the secret that I had been missing – that building a business is not just about maximising its value, it is also about finding the passion and purpose behind what you are doing. I found that passion and purpose in two things:

- The ability to pass on the insights I had gained about how business owners can buy, grow and exit in a way that maximises their financial outcomes. In a way that I feel could really make a difference to the lives and retirement of our clients, and indeed their experience of their business.
- I also found a wonderful philanthropic organisation called B1G1 that showed me how any business, no matter how small, can implement contributions to worthy global projects and start to make a difference.[43]

43　Check out www.B1G1.com

The point of all of this is a reminder to you. While there is a lot to do in business, and a lot you can do to change your endgame if you start with a bit of understanding and purposeful planning, don't forget also to step back every now and again and look at the bigger picture.

Don't forget to find the joy, find the balance, and find the meaning in what you do every day.

And don't forget to find the purpose.

Because not only will finding a purpose give you an energy for your business to help see you through the often tough work it requires to build it, it can also in and of itself create greater value. A recent study by Deloitte has highlighted that companies with a higher purpose outperform in valuation and performance. Purpose-driven companies have an average valuation multiple more than 4 × higher. They have 20% higher shareholder returns. And they double their value more than four times faster. Additionally the study revealed that 78% of employees are more inclined to work for a purpose-driven company, and indeed 50% of workers (and 75% of millennial workers) even said they would take a pay cut to work for a purpose-driven company.

So I would love you to leave this book remembering that success in business is not just about the mechanics of buying cleverly, growing safely and finding the levers to increase your multiple at exit. Because while those elements are of course incredibly important, it can mean little at the end of the day if you don't remember to enjoy the ride along the way. To have fun, to make a difference, and to find passion and purpose.

IT'S NOT AS HARD AS IT ALL MAY SEEM

There are many pages in this book full of information. Maybe you are now in information overload and feel it's impossible to get your head around the myriad things to do in the business, and the myriad considerations in each of these phases of acquisition, growth and exit. But it doesn't have to be hard. If you have the right team around you, they will guide you through these considerations. While this book provides you the framework, I am not suggesting by any means that this is something that can be nutted out on its own. Get the right advisers on board, the right checklists and action plan in place, and then execute hand in hand with people who have run through this fire before.

Chapter 23

JARGON BUSTER: TERMINOLOGY EXPLAINED

As you enter into this space it's easy to become overwhelmed by the sheer level of jargon. Interestingly, the jargon is often complicated within the industry itself. While there might be clear meanings in large M&A, here in our world of SME M&A, I often find the jargon is used by different people to mean different things!

Here are some fundamental terms that you will see used again and again through the book – these are the important ones to understand:

- **M&A:** Mergers and acquisitions. In this book, we use the term M&A to mean the sale or acquisition of a business, or shares in the company that runs a business, or units in a unit trust that runs a business. M&A sounds complicated, but it's definitely shorter to write than that last sentence!

- **SME M&A:** In Australia SME is a fairly broadly used term to describe small and medium-sized enterprises. There is a bit of a fuzzy definition. I use it in this book for businesses with less than 200 employees, and with annual revenue of less than $50m. However, the concepts I cover stand true for businesses with hundreds of staff, and annual revenue higher than this figure.

So let's not get too caught up on thresholds. Let's just say I'm using the term to differentiate your business from an international conglomerate with staff numbering in the thousands.

- **Asset sale, business sale or share sale:** This is not really jargon. But it can be confusing. I dig into the meaning and the big differences in part III, and also discuss examples and practical issues in chapters 5 and 8.
- **Acquisition:** Buying a business (or shares, or units, or whatever!).
- **Exit, divestment or sale:** Selling a business (or shares, or units, or whatever!). Sometimes also called 'realisation'.
- **Merger:** A combination of two or more businesses that results in the creation of a new entity.
- **Target:** the business (or company) that is being acquired.
- **Acquirer:** the buyer(s) or purchaser(s).
- **Vendor or seller:** The person, people or entities selling the business (or shares).

And here is a full list of other jargon in the book and in the industry (ordered alphabetically, not in order of importance!):

Adjusted EBITDA The EBITDA after add backs from the normalisation of the accounts (the EBITDA of the business after taking into account the adjustment of the non-recurring income and expenses). Also sometimes called normalised EBITDA.

Assignment The transfer of the rights, but not the obligations, under a contract. Often this can be done without the contracting party needing to sign anything as part of the sale process. See more detail in chapter 20.

Business sale agreement (BSA) The agreement between a buyer and seller for the sale of a business.

Chain of title This term refers to establishing and proving the ownership of intellectual property, which can often have been generated through a chain of people or entities (thus the 'chain' of title to the intellectual property). For example, website code may have been created by a series of individuals. If those individuals were contractors or even the founders of the business, you will need to ensure you have documentation that shows that the underlying intellectual property rights have been assigned from those creator/s (the individual contractors) to the business.

Change of control clauses A clause in a contract that is held by the target business, which allows the contracting party to terminate the contract if control or ownership in the target business changes and the contracting party has not consented to that change. This kind of clause is common in leases, and can also often appear in contracts with customers, suppliers, franchisors, licensors, and the like.

Commercial terms, terms sheet, NBIO, MOU, LOI, HOA This might look like a weird combination of letters, but the reason they are grouped is because in the sub-$50m deal size, these terms are all often used interchangeably to talk about the same thing. NBIO – non-binding indicative offer. MOU – memorandum of understanding. LOI – letter of intent. HOA – Heads of Agreement. They all mean a document that is generally a few pages long that sets out the main commercial terms of the deal (buyer, seller, price, terms, etc.) that are intended not to be binding, plus sometimes a few clauses for good measure that are meant to be binding (enforceable), such as a term of exclusivity for the buyer, or confidentiality.

Completion The point at which the business/company fully transfers over to the buyer. This is often when the balance of the purchase price will be paid, other than any retention or deferred payments. It can also sometimes be referred to as 'settlement', or outside of Australia is often referred to as 'closing'.

Data room A place where information about the business is placed for review by the buyer in their due diligence. This can be a physical room, or more generally for SME transactions, an electronic space.

Deferred payment The part of the sale price that is paid at some point in the future after completion.

Disclosures A seller may disclose (tell the buyer about) exposures or risks in the business that might be in contrast to warranties provided in the sale contract. The purpose is to avoid legal action by a buyer claiming that they were not aware of certain issues that may lead to future loss.

Drag along clause Drag alongs are clauses in a shareholders' agreements that enable one or more shareholders holding a major share of the company to force a minority shareholder to sell together with them – the majority shareholders get the right to 'drag along' the minority shareholders in a sale.

Due diligence The investigation into a business before acquisition to evaluate the risks and opportunities (and to confirm facts provided by the seller) from the perspectives of financial, legal, commercial, operational, organisational, environmental and insurance. This could include examining the business's records and inspecting its physical assets.

Earnout A future payment calculated based on the performance of the business after completion. Given the payment is based on future performance, much care needs to be taken with how these clauses work. This type of clause can be effective if the sale price is based on the future potential for the business, if the business is hard to value, if the buyer wants to incentivise the seller to help continue maximising the business value post-sale, or if there is some risk in the transfer or ongoing operation of the business that the parties have agreed to share.

EBIT (earnings before interest and tax) The profit in the business before interest and taxes. This is also called 'operating profit' or 'operating profit before tax'.

EBITDA (earnings before interest, tax, depreciation and amortisation) The profit before interest, taxes, depreciation and amortisation. EBITDA provides a gauge of the operating cashflow of a business.

Escrow An escrow is the use of a third party to hold assets (usually money) on behalf of parties who are in the process of completing a transaction. It is essentially a contractual arrangement where the third party agrees to receive and disburse money on conditions agreed to by the transacting parties.

EU GDPR European Union General Data Protection Regulation 2016/679 – regulation in the European Union and the European Economic Area on data protection and privacy that impacts not just businesses within the EU, but also businesses outside of the EU that have clients within the EU.

Exchange When the sale contracts are signed (but the business/company has not yet transferred over to the buyer).

FIRB approval This is approval that may be required from the Foreign Investment Review Board for certain acquisitions made by foreign entities or individuals.

IPO (initial public offering) Colloquially referred to as a 'list' or 'float'. This is where a private company lists (or 'floats') on a stock exchange and can then be traded publicly. It is a complicated and expensive route, but is where the headlines are made from business founders achieving eye-watering returns.

LBO (leveraged buy out) Where a buyer uses a significant amount of borrowed money to fund the acquisition. Often the assets of the target company/business will be used as all or part of the collateral for the funding.

MBI (management buy in) A transaction in which a new management group and an investor or investment fund become co-owners of a company.

MBO (management buy out) The management of the business buys the business. Often I hear this term also used where employees are buying the business.

Minority shareholder A shareholder who does not exert control over a company. Typically holding less than 50% of a company's shares.

Multiple A valuation method that is applied generally to the adjusted EBITDA to arrive at a sale price. The higher the 'multiple' used in a valuation, the higher the sale price. This is an important distinction for businesses to understand – that value can be arrived at by influencing not just the profit of the business but also the 'multiple' used.

NDA (non-disclosure agreement) Otherwise referred to as a confidentiality agreement, or deed of confidentiality – where the parties agree to treat information provided to them confidentially.

Normalisation of accounts (or add backs) Reworking the earnings of a company to take out the impact of unusual or one-off situations by adjusting non-recurring expenses and revenue accounts both upwards and downwards to illustrate the true earnings of a business.

Normalised working capital An adjustment of the working capital requirements of the business after taking out all exceptional and non-recurring items.

Novation The transfer of both the rights *and* the obligations under a contract. This will often require a document signed by the buyer, seller and the contracting party. Novation of contracts is an alternative to the more simpler process of 'assigning' contracts. See more detail in chapter 20.

Phantom equity An alternative to providing employees with shares in a company. Phantom equity provides a bonus that effectively 'shadows' the performance of the company. This can provide incentives to employees similar to share ownership (by giving them a benefit based on the increasing value of the business) without diluting the owners' voting power and control of the company.

Privacy Act *Privacy Act 1988* (Cth).

Retention Part of the purchase price that is withheld for a certain period after completion as security for ensuring the full transfer of all the key assets, or for the buyer's possible warranty and indemnification claims against the seller. Sometimes referred to as a 'holdback'.

Share purchase agreement (SPA) The agreement between a buyer and the seller for the sale of the shares in a company. The term SPA is very commonly used, however I have at times also seen it referred to as representing the words 'sale and purchase agreement' (rather than share purchase agreement) or 'stock purchase agreement'. Or it might also be called a share sale agreement (SSA). Same same, really.

Tag along clauses Tag alongs are clauses in a shareholders' agreement that enable a minority shareholder to sell their shares to a purchaser at the same price as any other selling shareholder – the minority shareholder gets the right to 'tag along' with the larger shareholders who are selling.

Vendor due diligence A due diligence process conducted for the vendor (seller) in advance of a sale, to identify early the risks that would be identified by a buyer in the due diligence phase.

Vendor finance Where the seller 'funds' the purchase by deferring payment for part of the purchase price after completion, allowing the buyer to pay off the balance of the purchase price over time.

This may be a short deferral of payment with the balance payable at a set date after completion, or a longer period with regular set instalment payments.

Working capital The amount of money a business requires in its day-to-day operations. It is calculated as the current assets minus the current liabilities. This is often an important element in share sales that can impact the actual price received by a seller, if the buyer requires that working capital is left in the business as part of the sale.

ACKNOWLEDGEMENTS

I am so grateful to the many people who have helped make this book a reality, and supported me along the path not just of this book, but of all the business and life experiences that led to it.

My deepest thanks go to my family – my husband for bearing with me and supporting me as I typed away every morning as I got lost in the book, my gorgeous children who often got up in the wee hours to come and sleep by me as I typed, and to my parents and sister who have always been a never ending well of encouragement. I feel eternally grateful for all of your love and support.

This book would not have been written without the incredible insight and assistance of both Andrew Griffiths, and Michael Hanrahan and his team at Publish Central. Thank you also for your huge votes of encouragement along the way that kept me moving.

Huge thanks must go out to the hard working team at Aspect Legal, who work hard every day to turn the ideas from this book into the reality of protection for our clients. And of course to our incredible clients who are living the reality of acquiring, growing and exiting – we adore working with you hand in hand to achieve your goals, and I am forever grateful for the trust you put in us to help you along the way.

Thank you also to my podcast subscribers. I am so often surprised by the lovely feedback our listeners have given me along the way, which gave me the energy to capture my ideas down in this book.

And finally, huge thanks to the many partners, referrers, supporters and my incredible mentors who have made Aspect Legal the business that it is today. And of course, to you, the reader, for making it this far – I truly hope the insights covered in this book help you to buy, grow and exit with the confidence and success you deserve.

ABOUT THE AUTHOR

Joanna Oakey was born in Sydney in 1978. A small town upbringing and the influences of her socially conscious parents helped Joanna form the foundations of a strong values base and a hard work ethic. It also fostered a penchant for doing things differently.

After achieving university awards and an honours degree in law, Joanna spent time working for some of Australia's top legal firms. She quickly built a loyal client base and became a known speaker in commercial and contract law.

Working with businesses in acquiring, growing and exiting for more than 20 years, Joanna has dealt with thousands of owners and business advisers. She has worked with small startups that have catapulted in value, through to large national and multinational brands. But she has also seen many people from both large and small organisations spend years and years building a business that has no value at exit, or worse, really good businesses that fall in a hole they never recover from.

Through all of this experience she has gained incredible insights into the mistakes that businesses commonly make when acquiring, growing and exiting. She has also seen what drives really great deals. She has spent the last four years sharing many of these stories in her top-rating podcasts, *The Deal Room* and *Talking Law*, and now brings them all to life in this book, *Buy, Grow, Exit*.

Today, Joanna lives in Sydney's beautiful northern beaches with her husband and two young children. She spends her spare time dreaming about ways to create the perfect business, one that breaks the traditional lawyer mould, delivers deep value to its clients, and has a positive impact on the community and the world.

RESOURCES TO HELP YOU IMPLEMENT

You've read the book, now you're ready to take your next steps.

Check out our Resources Hub at **www.buygrowexit.com.au/resources** for resources we have designed specifically to support business owners through acquisitions, growth and exit and implement what they've read in this book.

Including:

- Buy, Grow and Exit Scorecards – take the scorecard that relates to your current stage to help you pave the way to minimise risk and maximise success

- Choosing the Right Lawyer for your Deal ebook & checklist

- Due Diligence Checklist

- Rapid Contracting Process™

- Business Insurance health check

- Warranty and indemnity insurance overview

- On-demand webinars

- Articles

- Podcast episodes

- And many other checklists, tools and guides

We have all of these resources and much more

TUNE INTO OUR PODCASTS

Tune in to our top podcasts covering the top tips and tricks and what you need to know about buying, growing and exiting a business (plus some legals you'll need along the way).

The Deal Room Podcast provides information, interviews, tips and actionable strategies for buyers, sellers and professional advisors in the world of business sales and acquisitions. Joanna Oakey interviews seasoned professionals, industry advisors and business owners and managers to give listeners a unique perspective of both the Buy and Sell sides of the Deal Room.

Subscribe at www.thedealroompodcast.com
Also available on your favorite podcast platform

Talking Law provides clear and simple legal strategies and smart legal tips for businesses and their managers, with a view to helping them to be proactive in their approach to legals and avoid any lurking legal landmines before they blow up a business.

Subscribe at www.aspectlegal.com.au/talkinglaw/
Also available on your favourite podcast platform

BUY - SERVICES FOR ACQUISITIONS

Guiding great deals through acquisitions – the path to exponential growth

Whether you are acquiring to start a business or acquiring for growth, the success of the acquisition depends heavily on the quality of the approach in the legal phase.

At Aspect Legal we help buyers construct and execute great deals, ensuring thorough preparation and a focus on realising the value and minimising risk in the deal. Working through our 5-step methodology, we ensure our buyers are well equipped going into the deal-making process and are supported to ensure post-acquisition success.

The services we provide include:

- Ready to acquire: working with our buyers to get them ready for acquisition
- Legal audit and due diligence of a potential acquisition
- Advising on deal structure design
- Advising, negotiating, drafting and completing share and business acquisitions, and providing essential advice along the way so that you achieve the most successful commercial outcome

The end of a purchase is the beginning of a new chapter. We often continue to work with many clients long after an acquisition, supporting their operations through growth, ensuring legal protections are upgraded as they grow (and often as they acquire additional businesses along the way).

Aspect Legal – A Legal Firm
Dedicated to M&A in the SME Market

GROW - COMMERCIAL LEGAL SERVICES

Aspect Legal works with growing businesses to **identify** and **protect** the value in their business, and to **predict** and **prevent** risks before they deplete business value.

We provide a range of services to help businesses deal with **immediate** legal needs as they occur, and **proactive services** to build the legal foundations of a business to withstand the storms of business along the way.

Our services include:

- Legal advice

- SME insurance

- Negotiation and drafting on the full range of commercial legal areas, including:

  - Contracts
  - Brand Protection and IP
  - Employment
  - Structuring

  - Leasing
  - Disputes
  - Procurement
  - Asset Protection

"Businesses that have a regular legal contact at their fingertips have fewer disputes."

Check out our Resources Hub at **www.buygrowexit.com.au** to view our full services and offerings (including retainers, memberships, and ad hoc services).

Or visit our website at **www.aspectlegal.com.au** to book in a free initial consultation with one of our legal eagles at Aspect Legal.

EXIT - SERVICES FOR EXIT AND SUCCESSION

When you choose to sell your business, you may be walking into a legal minefield of issues you have not encountered before. It is essential you have an advisor that can support your ultimate exit and can strategically optimise your business for a sale that achieves it.

Aspect Legal has a range of exit services that are specifically designed to drive a great exit - one that achieves the business owner's ultimate financial dream. We prime the business to gear it up for sale and then work through the exit to achieve the best possible outcome, leaning on decades of industry experience to drive smart negotiation, tight systems and commercial nous.

Our services include:

- 'Exit Ready Consultation' to work through the imperative legal steps needed to prepare your business for sale (including initial legal searches to help you prepare for sale)

- Building employee share and option plans, for future succession

- Advising on deal structures at sale

- Advising, negotiating, drafting and completing share and business sales, and providing essential advice along the way so that you achieve the most successful commercial outcome

If you'd like to discuss preparing for a sale and your ultimate exit, our Resources Hub at **www.buygrowexit.com.au** has more information about these services, or book a free initial discussion with our legal eagles at Aspect Legal to find out how we can assist **www.aspectlegal.com.au**

Aspect Legal – A Legal Firm
Dedicated to M&A in the SME Market

ARE YOU LOOKING FOR THE PERFECT GIFT FOR YOUR CLIENTS?

If you deal with businesses that are buying, exiting or growing, and are looking for the ideal gift for your business customers, *Buy, Grow, Exit* is one of the most valuable presents you could possibly purchase.

Books are available to be purchased in bulk as thank you gifts, event gifts (such as birthdays and christmas), relationship-building tools, and part of promotional campaigns and incentives.

There are many options available for bulk book purchases, including special print runs that include your own personal message printed in the book, having your branding added, or having your own company message included as an introduction. You can also include bookmarks and other additions.

If this sounds like the ideal promotional opportunity for your organisation, please email Joanna's team at enquiries@buygrowexit.com.au